THE STARS
AND
STRIPES

An editorial conference between some of *The Stars and Stripes* staff in their Paris office. Left to right: T.H. "Tip" Bliss, Philip Von Blon, J.W. Rixey Smith, Robert I. Snajdr, and Hudson Hawley. *Courtesy of National Archives.*

THE STARS AND STRIPES

Doughboy Journalism in World War I

Alfred E. Cornebise

CONTRIBUTIONS IN MILITARY HISTORY, NUMBER 37

GREENWOOD PRESS
WESTPORT, CONNECTICUT · LONDON, ENGLAND

Library of Congress Cataloging in Publication Data

Cornebise, Alfred E.
  The Stars and stripes.

  (Contributions in military history, ISSN 0084-9251 ;
no. 37)
  Bibliography: p.
  Includes index.
  1. Stars and stripes (Paris, France) 2. World War,
1914-1918—Journalism, Military—United States.
I. Title. II. Series.
D501.S725C67 1984   071'.3   83-12863
ISBN 0-313-24230-5 (lib. bdg.)

Library of Congress Catalog Card Number: 83-12863
ISBN: 0-313-24230-5
ISSN: 0084-9251

First published in 1984

Greenwood Press
A division of Congressional Information Service, Inc.
88 Post Road West
Westport, Connecticut 06881

Printed in the United States of America

10 9 8 7 6 5 4 3 2 1

THE STARS AND STRIPES

I've seen it all the way from Havre
    And Bordeaux to the Rhine;
In trench, in camp, in hospital,
    In S.O.S. and line;
I've seen it where Yanks landed,
    Where they laughed and loafed and fought,
In barracks, billets, dugouts,
    And holes of every sort.
I've seen it stuffed in helmets
    That wobbled on the head;
As inner soles for issue boots—
    Sometimes I've seen it read.
What's this I've seen, in cold and wet,
    In mud and dust and heat?
The Stars and Stripes, the doughboy's "pape,"
    The Yanks' official sheet.

I remember out at Number Two,
    One day last summer—gee!
The way the wounded crowded in
    Would make you sick to see.
The fracture ward was worst of all,
    And worst of those trussed up
In slings and splints and pulleys—
    A little red-head pup.
The other boys knew why the nurse
    Stood wiping off his head,
And asked and watched and listened
    For news of "Little Red."
They thought the kid was going West,
    Until he sighs and pipes—
"Say, nurse," he grins, "you reckon
    I could get a *Stars and Stripes*?"

Another time, at St. Benoit,
      One gorgeous autumn day,
The M.G. boys were lying round
      In shallow holes and hay.
Way off, a mile or two in front,
      Where guns were going "bang"
Old Brother Boche's big ones,
      Could never fret this gang.
They lay quiet in the sunshine,
      A-shaving on their backs,
Or smoking, swapping insults,
      Or shaping up their packs.
One lad was sprawled out reading,
      And dreaming more or less;
One hand was hunting cooties;
      One held the S. and S.

You can't tell what these historians
      Will say about this scrap;
Of men, gas, guns and aeroplanes,
      With Heine off the map.
But I bet if they had been around—
      Had seen what I have seen—
They'd include *The Stars and Stripes*
      With them that licked 'em clean.

Daniel T. Pierce
American Red Cross
(13 June 1919)

Contents

Illustrations

Introduction

"Machines just started to print first number of *Stars and Stripes*. We all wish it Bon Voyage." With these words, P. A. Goudie, the editor of Lord Northcliffe's *Continental Daily Mail* in Paris, where the army paper was printed, announced to Gen. John J. Pershing, the commander-in-chief of the American Expeditionary Forces in France, that a remarkable journalism venture was safely launched.[1] Beginning publication on 8 February 1918, for seventy-one weeks, on every Friday, this weekly appeared, ceasing operations on 13 June 1919. The paper was established primarily for the purpose of improving morale among the troops. To these ends, it sought to encourage and inspire the fearful; to evoke a grin in the face of the horrors of battle; to stimulate the patriotism that was already present; in general to call forth enthusiasm and obedience in doing the many dirty, often boring, jobs associated with the waging of war. The paper also assisted AEF headquarters in managing the anomaly of a democratic army.

The sheet was published in Paris by a remarkable collection of newspapermen, most of whom had experience on American newspapers prior to their entering the army. Essentially civilians in uniform, the men clung to their civilian newspapermen ways, naturally having, on occasion, to take into account military constraints. Men who would be well-known in the future were present, such as Harold Ross, Alexander Woollcott, Grantland Rice, and Franklin Pierce Adams, to mention but a few. Among other things, this work undertakes a study of these people, and the manner in which they produced and managed the paper.

The Stars and Stripes proceeded to set a high journalistic standard for military periodicals—indeed, perhaps for journalism generally—and it comes down to us filled with information revealing much of how the AEF lived; something of what it thought; how it played and fought; certain of its attitudes regarding, for example, the changing status of blacks; how it worshipped and felt about its dead; how it considered its allies, foes, and its officers and buddies; something of the style and ambiance of service overseas. In short, the paper is a prism, providing us with useful and fascinating glimpses and insights, often presented in an amusing fashion, into the life of Americans soldiering in Europe, far from familiar scenes, under the conditions of a great war.

While a newspaper is hardly the complete historical source, it does reveal many things which cannot be ascertained from having perused and studied reams of official documents, important though the latter are. To the social and cultural historian, in particular, the paper is a valuable help in conjuring up the spirit of its age in a most interesting and satisfactory fashion. Diaries and memoirs serve the same function, and as such are naturally of interest to the historian. However, these, more often than not, were written by relatively few, usually the more articulate and the better educated. Far more soldiers wrote letters to the editor than have left us more extended accounts of their war experiences, opening up additional avenues of experience largely overlooked. For readers brought up on the literature of despair and disillusionment which so soon followed the Great War, a consideration of letters, poetry, editorials and articles written during the conflict serves as a corrective, revealing what at least some of the men felt at the time, not what they may have felt later. Undoubtedly, *The Stars and Stripes* did accentuate the positive; that was one of the reasons for its existence, and the editors were certainly selective in what they published. At one level, then, *The Stars and Stripes* was skillful propaganda. Still, there is little doubt that the paper's tone and content corresponded closely to what the men felt. Their numerous letters and poetic contributions, coming into the paper's offices in a veritable blizzard, and the paper's almost universal, perennial popularity is evidence of that. Furthermore, the men would hardly have read a paper that did not reflect their own feelings, desires and aspirations, or that significantly deviated from the truth as they knew it.

Indubitably, the paper was more than journalism; it also produced literature of some merit. An unknown writer at *The New York Globe* once observed that "a favorite occupation of the American public used to be to make guesses as to when, where, and how the Great American Novel would be born. Well, it is being born now—once a week—and not here, but in France [as *The Stars and Stripes*]."[2] This was certainly an exaggeration, but the paper did in fact contain much that might be regarded as stimulating—if not great—literature. In this respect, the paper served as a literary outlet for many doughboys, some of whom would be later better known in the fields of literature. Others would never be heard from again, but they have left behind some engaging poetry and arresting, thoughtful prose. Yet, not all the poetry that they produced was first-rate. Though studies have been made of the poetry of the trenches, these have mainly focused on verse at a more elevated plane. "Doughboy doggerel," at a more elemental level, has not received the attention it deserves. In this book, some tentative steps are taken in this direction. Herein, traditional literary criticism is eschewed, the poems and narrative pieces being offered as the doughboys themselves presented them, frequently of the moment, within a certain context, sometimes with a light, even frivolous touch; often as cries of the heart.

It should be obvious that a newspaper is neither written nor read as a narrative. It remains episodic and impressionistic. Nevertheless, an account of it need not therefore be simply a series of clippings or excerpts. Some discernible themes are present and can be identified and presented as separate chapters. The topics have been arbitrarily selected, necessitating that others will be excluded. Assuredly, this book does not purport to be the last word regarding either *The Stars and Stripes* or U.S. involvement in World War I. Its aims are more modest: to serve as a piece of reportage on an interesting journalistic undertaking, as a sampler of AEF life.

In this work, direct quotations and poems have been liberally used so as to retain the paper's essential character, and the date of the issue of the source of these, as well as that of other references, quotations, and paraphrases, are either given parenthetically in the text or acknowledged in the notes.

Not the least of the paper's importance is the precedent that it set for the similarly famous World War II editions of *The Stars and Stripes*. Nevertheless, it can well stand on its own merits as a stimulating historical source which deserves the attention of anyone interested in the American past at a particularly significant point in its passage.

THE STARS
AND
STRIPES

1

Origins, Personnel, and Operations

The Stars and Stripes is, as far as we know, the only subdivision of the A.E.F. that does not claim to have won the war single-handed.

(13 June 1919)

The editors sure have spizzerinktum and every word of the paper is darned interesting.

Pvt. Howard W. Butler
(5 April 1918)

Your paper has the real American jump.

Charles H. Grasty
(5 April 1918)

It was only an eight-page weekly. Many a village could boast as much. But this paper's beat was a Europe in conflict, and its main clientele a body of American military men eventually 2,000,000 strong. From 8 February 1918 to 13 June 1919—for seventy-one weeks—the paper appeared every Friday. Its circulation began with less than 30,000 copies; it eventually reached more than 526,000 produced by a staff of over 300 men.

Undoubtedly, *The Stars and Stripes* is the best-known army newspaper of all time.[1] It originated in the offices and corridors of General Headquarters of the American Expeditionary Forces at Chaumont, France, perhaps in the office of the commander-in-chief himself, late in 1917. The provenance of the initial spark is lost to history, but in November, a second lieutenant of infantry, Guy T. Viskniskki, who was then an assistant press officer in the AEF, was charged with reporting on the need and practicability of establishing an official newspaper published by and for the AEF.[2] His report—which was also a piece of special pleading by an ambitious believer sensing an opportunity for himself—asserted that in his investigation, conducted among officers and men at representative units at Neufchâteau and Condrecourt, one universal complaint was met: there was no reliable news from home and no indication as to what the nation was doing or thinking. Certainly, they were adamant that the Paris editions of *The Chicago Tribune* and *The New York Herald* did not suffice: "They don't give us what we want; we don't want hotel arrivals in Paris and society news." As a typical complaint went, "the army is doing the best it can by us in everything except giving us the news, and we want that more than anything else." It was obvious, then, as Viskniskki observed, that "by giving the soldier the news he wants from home, in the newspaper form in which he has been accustomed to getting the news, he would be better satisfied with his lot—his morale would have an additional substantial prop under it."

Viskniskki also recognized that the General Staff could use the paper "as a medium for the dissemination, and driving home, of such orders as could with propriety be given such publication; for example, orders relating to the necessity of strictly observing the rules of military courtesy; the rules of personal and collective hygiene . . . and the reasonableness of these orders could be made plain to even the least understanding by editorial . . . comment thereon."

The paper would also include news of events within the AEF; the football scores could be reported; articles would feature accounts of medal winners to encourage others; what was being done on behalf of the rank and file by those in authority could be stressed, such as descriptions of the well-equipped hospitals ready for all eventualities. There would be cabled reports from home and perhaps the gratis use of comic features such as "Mutt and Jeff." Fiction might be published in its traditional installments, and maybe such special features as "an authoritative military summary of the past week's events in the war on both sides, with an interpretation thereof in popular terms," could be included. Further, since "the average American has become accustomed to editorial comment, the proposed newspaper would have an editorial page, written with the firm purpose in mind of keeping every soldier reader high-minded in the performance of his duties."

The cost of the proposed six- to eight-page weekly would be covered by subscriptions, advertising and perhaps by Red Cross contributions if necessary. The paper could be produced in Paris on presses of some established newspaper. Viskniskki felt that American circulation methods, "adapted to wartime conditions in France," would work nicely. The French, he ventured to conclude, would also come up with the paper supplies when the proposal was presented to them.

The paper would be censored, of course, denying information to the enemy, and also to counter "any feeling of discouragement" which might creep into the army.[3]

Adding to his report, Viskniskki instanced his own recent experience as founder and editor of *The Bayonet*, an eight-page weekly produced by the 80th Division at Camp Lee, Virginia.[4] The paper was printed at the plant of *The*

Richmond Times Dispatch, the night before its date of publication. He suggested that the paper—a copy of which he attached to his report—could serve as a model. It had been a success, he maintained, and quoted the division's chief of staff to the effect that *"The Bayonet* [would] be one of the most powerful influences in the Division for creating esprit de corps and assisting in disseminating military information to the command." Viskniskki could only conclude that these positive aspects would be so much more effective on the entire AEF, and "week after week it would prove itself a potent factor in bringing about that ultimate victory for our country, and for Democracy everywhere, that we are all striving and working for, every man according to his ability and light." In truth, he felt that "the coming Winter months will be particularly trying to the morale and spirits of the soldiers. The proposed newspaper, edited as herein outlined, would do much to bring them through the Winter in good fighting trim and spirits, keyed up for the work of the Spring, mentally, morally, physically."

The strictures of an official report scarcely masked Viskniskki's personal enthusiasm and eagerness in seeing the project launched, and one suspects that he told his superiors what they wanted to hear as well. Indeed, his report was prophetic in many respects, though not all of his plans materialized. In any event, Viskniskki was no doubt gratified when, on 10 December, Lieut. Col. Denis E. Nolan, Chief of the Intelligence Branch of the General Staff—soon to be referred to as G-2—directed him to work out the details and on 30 December, Viskniskki submitted his report.[5] He had lined up the paper supply from the French, until he could be supplied from the United States, and had persuaded the owner of the Continental edition of *The London Daily Mail*, Lord Northcliffe, to grant the Americans the use of their presses, located in Paris. Viskniskki felt that a three-month subscription at four francs would be adequate, and he suggested that the profits go into a fund to supply the AEF with tobacco, then in short supply. He was confident that were he to be placed in charge, that with only five or so printers from the AEF's base printing plant at Langres, and with motor transport for distribution of the paper, he could be in business by 1 February 1918.

With Nolan's indorsement, Viskniskki awaited official approval. This was soon forthcoming; Pershing expeditiously approved the publication of a weekly newspaper under the direction of the Press Section of the Censorship and Press Division—G-2-D—of the Intelligence Branch of the General Staff, with the title *The Stars and Stripes.*[6] On 7 January, Viskniskki was authorized to sign an agreement with the French firm of Darblay for the print paper and plans were speedily implemented to launch the paper in early February.[7]

Two other things remained: a grubstake and an official bulletin bringing the paper's existence to the general attention of the AEF. The former took the form of a loan of 24,724.65 francs secured from G-2 funds.[8] The latter was accomplished by means of Bulletin No. 10, G.H.Q., series of 1918, of 8 February 1918.[9] This document, which closely followed the wording of Viskniskki's report of 28 November 1917, indicated the paper's official authorization and set forth the rationale behind it and its basic modus operandi. It was emphasized that the paper was "the only official publication of the A.E.F.," of this sort. It was to be published every Friday, beginning on 8 February 1918, promising to bring the men the latest news from home by cable, through its American staff correspondent, "a lifelong newspaper man of national reputation." He was also charged with cabling the AEF the latest news of sports at home. The paper was also instructed to give the AEF news about itself, "keeping every unit as fully informed as possible as to what the entire AEF is doing." In addition, the bulletin continued, the paper would serve "as a medium of publication for poems, stories, articles, caricatures and cartoons of army life produced by members of the A.E.F." In short, *The Stars and Stripes* "will be strictly and solely an A.E.F. newspaper, bringing to its members regularly every week the news which up to now it has received at best irregularly and in an unsatisfactory manner."

The document also set the price of the paper at four francs for a three-months' subscription, paid in advance. As an incentive, a proportional part of the four francs—up to a franc—would go directly to the company funds, determined by the number of subscribers in each unit. In fact, in this way, many company funds in the AEF were created.[10] With this description, Pershing also stated that "the heartiest and promptest co-operation of all organization commanders is desired in order that *The Stars and Stripes* may reflect the greatest possible credit on the A.E.F." It is safe to conclude, however, that even without this exhortation from the commander-in-chief the paper would have become popular.

The American correspondent alluded to in Bulletin No. 10 was Julius W. Muller, a man Viskniskki had known at the Wheeler Syndicate and earlier at *McClure's Magazine*.[11] Muller agreed, without any cost to the paper, to transmit each Wednesday a cable of 2,000 words, along the lines of the request that it tell "optimistically" what the nation was doing, "explaining for [the] army over here in [a] way to increase its fighting morale the week's big happenings and trend at home and spirit of [the] nation."[12] It is noteworthy in this respect that neither Muller nor the paper's staff desired to tap the Creel Committee's news sources. Muller was opposed "to the whole conception and the . . . loose and reckless activities of the organization." Others did not desire that *The Stars and Stripes* bear any evidence of being inspired from Washington, which would materially lessen its usefulness.[13]

The aims of the paper were fairly clear, its main purpose being for internal propaganda, "to stimulate a healthy morale among troops of the A.E.F. by giving them news of the war and of America attractively and interestingly presented."[14] It was further intended that the paper would help consolidate the AEF, which at that time was "a rather bewildered force of some 300,000 men scattered all the way from Bordeaux to Lorraine and heartily echoing the sentiments of the late William Tecumseh Sherman" (13 June 1919). In short, it was a "green and none too self-confident Army, . . . in serious danger of losing all sense of belonging to a single [force]." The paper would give this army a voice and stimulate its morale. Thus, "to write for the Yanks training with the British, the Yanks brigaded with the French, the Yanks loaned to Italy, and the Yanks venturing a bit on their own northwest of Toul—to tell each separate part and group that the others were helping that was the idea" (7 February 1919).[15]

Certain features of the paper's first issue amounted to a prospectus detailing what the paper was and what it intended. Pershing himself set the tone, emphasizing that the new paper's readers would mainly be "the men who have been honored by being the first contingent of Americans to fight on European soil for the honor of their country . . . which makes them fortunate above the millions of their fellow citizens at home." Yet, "commensurate with their privileges in being here, is the duty which is laid before them, and this duty will be performed by them as by Americans of the past, eager, determined, and unyielding to the last." *The Stars and Stripes* was created to assist in attaining these lofty endeavors, and "written by the men in the service, should speak the thoughts of the new American Army and the American people from whom the Army has been drawn."

The editor elaborated, emphasizing that this "is *your* paper, and has but one axe to grind—the axe which our Uncle Samuel is whetting on the grindstone for use upon the august necks of the Hapsburgs and the Hohenzollerns." The paper was also unique in that "every soldier purchaser, every soldier subscriber, is a stockholder and a member of the board of directors. It isn't being run for any individual's profit, and it serves no class but the fighting men in France, who wear the olive drab and the forest green." Readers were urged to write the editor about their concerns, and an invitation was extended to artists, writers and poets in the AEF for contributions. The paper promised to keep "at the top o' the mast for the duration of the war," and would endeavor "to reach every one of you, every week—mud, shell-holes and fog notwithstanding." It would "yield rights of the roadway only to troops and ambulances, food, ammunition and guns, and the paymaster's car." Having taken on a considerable job, the paper's staff assured the readers "in good old down east parlance, [to] 'do its golderndest' to deliver the goods." Finally, Viskniskki promised that the paper would be "lively, slightly irreverent, [and] plain-spoken," one "which did not smell to Heaven of propaganda and which was not choked up with deadly official utterances." This approach was needed, he declared, "as Yanks are all sceptics who can smell bunk a mile off." This being the case, "truth must and should serve" (7 February 1919).[16]

It became an article of faith—and something of a myth—assiduously cultivated, that *The Stars and Stripes* was strictly its own master under the complete control of the enlisted staff. In fact, the final issue of the paper expressed the warmest appreciation for "the generous policy of non-interference, of non-dictation, which the General Staff, A.E.F., has held to from the start in the dealings with us." In this regard, a special note was taken of a memorandum, which was the outcome of "a little difference as to whether the paper was going to be run for the enlisted man or not." Coming from the top at G.H.Q., it read in substance: "The style and policy of *The Stars and Stripes* is not to be interfered with.'' In short, the General Staff left the paper ''severely alone,'' enabling it to achieve ''whatever measure of usefulness, whatever place in the hearts of its fellow Yanks it may be credited with, now or in times to come'' (13 June 1919).

Later, when a doughboy returning to the United States reported to an American newspaper that *The Stars and Stripes* was the General Staff's propaganda sheet, the editor took him to task. ''The facts are these: There *was* censorship on *The Stars and Stripes*. It was made up of some three privates and one fat sergeant.'' These men carefully considered every article, and ''if they caught the scent of the press agent, the promotion-hunter, or the officer who wanted to explain all about what the enlisted man really thought, they threw the said contribution into the waste basket and Rags, the credulous office bloodhound, swallowed it. . . . Once in a while some joyful enthusiast put over some Pollyanna-keep-smiling rubbish, but it wasn't often'' (13 June 1919).

These assertions are not altogether wide of the mark; neither are they altogether true. The facts are somewhat at variance with these commonly-held viewpoints. While it is true that especially Capt. Mark S. Watson, the second (and last) officer-in-charge, allowed his enlisted staff to run on a loose leash, the leash was there nonetheless. In the first place, there was a Board of Control in existence at G.H.Q., charged with determining and directing the paper's policy and taking full responsibility therefor.[17] The original members were Lieut. Col. Walter Sweeney, Maj. Bruce Magruder, and 2nd Lieut. Mark S. Watson, at Chaumont, with Capt. Earl H. Smith and Viskniskki in Paris. The Paris representatives were to edit all copy of the following Friday's issue and send it to G.H.Q. by courier every Monday morning. The Board met regularly every Tuesday afternoon at which session one or both of the Paris members were expected. In all of the deliberations certain guidelines were to be considered. Prime interest was placed on the problem of maintaining a high morale in the AEF. Secondly, consistent with the exigencies of the war, news, with the widest possible appeal was to be published. Finally, it was stipulated that ''every issue of *The Stars and Stripes* should interpret the spirit of a great Democracy at war for a just cause, in the encouragement of individuality of expression consistent with tolerance and sanity of view.''

The minutes of one of the board's early meetings reveal interesting policy positions. Specifically for meeting the needs of maintaining high morale, it was decided to publish extensive features giving news of the Army. News from home would not only include a general news coverage, but special articles, such as those detailing the punishment of profiteers, would appear, as would others emphasizing the great speeding up of production, which well demonstrated the support that the United States was giving the AEF. Then, too, there would be ''small doses of propaganda, [though] not so obvious as to make [the] reader suspicious.''[18] *The Stars and Stripes* could also raise morale by furnishing the men with an outlet for expressing their own thoughts and through emphasizing that the paper was their own. The emphasis would be on plenty of light, humorous contributions of all sorts. The paper would also draw no class distinctions; for example, there would be no special departments for college associations, fraternal orders and the like. The AEF was to be treated as thoroughly democratic.[19]

Not only was there a board of control, the officers-in-charge of *The Stars and Stripes* recognized that they could always expect that G.H.Q. would insist upon having certain items printed, i.e., some "must-go stuff." To be sure, in this area lay a battleground between the management of the paper and higher authority, and it saw some skirmishes if not major engagements; indeed, the latter were rare, but they did occur, and some instances remained, for the staff, part of the paper's lore and significant history.

Some of the "must-go stuff" included President Wilson's Labor Day speech of 1918 which Nolan simply instructed Viskniskki to run.[20] And later in the paper's career, Watson, then the officer-in-charge, bucked the reprinting of an article by the British military commentator, Lieutenant Colonel Repington, which had appeared in *The London Morning Post*.[21] The colonel had warmly praised the American war effort in general and Pershing's leadership in particular. The latter especially made the article suspect as far as Watson was concerned. Accordingly, he resisted its republication. He was of the opinion that a favorable review of America's efforts was appropriate in British or French papers but "it appears immodest in the American soldiers' own paper and the same applies to praise of the Commander-in-Chief." Watson also feared that the reprinting would only add fuel to the fire then raging as to who had won the war and would increase friction between British and American armies. He further argued that it was standard newspaper practice to reduce reprinted matter to a minimum because this implied "either that the paper was unable to write its own material or that the article in question was 'inspired.' " Since Watson was allowing the editorial staff to run the paper, and the office force was firmly opposed to printing the article, he did not feel like overruling them on the point unless necessary.[22] In the event, he had to overrule his staff, but not without a compromise: the praise of Pershing was watered down.

However, Nolan could sometimes be counted on to defend the paper from pressures from other quarters. Brig. Gen. W. W. Harts, the commander of U.S. troops in the Paris District, was a case in point. Harts observed that *The Stars and Stripes* "which is generally considered by our Allies as being the representative paper of the American Expeditionary Forces is being more or less criticized for the general use of slang in virtually all of its articles." This had created a bad impression since "English speaking Frenchmen read this paper and they endeavor to familiarize themselves with the American Army news, and the statement has been made that the general use of base-ball slang in relation to military subjects has not had the desired result. The average Frenchman does not understand base-ball terms, particularly when used in connection with other matters."[23]

The riposte was obvious, and Nolan did not hesitate to deliver it. In his indorsement of Harts' memorandum Nolan replied that "*The Stars and Stripes* is essentially by the soldiers and for the soldiers." That being the case, "the strongest effort has been made to avoid confining its language to the language of the public forum. The use of slang in the interpretation of subjects in themselves serious is the surest way of getting the average soldier to read the article. This applies particularly to certain general orders. . . . '' While it was desirable to have the paper read by ''American reading Frenchmen and by British troops,'' this in no way affected the principal mission of the paper, he concluded.

But the most celebrated incident of conflict between the paper's management and higher authority was triggered by a memorandum from Lieut. Col. Aristides Moreno, then acting secretary of G-2, to Watson.[24] Its words were long remembered: ''The Commander-in-Chief has noticed recently that *The Stars and Stripes* is criticizing the A.E.F. Some of these criticisms have appeared in a humorous vein. You will take proper steps to the end that no article containing a criticism of any kind appears in *The Stars and Stripes*.''

The paper was ably defended by Watson whose reply was both loud and long.[25] He began by describing once more his successful editorial policy which was ''to let the enlisted men run the paper and feel thereby a sense of responsibility for it.'' As he noted, in every case which has not been based on faulty grounds, ''or sure to produce results injurious to the Army, I have approved the recommendations of this group of very intelligent men and propose to continue doing so.'' He only on rare occasions suggested any of the paper's content, ''preferring that inception come from the men.'' As he saw it, his fundamental role was acting as a buffer between the editorial staff and G.H.Q. His sympathies more often than not rested with the paper, and he tried to combat higher authority when it ''directed the printing of something which the editorial board regarded as poor stuff for *The Stars and Stripes*,'' or which he knew, ''as only a newspaperman can know to be injurious [to the paper].'' But this attitude worked in the best interests of all, especially that of the commander-in-chief. He instanced several occasions of successful ''bucking'' which he felt illustrated the point. He had resisted printing Pershing's final report in the paper, ''except in short installments, knowing that a single document would be clearly recognized as something dictated from above and not coming spontaneously from *The Stars and Stripes*.''[26] He was likewise opposed to praising the Postal Service in print, ''in view of the fact that almost every mail brings into this office the most bitter complaints against that service—complaints that I cannot believe are without foundation in fact.'' Just as soon as the paper departed from its well-developed modus operandi, and failed to print ''humorous, harmless grouches of the soldiers, just at that time will *The Stars and Stripes* be regarded as a G.H.Q. organization, or more serious, as a J.J.P. organ, and when that time comes there is one man who will suffer and that is the commander-in-chief.'' He went on in even stronger terms, observing that he had never presumed to advise G.H.Q. on the handling of combat operations or about supply problems, but ''I do, however, presume to advise you about the technical work with which I am familiar. . . . I do know newspaper work and without blushing I state that I know more about it than an officer whose entire life has been spent in the Army and who, with the exception of certain rare individuals, knows very little about newspaper work and the reaction of the public mind to what is printed in news-papers." While he did not wish to appear insubordinate, he wanted, "in the strongest possible terms," to put his conviction that *The Stars and Stripes* must remain as near as possible, "a means of free expression for the soldier." This was necessary, because as matters stood, "every soldier swears by this paper. He does so because he knows that it is his paper. He knows that no officer and especially no commander-in-chief is dictating what this paper shall contain." He could recite "for hours" enthusiastic comments on *The Stars and Stripes* from officers and men alike, and one man had even stated that "he never believed a general order until he saw it reprinted in *The Stars and Stripes.*" Watson urged that his remarks be presented to high authority in such a way that the paper might remain "unimpeded by interference from . . . high authority." If this could not be accomplished, Watson respectfully submitted that in his opinion, "*The Stars and Stripes* has outlived its usefulness and publication should be immediately suspended."[27]

The enlisted men of the paper remembered the incident differently, and the final issue of the paper recounted their version. It seems, the account began, that a certain lieutenant colonel attached to G.H.Q. [Moreno], "who took himself very seriously," some time after the Armistice sent the editors a formal letter in which he officiously demanded that criticisms of the AEF in the paper—though some had been of a humorous nature—cease forthwith. The immediate consequence of the receipt of this missive was that "the then somewhat violent buck-private-managing-editor [Private Harold Wallace Ross, late of the 18th Engineers (Railway)] phoned the lieutenant colonel's boss," who apparently led his charge "out behind the headquarters caserne, and quietly told him that a Boche named Gutenberg discovered the art of printing in Sixteen-something-or-other; that it had later been perfected by a bleedin' Tommy named Caxton; that a wild Irishman named Burke . . . once uttered some poignant remarks about the Fourth Estate, and that, to conclude with, this was the year 19 of the twentieth century—together with some elucidating remarks upon the law of gravitation and the square of the hypothenuse." This had its desired effects, and the editors gratefully acknowledged that "after that we were able to work our own sweet will practically unruffled" (13 June 1919).[28]

For all the manner of its launching, the paper had humble beginnings; it was in fact "born in a log cabin," as one account has it, but this was not scorned for "what candidate for the Presidency ever suffered from having been born in a log cabin?" The "log cabin" office was in the back room of a small converted shop on the Rue St. Jean in the French town of Neufchâteau, Haute Marne, then the site of the Field Press headquarters of the AEF. "There, amid the constant coming and going of great but deeply grieved war correspondents, the plaintive pleas for mercy from the cruel, cruel censors, the urgent demands for more wood for that damned old stove by (Censored), and the rigors of the Vosges climate in late January, *The Stars and Stripes* was born" (13 June 1919).[29]

However, while the paper was launched in Neufchâteau, it soon migrated to Paris, taking up quarters in a small hall bedroom on the second floor of the Hotel Sainte Anne, at 10 Rue Sainte Anne. Its staff was to be drawn from experienced newspapermen from throughout the AEF, some of the men being recommended by their commanding officers while others volunteered. Its initial staff consisted of the "frantically energetic and everlastingly pepful" Viskniskki; another "equally energetic but much more restful second lieutenant of Marines," Charles Phelps Cushing; one "never energetic" buck private of Leathernecks, Abian A. "Wally" Wallgren, one of the paper's cartoonists, who was with it from the first issue to the last; "one forced-to-be-energetic" buck private of machine guns, Hudson Hawley; and 1st Lieut. William K. Michael, an infantry officer, who was the paper's first advertising manager (13 June 1919).

The first issue or two were hurriedly written between errands by Hawley, and the first few cartoons "were done at odd times on still odder scraps of paper, . . . " on one beer table, while the newly arrived treasurer, Lieut. Adolph S. Ochs, Jr., a cavalry officer, counted the paper's first francs on another. But as the paper began to flourish, like the proverbial green bay tree, the staff grew and operations were stabilized. The room at the Hotel Sainte Anne was clearly inadequate and a move was made in early March 1918, to 1 Rue des Italiens, where space on the fifth and sixth floors of an office building was obtained.[30] The paper finished its career in offices on an entire floor in a larger building at 32 Rue Taitbout, Paris, above the Credit Mobilier offices, making that move in early December of 1918.[31]

The editorial staff had few doubts as to its importance. The department "has from time to time been somewhat taken aback by encountering a rumor that it consisted of a detachment of General Staff colonels or a committee of YMCA secretaries."[32] To all such charges, the editors retorted, "we can, and always do, reply, 'Liar.' " Four men, three privates and a sergeant, all of whom had earlier newspaper experience, formed the main editorial staff almost from the beginning. Private Hudson Hawley, from Connecticut, formerly of *The Hartford Times*, *The New York Sun*, and *The Yale Record*, had been with the 101st Machine Gun Battalion. He wrote the first few issues of the paper almost singlehandedly. He later introduced columns which had a short run, such as "Bran Mash," and "Miss Information." He then concentrated on articles pertaining to the Services of Supply, the much-maligned "S.O.S."

Another prominent member of the editorial staff was Pvt. John Tracy Winterich, of Rhode Island, who had earlier been on the staff of *The Springfield Republican*. "Escaping" from the 96th Aero Squadron, he was recognized as "a splendid all-around newspaper man discovered by . . . Watson at Chaumont. Winterich's modesty is characteristic," as Katz stated, "but his associates on the paper realized the tremendous work he performed, and gave him credit for a major part of the paper's phenomenal success." He could write heads and feature stories with equal facility and he also assumed the responsibility for the final make-up of each issue.[33]

1. Pvt. Abian "Wally" Wallgren, U.S.M.C., at his drawing board. *Courtesy of National Archives.*

2. *The Stars and Stripes* offices at 32 Taitbout, Paris. *Courtesy of National Archives.*

3. Interior of *The Stars and Stripes* office at 32 Taitbout, Paris. *Courtesy of National Archives.*

Certainly one of the most interesting of the characters drawn to the new paper was Pvt. Harold Wallace Ross, who later founded and for a long time directed the fortunes of *The New Yorker* magazine. Born in Aspen, Colorado, he had earlier served on *The San Francisco Call*, and "some 78 other American newspapers (one at a time)," joining *The Stars and Stripes*' editorial staff from the 18th Engineers (Railway). Ross was known for his energy but also for his rather abrasive character. It is noteworthy that later Watson recommended Ross and only one other enlisted man for the Distinguished Service Medal, observing that his work "stood out so conspicuously as to entitle [him] to special mention above even the admirable work performed by [his] associates." However, as it transpired that the DSM was rarely awarded below the rank of colonel, Ross did not receive his medal, but then Ross had never asked for credit, though Watson clearly felt that he richly deserved it.[34]

The sergeant of the quartet was Alexander Woollcott, from New Jersey, who had been a drama critic for *The New York Times*. In the army, he had been "safely ensconced in the registrar's office of Base Hospital No. 8, when captured and borne off to Paris." But, "when the war suddenly became warlike last spring [1918], he was sent to the front, where he remained for the most part until the armistice was signed, serving as chief war correspondent of *The Stars and Stripes* and living in constant danger of death at the hand of some division that thought he was giving too much attention to the wretched craven divisions on either side."[35] Soon others joined him in working the front, "for it took many men to cover that fairly lively beat." Woollcott was later put in charge of the amusement column, which became a regular, rather lengthy, well-written feature of the paper.

These four men long remained in charge of the paper's editorial destinies. From December 1918 to April 1919, Ross functioned as "probably the lowest paid managing editor in the history of journalism." The four were also responsible for nearly all of the editorials—which were unsigned—making it virtually impossible to ascribe authorship to any particular piece. Many of them are brilliant pieces of sparkling journalistic prose, some certainly attaining the level of essays of marked literary merit. The role that these editors played had another dimension also: "They have helped make the world safe for democracy by serving as models for Wally's cartoons," as one account playfully recorded.[36]

These four editors, sometimes joined by the cartoonists, for fourteen months of the paper's sixteen and one-half months of life, formed the main editorial board at Paris—not to be confused with the Board of Control at Chaumont—which "X-rayed every article that came in," in the process of which "they brought many limelight seekers and overzealous promoters to grief, shocked many a chaplain, Y.M.C.A. man and visiting congressman by their deafness to pleas that *The Stars and Stripes* should run a religious column . . . [or one] . . . entitled 'Happy Thoughts' (or something killingly funny like that), enraged many a divisional publicity officer, and in general thumbed their collective noses at the martial universe." In so doing, they naturally "worked always with one foot in the hoosegow, for practically every one of their callers and advisers ranked hell out of them." Their attitude was necessary, however, since they "from start to finish. . .held the paper to its original intention of being 'by and for the enlisted man.' " Since the editorial staff were enlisted men themselves, who had done their share of KP along with everyone else, they insisted that they knew what the enlisted men wanted in their paper and that, "by the shade of George Washington's spurs, they were going to give it to him" (13 June 1919).

Viskniskki was at some pains to emphasize the role of the enlisted men. "Barring an officer or two, who had to be around to satisfy Army tradition," he once stated, the paper was produced by the men, "many of the lowly, or buck, variety." He went on to explain: "A handful of enlisted men has written and illustrated the greater part of the paper—I believe, for its size, the most brilliant and—er—erratic editorial staff ever possessed by an American newspaper." This fact did not dismay him because, in his view, "the American private is the greatest man in the world at fighting or writing or anything" (7 February 1919). To be sure, the officer-in-charge, as commander of the men attached to the staff, had something to say about the paper's operations, but the enlisted editors mainly ran the production side of the sheet.

The number of editors grew so as to keep up with the paper's steadily expanding operations. Other prominent members later included Sgt. Seth T. Bailey, of the 162nd Infantry, part of the "Sunset Division." A native of Portland, Oregon, he had served with *The Portland Oregonian*. Bailey, "a peculiarly hard-boiled doughboy, [had] descended on the sanctum in column of squads, sporting a Mexican [campaign] badge." His greatest claim to fame was the humorous column of ficticious letters that he introduced, entitled "Henry's Pal to Henry," which were later collected and published by *The Stars and Stripes* as a paperback book.[37] The letters made "many otherwise dull moments for the doughboys bright by his ridiculous letters supposedly written by the pal of a mythical Henry, who had enlisted in the Army early in the game and who insisted on keeping Henry informed of his personal adventures in a manner that brought mirth whenever read."[38]

Another editor was Sgt. Philip Von Blon, of Ohio, and of Base Hospital No. 4, who had received his newspaper experience on *The Cleveland Plain Dealer*, and who replaced Ross as managing editor in the paper's last few weeks of life. He had also served as a front-line correspondent. Pvt. ("Third Lieutenant"), later 2nd Lieut., Hilmar R. Baukhage, formerly of *Leslie's Weekly*, served as an editor, and often contributed verse to the paper as well.[39]

Army Field Clerk George W. B. Britt, the "most melodious man on the paper," and initially on the editorial staff, wrote a few articles for the sports page and then established the Soldier's Service Department, which answered thousands of queries from soldiers, such as " 'How can I match the enclosed sample of a broken tooth?' (We bite. How can you?) or 'Has Mary Pickford died of the flu?' (Referred to Graves Registration Service)." Katz, at least, was of the opinion that the Service Department rendered better service than the information departments conducted by the welfare organizations. The extent to which this feature was used by the men is indicated by the fact that during the life of the paper the Department answered more than 500,000 inquiries. Several men were required simply to answer the mail.[40]

Other men of note included Frank Sibley, "the Boswell of the 26th Division," who, in the early issues, was rewrite man for the copy that came in from the foreign correspondents. Sgt. Nathaniel T. Worley, of the 11th Engineers, was the Sporting Editor after the Armistice. He had learned his trade at *The Washington Herald*.[41]

The editorial department also listed the two members of the art department: one doughboy and one Marine. Pvt. Abian A. "Wally" Wallgren was "formerly of any Philadelphia newspaper you can think of," and *The Washington Post*. He had been "pried loose" from the Supply Company, 5th Marines, then near Damblaine just as they were getting ready for their first trip into the trenches. Wallgren's first strip was drawn there and sent to Neufchâteau. He was soon acknowledged as "the best advertised and worse behaved enlisted man in the A.E.F. At least he is the best-advertised Marine, and that is going some." Indeed, Wally's cartoons from the start were a staple of the paper and excited much comment. He later had them published separately as a book by *The Stars and Stripes* and in 1933, they were reissued by a commercial press.[42] Indeed, perhaps no other man on the staff became as well known to the soldiers of the AEF, as this sometimes-styled "Scandinavian cartoonist and enemy of prohibition" (7 February 1919). His cartoons were described as "undoubtedly the funniest drawings of army life ever conceived," reflecting the fact that he was a soldier himself and "his sense of humor and his powers of observation were so keen that he readily grasped the things which the men considered humorous." His powers were sharpened by his constant trips to the front where he carefully studied conditions and gathered material for his cartoons. It is also true that he made life miserable for certain members of the staff who had some conspicuous physical characteristic which made them good models. One of his favorites was Hudson Hawley, "whose dome was devoid of any hirsute adornment," and W. B. Britt, "offered good material with his 300 or more pounds of avoirdupois."[43]

The "respectable half of the Art Department" was Pvt. Cyrus LeRoy Baldridge, an infantryman. This native of San Diego, California, had earlier observed the operations of the German Army in Belgium in 1914 as a combat artist. He then returned to the United States, participating in Pershing's Mexican venture as a stable sergeant. Ever restless, he again went to France, joining the French Army as a *poilu*. Having later "discovered the A.E.F.," he entered that, transferring to the staff of *The Stars and Stripes*, and "ever since, his drawings of the doughboys have been famous the world around." One of the great American daily newspapers asserted on one occasion that, "if *The Stars and Stripes* accomplished nothing more it served to bring to the front a truly great American artist in the person of C. LeRoy Baldridge." Unquestionably, "Baldridge caught the spirit of the American fighter in a fuller sense than did any other man who attempted to do so, and . . . he drew stories, morals, and doctrines into his cartoons which not even the most indifferent could fail to see.''[44]

The enlisted editors once admitted that it was ''only fair to add . . . that from time to time, some officers did have something to do with *The Stars and Stripes* . . . '' (7 February 1919). Viskniskki, of course, launched the venture, remaining as officer-in-charge until 29 November 1918, when Capt. Mark S. Watson took charge. But despite the importance of Viskniskki's role, however, he was replaced rather precipitately. The exact reasons are not clear, but it is certain that trouble and tension had long been present at the office between the officer-in-charge and the paper's staff. In the upshot, Viskniskki, apparently without warning, was relieved of his duties with the paper. An investigation soon followed, conducted by Lieut. Col. Bruce Magruder, of the paper's Board of Control at Chaumont. The men he most closely questioned were 1st Lieut. Milton J. Ayers, of the circulation department, and 1st Lieut. Adolph S. Ochs, Jr., the paper's treasurer—who was also relieved on 4 December, being replaced by 1st Lieut. William E. Miltenberger, who, unfortunately, died of a respiratory ailment before the month was out.[45] Ochs and Ayers were in substantial agreement that Viskniskki was not the right man for the position that he had held. Ignoring his considerable exertions in founding the paper, and his undoubted abilities, his two major critics charged him with a whole catalog of faults and shortcomings: He was guilty of bullying the enlisted men; he meddled in all departments' business, down to the last detail; he often reprimanded officers in the presence of enlisted men; he bribed his favorites with favors and promises of promotion; he was said to be imbued with grandiose schemes of making a name for himself in journalism in France so that his postwar future might be secure. It was further alleged that he had no business sense, and had recently capriciously raised advertising rates, causing consternation among the agencies who were handling the paper's advertising. Beyond this, he had no sense of personal ethics, and was certainly dictatorial and bigoted; Ayers categorically asserted that he was ''drunk with power.'' He had fired one of the paper's early acquisitions, the well-known journalist Capt. Franklin P. Adams, on the grounds of religious prejudice, so it was said, though this was not explained. He had shunted Capt. Richard Waldo to the London office of the paper, apparently fearing that that competent man would ease him out of the front office. This Viskniskki could not stand, Ayers and Ochs charged; he wanted all of the credit. These men, in short, felt that he had no support on the paper's staff, who were kept in line only by the fact that he was officer-in-charge with the rank of captain. He was also allegedly disloyal to the commander-in-chief; was said to be anti-French, and even worse, anti-Belgian, and vehemently opposed to the AEF's auxiliary organizations, i.e., the YMCA and the Knights of Columbus in particular. Both Ochs and Ayers were of the firm conviction, then, that Viskniskki was in no way qualified to be in charge of ''the most powerful and most influential periodical in the world.'' He was ''temperamentally unfit'' to command other men.[46]

It is not clear as to all of the results of the hearings nor to what extent Ochs

and Ayers were correct in their heavy attacks on Viskniskki. There is no documentary evidence located in the paper's files shedding any more light on the
charges. What is certain is that Viskniskki and Ochs were replaced; Ayers,
however, continued to render substantial service to the paper. There was no
doubt some truth to the allegations against Viskniskki. Ambitious he certainly
was and when some of his carefully nurtured schemes failed, as several did in
November of 1918, he may have made no secret of his disappointment, perhaps
blaming others for the failure.

In any case, the paper's new officer-in-charge—and several documents make
it clear that he certainly did not seek the post; for one thing, he was Viskniskki's
close friend—was the much cooler, and very competent, Captain—soon to be
a major—Mark S. Watson, summoned to Paris from Chaumont. There, as a
member of the Board of Control, he was closely in touch with the paper's affairs.
The documentation of this period makes clear that Watson had the respect of
his subordinates, his peers and superiors; his intellect, personality and indus-
triousness were widely remarked upon.[47] He patently did not merit the sally, no
doubt made in jest in the anniversary issue, that he was simply a "mysterious
figure . . . who sort of stands around to see that the show isn't pinched." His
presence was clearly felt.

Watson's assistant officer-in-charge was 1st Lieut. Stephen T. Early—shortly
to be a captain—of Washington, D.C. He joined the staff on 12 December 1918
from the 317th Infantry, and quickly demonstrated his own considerable abilities.
Another man who assisted Watson was Army Field Clerk John M. Bucher, also
of Washington, D.C., who joined the paper's staff on 27 February 1919. These
men were all ex-officio members of the paper's editorial board, but Watson in
particular usually permitted the enlisted members thereof to have the final say
in the paper's day-to-day operations and local editorial decisions.

Another officer of importance was 1st Lieut. Charles Phelps Cushing, who
had shared the work of launching the paper, and served the new creation as its
first managing editor. From New York City, Cushing was a Marine officer. Capt.
Franklin P. Adams, another New Yorker, and formerly with *The New York
Tribune*, for a time wrote a column for the paper, submitting verse as well.[48] A
good example of the latter well illustrates the feelings, no doubt, of many staffers
attached to *The Stars and Stripes*:

Lines on Taking a New Job

When I was a civilian in the typing days of
        peace,
I spilled a column daily, *sans* vacation or sur-
        cease,
I whittled many a mournful wheeze and many
        a halting rhyme
To cop the fleeting jitney and to snare the
        elusive dime.

4. At the head of *The Stars and Stripes* in late 1918 and 1919 were (left to right): Maj. Mark S. Watson, Field Artillery, officer-in-charge; Maj. P.G. Mumford, Quartermaster Corps, financial advisor; and Capt. Stephen T. Early, assistant officer-in-charge. *Courtesy of National Archives*.

I jested by the carload and I frolicked by the
     bale,
When I used to write a column on the
                    New
                              York
                                        Mail.

The years continued flitting, as the years are
     wont to do,
Until one New Year's Eve I went and shifted
     my H.Q.
I wrote a ton of trifles and a mass of metric
     junk
To give me daily ammunish for my Barrage of
     Bunk.
Oh, many a paragraph I pulled and many a
     sassy squib,
When I ran a daily column on the
                    New
                              York
                                        Trib.

Goodbye, O dull serenity! Ye days of peace,
     farewell!
I went—Oho!—to fight the foe and hear the
     shot and shell.
Yet once again I find that I must hurl the
     merry josh,
Though I now command a column set against
     the beastly Boche.
But the grandest, proudest job I've ever had
     among the types
Is this job to run this column in
                    THE
                              STARS
                         AND
                                   STRIPES
                                        (29 March 1918)

First Lieut. Grantland Rice, another veteran of *The New York Tribune*, and of the 115th Field Artillery, and who also wrote verse, was at the time, in *The Stars and Stripes*' circles, best known for having taken over the sports page, only to kill it for the duration of the war on the grounds that there was more important news to report. He then became a reporter at the front.[49] More on the story of the sports page will be recounted later in a separate chapter.

Another ongoing feature of the paper was the much-discussed divisional histories launched after the Armistice which often elicited heated responses in the
letters column, when it seemed that their author, Capt. Joseph Mills Hanson,
had erred or had failed to give the "Umpty" division its proper due. These
articles collectively provide a detailed history of the AEF's operations.[50]

Capt. Harold W. Clark, late of *The Boston Herald*, aided *The Stars and Stripes*
in its work in the area of the S.O.S. and at the major French base at Tours.
Liaison at G.H.Q. was performed by Lieut. Robert S. Fendrick, who also assisted
Watson briefly, and Lieut. Earle Wingart.

Several officers contributed to the art production of the paper. Capt. Wallace
Morgan and Capt. Otho Cushing were among these, as were Lieut. Ray N.
Crosby, Lieut. Herbert Morton Stoopes, and one of the eight official AEF artists,
Capt. Ernest Peixotto. From the British Army, Capt. Bruce Bairnsfather, creator
of the famous "Old Bill" cartoons, provided the American paper with examples
of art. A contribution of the civilian Rube Goldberg appeared in the 7 February
1919 anniversary issue of the paper.[51]

From beginning to end, the paper was made up and composed in the composing
room of the Continental edition of *The London Daily Mail*, at 36 Rue de Sentier
in Paris. To accomplish this duty, four Yank printers were initially dispatched
from the 29th Engineers. These were Sgt. Richard S. Claiborne, who at age
forty-nine, was the oldest man on the paper. He had served in Cuba in the
Spanish-American War. The others were Pvt. Frank J. Hammer, Pvt. Herman
J. Miller, and Pvt. 1st Class Sigurd U. Bergh. These men were later joined by
others as the paper grew. Day and night shifts were operated by the British
paper. The day shift was supervised by James W. Faithful, a former corporal
in the Second London Rifles. The night shift was in the hands of Harry Layland.
Both of these men were supervised by John H. Roscoria, "a genial Cornishman,"
the *Daily Mail*'s master printer in Paris. The British paper, then, was "the first
of journalistic friends to extend a helping hand in the days of our recent infancy,"
as one account warmly expressed it (18 October 1918).

Until September 1918, the printing was also done at the *Daily Mail* plant, but
after that, when the circulation exceeded the *Mail*'s capacity, the printing was
taken over by the plant of *Le Journal* at 100 Rue de Richelieu, "a wonderfully
complete newspaper plant to which even our half-million press run [was] no
serious problem," one account explained. Indeed, the *Journal* "was unquestionably the finest newspaper plant in France."[52] This change was by courtesy
of *Le Journal*'s general manager, M. Le Page, whose gesture reflected the
"helpfulness and cooperation that exists among the Allied nations in other respects" (18 October 1918). Since the paper continued to be made up at the *Daily
Mail*, an Allied team of American, British and French printers and engravers
was responsible for the paper's production.[53]

The question was sometimes asked why the U.S. Army did not do the entire
task itself—and there is indication that Viskniskki thought that it eventually

5. Majors John W.F.M. Huffer (left) and Raoul Lufbery (right) talking to Capt. F.P. Adams (center), 18 April 1918. *Courtesy of National Archives.*

would—the answer was that though there were hundreds of presses in the Army and more than enough "olive drab" printers to do the job, there was not an issue press of sufficient size to print a half-million copies of an eight-page paper.

To be sure, when in July 1918, the Huns began shelling Paris with the famous long-range "Big Bertha," the sensation of the day, since no one could understand how the Germans could shell from such long distances, and the big newspapers contemplated leaving, a group of emergency printers was gathered and prepared "to publish *The Stars and Stripes* in Paris until the Boche should come in and stop us with bayonets, at which time it was planned to drop the pen, if need be, in favor of the sword" (7 February 1919). It never came to that and the would-be printers became field agents in charge of distribution.

The French also provided other assistance. *The Stars and Stripes*' "insatiable appetite for white paper"—precious stuff in wartime—was supplied by the Société Anonyme des Papeteries Darblay until late in the paper's career, when supplies came in from the United States.[54]

The Stars and Stripes was admittedly a rather expensive paper. At a time when an American paper could be purchased in Paris for fifteen centimes, *The Stars and Stripes* cost an unvarying fifty centimes (worth about ten cents) an issue. There had been some debate as to whether or not to charge at all. The decision to do so was based on the consideration that "it would have been a long and uncertain project to start the paper unless it had promised to be self-supporting." This it indeed was almost immediately and went on to amass very considerable profits. "Then the fact that the doughboy paid his ten cents for every issue made it possible for us to remind all and sundry from time to time that the paper was his and that every one else in the world could keep hands off." A final reason was that "no American ever did or ever will respect reading matter that is thrown at him like a department store bulletin" (7 February 1919).[55]

It was widely acknowledged that were the paper to be successful an effective distribution and circulation scheme must be devised, since difficulties in this regard had proved "insurmountable with other armies." What seemed to be required was to bring in someone with wide experience in American distribution practices. That man proved to be Capt. Richard H. Waldo, who had been with *The New York Times* and *Good Housekeeping* magazine. Arriving in April of 1918, he closely studied the problem and concluded that the paper must be distributed through selected centers. In the United States, every town with a railroad station was classed as a center and the key to rapid distribution. Waldo had closely studied the successful methods of circulation developed by *The Saturday Evening Post* which employed the method of focusing on distribution centers. In the AEF, natural centers were the Army Post Offices. Waldo proposed to place field agents at each APO to which the papers would be sent either by rail or by truck. The agent would be responsible for servicing all units served by their particular APO. As to the individual soldier, Waldo devised a coupon plan consisting of twenty-six coupons which the purchaser bought in advance for eight francs. The coupon permitted the bearer to obtain a copy of the paper from the nearest source of supply. The coupon sheet lasted for a longer period than twenty-six weeks, giving the soldier time to consume his coupon sheet before the expiration date. For example, the first series were from May to 31 December 1918. If the purchaser failed to expend his coupons in the time limit, he would be reimbursed for the unused coupons. The advantages were that the cash received in advance enabled the paper to underwrite or expand operations. Further, it lightened the burden on the field agents, since collections were simplified. Finally, the readers profited because paydays were uncertain in the AEF, and they could be assured of their paper even when they were broke, a common occurrence apparently.[56] Waldo's scheme received the prompt approval of the Board of Control, and the high command issued Bulletin No. 26, which modified the subscription plan outlined in Bulletin No. 10.[57] The plan was immediately successful, and Viskniskki asked that a note of commendation be sent to Waldo, "so that this paper may be placed before him as a concrete evidence of appreciation of his work." Lieutenant Colonel McCabe, then chief of G-2-D, complied, stating that "this officer's untiring efforts in organizing and building up the circulation of our splendid official paper are recognized and highly appreciated by these Headquarters."[58] Viskniskki's appreciation did not stand in the way of his summarily relieving Waldo of his duties in Paris and sending him hastily to the London office, which Waldo did not understand. However, when in certain quarters inquiries were made and attempts were made to bring Waldo back to the Paris office, Watson stated that he was opposed to it, and furthermore, "a cursory inquiry at the paper . . . indicated that almost all of the business office personnel was extremely well pleased to have him gone."[59] In any case, Waldo had served the paper well and was to continue to attempt to do so from London, which will be discussed later.

One by-product of the paper's efficient distribution and collection system, and its high profits, came on 16 August 1918: the instituting of a special service to the sick and wounded in the hospitals. The paper was henceforth provided to these patients at the rate of one copy to each three cots. The cost was equally shared by the American Red Cross which also distributed the paper. The editors pointedly asked that "the colonel, . . . [and] every man and woman at work in the hospitals, help us by seeing that when the gift edition arrives each week, not a needless minute is lost in distributing every copy of it . . . to whom it belongs—the Yankee sick and wounded." Members of the staff were enjoined to wait until they had read their copies before taking them, or, perhaps better still, subscribing to their own (16 August 1918).[60]

To be sure, the tasks of the circulation department were never ending, largely because "*The Stars and Stripes* could not do its papers into bundles and dump them on the government for distribution." In fact, it had to do its own, "even to the uttermost reader, and it had to send out its copies to a constantly moving public, which complicated the problem by always shrouding each move in the most baffling secrecy" (7 February 1919).

The man who replaced Capt. Waldo was 1st Lieut. Milton J. Ayers, an infantry officer. He had to supervise the activities of the field agents, numbering eventually 121 men and one lone officer, which were attached to each division and other major units as well as the APOs. They handled the paper's affairs for subscribers and usually about midnight met their shipments at the train station or received them by auto or truck. *The Stars and Stripes* owed an inestimable debt to the field agent, who, "in good weather and in bad, over shelled and unshelled roads, day after day, rainy night after rainy night, week after week," plugged along and got the paper to the men (13 June 1919). This was accomplished, "no matter how much the units may have moved about since the last issue, and often he moves along roads where shell pops send his heart into his mouth because he thinks they are blowouts. He is up against a circulation problem unique in the history of printing. But he delivers the goods" (26 July 1918). On at least one occasion, at the height of the action in the Argonne Forest, on 4 and 5 October 1918, American pilots dropped 2,200 copies of the paper by aircraft since the shell-torn roads were in such bad shape that even the trusty Fords were hard put to travel. Also more urgent traffic was traversing the roads that were passable. The American ace, Capt. Eddie Rickenbacker, was one of the aerial newsboys. This venture also led to some speculation about the reception of the paper in the German lines, as some of the air-dropped copies drifted into their territory at Mouzon and Sedan (18 October 1918).

There were no casualties among the intrepid agents, though there were opportunities enough, and many thrilling tales were told by some of them. One story has it that on the very day of the Armistice, two field agents on their rounds proceeded a little too far in looking for their customers, men of the 90th Division. As the paper recounted it, a "more or less muddy and decrepit Ford motor truck," blundered into the German lines a short time before 11:00 A.M., the magic hour for the cease fire, and was captured. The Germans "searched the bus, but found, to their sorrow, that it contained merely two large, fat mail sacks containing the latest editions of *The Stars and Stripes*." While being held, the men, being Americans, "effected a few investments in first-class Boche souvenirs." They were released at eleven o'clock and continued with their errand.[61]

Obviously, "the business department of *The Stars and Stripes* [had] been a somewhat wild and woolly affair. . . . But how could the . . . business department of a newspaper with a 550,000 circulation in a go-getting Army be anything else?" (7 February 1919).[62]

The circulation department was also assisted in its mighty efforts by the largest French distributor of periodicals, Hachette et Cie., which circulated *The Stars and Stripes* to news dealers throughout France and handled express shipments to military field agents and the YMCA huts. In this, the company did more than was strictly necessary from a business standpoint, acting "with a sense of that international courtesy that is helping materially to win the war" (26 July 1918).[63]

Closely related to the circulation department was that of transportation, which provided the field agents with their autos and trucks. This department was run by Sgt. Joseph G. Daly. He was responsible for the ninety-one government vehicles used, which included eighty-one "humble" Fords; five Sunbeams; three Cadillacs; one National; and a motorcycle, driven by one of the paper's characters, "Motorcycle Mike" (13 June 1919).[64]

Two other departments were responsible for getting out mailings. The Addressograph department had the weekly task of addressing the more than 70,000 single subscriptions to persons in the United States. This job was done originally on typewriters but soon became impracticable. The Addressograph system used machines made in France and proved highly satisfactory. Sgt. Nestor J. Born was the first in charge; he was later succeeded by Sgt. Thomas R. Healy, who remained to the end of operations. The mailing department also had much to do and required a force of from ten to fifteen men to keep pace with the work load. Sgt. Earl E. Riley first headed the department. He was later replaced by Sgt. Harry L. Katz. Both of the men had many years of experience with various publications in the United States prior to their entering the Army.[65]

Given the paper's success, it is only natural that plans were made to expand its operations. As early as June 1918, Viskniskki was sufficiently impressed with the rapidly increasing circulation to propose converting his weekly to a daily. Through twenty issues, the paper's run had reached almost 100,000 copies. He anticipated—correctly as it turned out—a circulation of over 500,000. He suggested, therefore, that the Army take over the plant of the Paris edition of *The New York Herald*, for the exclusive use of *The Stars and Stripes*. He justified his plans by observing, somewhat implausibly, that "a million persons in civil life back home not kept in constant touch with one another and events by means of the daily newspaper, would speedily deteriorate in civic morale." This would be the case for an army of a million men, he asserted, fighting thousands of miles from home, which in far greater measure needed "the stimulus and comfort of a daily newspaper of its own."[66]

Even Watson, at a later time, recognized that after the Armistice, with more leisure time for reading available to the men, the paper's circulation could easily top 700,000. He likewise felt that an enlarged paper was in order. Though he did not contemplate its becoming a daily, largely because of the paper shortage, he did conclude that the paper could easily be enlarged to twelve pages since, as he observed, "we throw away barrels of stuff every week because of lack of space." He also desired to limit advertising so as to print more news.[67]

But two of Viskniskki's most ambitious schemes were the creation of American and British editions of *The Stars and Stripes*. As to the former, he found enthusiastic allies in Muller and A. W. Erickson, the paper's advertising manager in the United States. Erickson seems to have been motivated, at least in part, by the desire to control the paper's advertising content more closely since many American advertisers vociferously complained that they had to compete, unfairly, for space in *The Stars and Stripes* with European advertisers. The paper, in short, was too "foreign" for their taste.[68] Erickson had written that "*The Stars and Stripes*, I think, is more popular in the United States today than ever before. . . . We have a hundred letters a week or more inquiring . . . especially about how they can subscribe. In fact, *The Stars and Stripes* is quite a proposition in this office at the present time.'' This went into Viskniskki's brief, and was "of itself a splendid argument for the speedy establishment of the American Edition,'' he argued.[69]

Erickson did not simply encourage the edition; he obtained permission from the War Industries Board for the necessary paper to reprint it. This procedure was in fact felt to be logical: Why send paper to France to publish the paper only to have it sent back to subscribers in the United States? Viskniskki happily concluded that the U.S. Government, "to all intents and purposes, had given its consent,'' and he perceived that the path was clear for a "go ahead'' order on the American Edition.[70] Also, the Red Cross, through Col. Harvey Gibson, its head in France, promised to take over sales and distribution of the new paper in the United States, all profits of which would go to care for sick and wounded U.S. servicemen.[71]

The plans were that the paper would be printed from a set of matrices sent from Paris to New York by a weekly courier and placed in the hands of Muller, who once more offered his assistance without charge. The first issue was expected off the presses by 1 December 1918. All that remained was for the final order to be given, and Nolan recommended that Pershing wire Washington for permission to proceed.[72] Unfortunately for Viskniskki, the Armistice intervened and, together with the Hohenzollern dynasty, one of its casualties was the American Edition of *The Stars and Stripes*, now quietly dropped.[73]

Simultaneous with Viskniskki's maturing plans for an American Edition were those for a British Edition. The paper had already opened a London office, headquartered at the Goring Hotel, on 15 June 1918, to handle circulation in the British Isles. It was in the charge of 2nd Lieut. William Carl Cartinhour and a small staff. By September, the paper's subscribers there numbered over 9,000. Cartinhour reported that the opportunities for growth were considerable. There were about 20,000 U.S. troops then stationed there and some 43,000 U.S. sailors and officers at five major bases. There were numerous hospitals and rest camps there as well. Furthermore, the men then being sent to Russia were being equipped in England and Col. George Stewart, commander of the 339th Infantry Regiment, the main force being assembled for service in North Russia, had firmly asserted: "We must get the paper."[74]

In the meantime, though, there seemed to be other reasons for Viskniskki's actions. On 19 August 1918, he abruptly ordered Captain Waldo to London to prepare for the launching of the British Edition. Despite his bewilderment and chagrin at this turn of events, since he felt that Cartinhour was more than qualified to handle the matter, Waldo complied and soon had things well in hand. He had obtained Northcliffe's consent to use certain of his newspaper presses in London which could easily handle the press run of 100,000 copies which would soon be needed. The British Paper Controller promised up to five tons of newsprint weekly at the attractive price of ten cents per pound. He had lined up the news agencies, as W. H. Smith and Sons, Ltd., to circulate the paper in England and

Wales, and expected that Charles Eason and Sons, Ltd., would do the same in Ireland as would Menzies, Ltd., in Scotland. He had obtained the cooperation of Adm. W. S. Sims, the U.S. Navy commander-in-chief in Britain, who agreed to set up a field agent system at naval bases.

As was the case in the United States, it was planned that a complete set of matrices of the Paris Edition of the paper would be sent to London by courier each Thursday, arriving by noon Friday. This would permit the printing of the paper on Friday night, and its circulation throughout Great Britain on Saturday. Waldo suggested that the process might be speeded up if the matrices came by airplane.[75] Viskniskki promised a quick decision by G.H.Q., with which Waldo was in firm agreement, as many people were "on hold, . . . all of whom have shown embarrassing interest in the matter."[76]

These hopes were soon realized. Maj. Gen. John Biddle, commanding general of Base Section No. 3, S.O.S., AEF, in England, the senior Army officer present, telegraphed G.H.Q. his approval and Chaumont soon concurred. Viskniskki happily cabled Waldo "English Edition authorized," and placed him in charge. The first issue was to roll off the presses on 15 November, Waldo being exhorted that "there will be no change whatever in the wording of the English edition from that of the French edition." All business and editorial functions were to remain in Paris; Waldo's main job was in printing and distribution.[77] To assist him in his now pressing tasks, Lieutenant Ayers sent him four men from the Paris office, skilled in printing, mailing and circulation matters.[78]

Once again, the Armistice interposed its considerable presence. Before the first issue could appear, upon being ordered to do so, Biddle withdrew his permission because "85% of the personnel in England will be en route for the United States within 10 days." They did not leave quite that quickly; in any case, the British Edition was dead. Waldo was ordered to return the four men to Paris immediately, and to remain in charge in London until further notice, marking the last that we hear of Waldo.[79]

Viskniskki's exertions in these failed ventures must have demoralized him considerably and no doubt contributed to his being relieved from duty only a matter of days later on 29 November 1918. He had been more successful, though, in fending off would-be rivals to his paper's exclusive rights as the official publication of the AEF, as Bulletin No. 10 had specified. There were at least two major challengers, however. For a time, the U.S. Navy toyed with the idea of producing its own official paper. When one considers the paucity of news published in The Stars and Stripes on naval matters, one does not wonder at the Navy's interest. Nevertheless, The Stars and Stripes' Board of Control was able to thwart this ambition.[80]

More formidable was the earlier threat posed by the U.S. Air Service which had succeeded in launching a publication at Issoudon, the great training and repair base, under the title, The Plane News. Made aware of the challenge, Viskniskki made haste to inform G-2-D that were the paper to receive authorization, all other arms could logically follow suit, "until there would be a plague

of official publications, even down to regimental and company trench papers,''
leading to much confusion, misunderstanding and embarrassment. He strongly
recommended, therefore, that ''those who desire to ape *The Stars and Stripes*
as being official should receive no encouragement.''[81] Viskniskki was promised
that such developments would be ''closely watched,'' it being recognized that
''more than one official publication of the A.E.F. would . . . lead to confusion
of considerable magnitude.''[82] To be sure, numerous newspapers did spring up,
eventually like mushrooms, but none was able to attain official status until later.

In the meantime, *The Stars and Stripes* developed apace. It became famous
for many of its features, notably its editorial page, its cartoons and artwork, and
its poetry. Indeed, the column devoted to ''The Army's Poets,'' was perhaps
the most widely read of all. It seemed to some observers that almost everyone
who served on the staff of the paper wrote poetry. Certain it is that the AEF,
''the most sentimental outfit that ever lived,'' read much poetry and sent in
thousands of poems to the editors. The men also cut out poems, sent them home
or pinned or pasted them up in dugouts, in Adrian barracks and mess shacks,
and laughed or wept over them. And even though often faulty as to the standards
of good poetry, the typical poem ''rang true, every syllable of it,'' since ''it
was inspired by mud and cooties and gas and mess-kits and Boche 77's and
home and mother, all subordinated to a determination to stick it through whatever
the time and pains involved.''[83] To be sure, some of the poems were written by
some established writers of verse, but the bulk were from the field. In any event,
the poems reveal that ''under the stress of war the literature of a country receives
an impetus.''[84] This was certainly true of the men most directly under the impress
of war and its horrors, the rank and file of the AEF. This being the case, the
Army's poets were regarded as its true interpreters, and poetry was not considered
by the paper's staff as a mere fad; rather it was ''a *Stars and Stripes* necessity''
(7 February 1919). The paper received enough verse every week ''to fill a volume
as thick as Browning's Complete Works,'' in actuality about 500 per week. Of
the 384 poems published in the paper's first year, about forty were written by
the staff; the remainder were contributed by the AEF at large. Only about a
dozen were not the work of soldiers (7 February 1919). Obviously, it all could
not be used, not even all of the best, which simply had to be skimmed. By the
best, however, was meant ''not the most rhythmical, the most polished, the most
felicitously phrased verses.'' In truth, ''many a poem printed in these recent
tumultuous weeks has limped along on crutches and been linked together with
questionable rhymes. Sometimes these little bits of awkwardness, before being
printed, have been camouflaged as well as might be without hurting the sentiment.
Sometimes they have been allowed to stand.'' This was the case, ''for the
sentiment must not be touched. And it is sentiment—heart, if you care to call
it that—that all of this verse possesses as verse seldom possessed it before. The
Army's Poets are the spokesmen of the Army's soul.'' And that soul had a
message, the same message, ''whether it comes from base port or front line. It
speaks the Army's longing and love for things and friends across the seas, of

slum and cooties and mud; it speaks the Army's determination to see this thing through, to keep at this bitter and glorious business of war until the high aims for which it is fighting are achieved, when the Army's Poets in unison shall interpret the Army's soul in a paean of victory."[85]

However, one problem regarding poetry constantly plagued the editors, that of plagiarism and the submission of filthy poems. An editorial, entitled "Naughty! Naughty!," attempted to shame the men about both. As to the latter, the policy was that smutty verse would simply not be considered, despite the "Rude Voice From the Rear." The paper also would manage to suppress its desire "to publish a submitted poem because it is so very good it was printed somewhere else long before we ever got a chance." All of this was said "by way of a gentle warning" (10 May 1918).

But gentle warnings did not suffice and the editors could be forthright, especially regarding plagiarism. An editorial in the 17 May 1918 issue, headed "Private Gaugler To The Bar," singled out Pvt. Clarence W. Gaugler of the Quartermaster Corps for strong rebuke since he had signed as his own a poem sent and published in the paper on 3 May. A reader had seen the poem earlier in *The Literary Digest*, and wrote in to complain. The editor's parting shot was, "what have you to say to the charge that you are a thief?"[86]

Another development in the history of *The Stars and Stripes* should be discussed, that of how the personnel lived in Paris. For administrative purposes they were eventually organized as the Censor and Press Company No. 1, commanded by Capt. Harry L. Parker, assisted by 2d Lieut. Donald R. Brenton. Some of their supply and commissary needs were met by their own supply department and canteen.[87] However, the matters of billets and messing remained a problem from start to finish.

The men were at first billeted and messed in the Hotel Sainte Anne, with many of the men on commutation of rations and quarters, where the paper's small office was located. However, the hotel was used to house prisoners awaiting trial and transients. Many of the prisoners worked on K.P., but were dirty, and the food was exceedingly bad.[88] A decision was accordingly made to transfer the men to two other hotels: the Méditerrannée and the Alexandria. These were not satisfactory either, as the men were too far from the paper's office and again were associated with prisoners and transients. There were numerous complaints of the loss of private property as many men were quartered in the same room and some even slept in the halls, sometimes on cots and often simply on the floor. These bad conditions were apparently responsible for the death of Pvt. Carl McIntosh of the paper's staff from bronchial pneumonia.[89] This intolerable situation resulted in preemptive orders from Pershing to Harbord, then head of the S.O.S., immediately to find suitable quarters for the men on the paper.[90] In the meantime, Viskniskki was able to quarter and mess his men at the Hotel Russie, which was only a five-minute walk from the offices of the paper and had more room space which could also be locked by the residents, thereby protecting their private property.[91]

These arrangements proved to be shortlived; the Russie Hotel was soon abandoned, and by January, the personnel of *The Stars and Stripes* were once more adrift. The solution seemed to be to house and mess all of the paper's personnel at the Clignancourt Barracks, on the outskirts of Paris, which had, in the meantime, been provided by the AEF as a transient barracks for men on leave in Paris and for the men stationed there. But the paper's staffers were unanimously opposed to living there. They once more found themselves in a transient barracks with the attendant loss of personal effects.[92] Furthermore, the men had to stand guard; were subject to unannounced physical examinations; there was often no hot water; the barracks were too noisy for sleep, and many of the men worked night shifts; and the barracks were so far from the offices as to make taking meals there impractical. The loss of morale was great and Parker argued that "the men of this Company are on the average a higher type of man than the ordinary soldier," and simply should not be left in such a debilitating environment.[93]

Watson could only agree. He had attempted to improve conditions for his men through the barracks commander, Col. John H. Parker, with little result. Capt. Harry Parker thereupon decided to live at the base so as to help the men where he could, but this seemed little enough, and Watson bitterly complained that the paper was being provoked by people who did not understand that *The Stars and Stripes* "cannot be run as a Labor Battalion." The paper had been brilliant, he continued, "because G.H.Q. [had] protected [it] from influences, which fail to understand its purpose and the manner of achieving this purpose." But, if, "as is now likely in spite of G.H.Q. and in spite of common sense, the paper is to be harassed and its personnel subjected to treatment which cannot be described except as positive stupidity, *The Stars and Stripes* will immediately lose its character and the loss to the A.E.F. . . . will in my opinion be extremely serious."[94]

The solution seemed to be to place as many men as possible on commutation of rations and quarters, especially those on night shifts and on such as the editorial staff who worked irregular hours. Some already enjoyed this status. However, one difficulty was that the government allowance of $1.75 per day was not adequate. Watson, therefore, asked that as many men as possible not only be placed on a commutation basis, but that the paper's treasurer be allowed to pay them a supplement of $1.25, already being paid to some, giving the men $3.00 per diem expense money. Were this not permitted, the men simply could not live in Paris, "and *The Stars and Stripes* consequently will be unable to publish."[95]

Meanwhile, Nolan also attempted to obtain the special commutation payments for them, citing the staff's low morale over the issue.[96] However, the Judge Advocate of the AEF ruled that no special treatment would be permitted and hence the commutation payments must revert to the authorized allowance of fifty cents per day for quarters, and $1.25 for food. The paper complied but failed to see how it could continue to function.[97] Chaumont thereupon decided upon what it hoped would be a solution. The major problem was the high cost of food in Paris. Hence, all men on commutation of rations were to be provided with messing facilities at the Duval restaurant, located at 11 Boulevard Poissonnière. A contract was draw up, and by late March this arrangement was functioning. This provided that the Duval restaurant serve *Stars and Stripes*' personnel three meals per day at regular prices, those being three francs for breakfast, five for dinner and seven for supper. Special tables on the second floor of the establishment were permanently reserved for the men and special employees were to cook and serve for them. A sergeant was detailed to Duval's staff to see that the meals were properly prepared and that the commissary supplies, which were made available to the restaurant, were only used for soldiers' meals. The men on commutation of rations must surrender the payments and sign for their meals, the tickets for which were to be redeemed by *The Stars and Stripes*. If the men ordered additional food in excess of the usual fare, that had to be paid for by the individual. Officers were not included in the arrangement, since they had the privilege of eating where they pleased.[98]

This solution seems to have satisfied the men on commutation of rations. However, Watson could not justify putting the entire staff on this basis as their regular daytime hours made it possible for them to continue on at the Clignancourt Barracks, much to their dismay. Watson did not continue to fight for their transfer because the paper was almost at the end of its career by this time. In any case, those men who could subsequently convince Watson or Parker of the need to be placed on commutation status were done so as several orders to this effect reveal.[99]

Other aspects of the paper's operations of a somewhat lesser importance are nevertheless worthy of inclusion in this narrative. From its beginning, Cpl. George P. Wrench was the paper's courier. He made numerous trips across the English Channel in tug boats, submarine chasers and other vessels in order to carry copies of the paper to American soldiers stationed in England. He also carried official documents between bases in England and Paris.[100] Though some members of the staff spoke tolerable French, it was necessary to employ an interpreter. He was Pvt. Robert S. Dilly of the French Army, a disabled soldier and a Parisian. Beyond his skills as an interpreter he was a good source of information regarding his native haunts which the staff often desired, for various reasons.[101]

Subsequently, when the AEF began to move homeward in ever greater numbers, the staff of *The Stars and Stripes* most decidedly wanted to join the parade. As early as March of 1919, Watson advised that office morale was being maintained largely on the understanding that the paper would suspend operations about 1 May; even at that, the men had "to be goaded to mental effort." The major reason was that the editorial staff in particular had excellent offers for positions in the United States and were anxious to get back.[102] Several other developments also occurred. One was a dwindling circulation. In addition, many newspapers had begun to spring up in all sorts of units, one of which served the interests of the Third Army in Germany which was soon to be the most significant

American military group in Europe.[103] It was felt that these sheets would better serve the interests of the American doughboy in the months ahead. Furthermore, orders came on 30 April discharging key people such as Ryder, Woolicott, Baldridge, Ross and Winterich. Seth Bailey also hastily departed since his sister was dying and he was rushed home.[104] Woollcott, Baldridge, Ross and Winterich took their discharges in France at St. Aignan and according to Watson, in a letter to A. W. Erickson, made their way home "in civilian clothes on a weird sort of a tour, touching North Africa, Gibraltar, and the Azores." He hoped with Von Blon, who had replaced Ross, and "Tip" Bliss and Hawley, and a few of the other old hands, to continue to publish the paper, it by then having been anticipated that production would only end on 4 July. This termination date corresponded with the winding up of the athletic program, "which seems to have become the most important activity of the A.E.F.," Watson rather contemptuously concluded.[105]

However, a few days before Watson wrote his letter to Erickson on 6 May, Pershing visited the paper's office and addressed the men, assuring them that he wanted to chop off the paper in its prime rather than see it dwindle and was willing to see this done even before 4 July.[106] Shortly thereafter, Nolan received orders that the issue of 13 June would be the last, and on 10 June he issued his own orders. The document transmitting these also observed that "certainly, no other newspaper was ever born of a greater need than was *The Stars and Stripes.*" It was also certain "that no other newspaper ever served its needs with more loyalty and ability. To bring cheer, smiles, news from home, news from places of interest in the land they were fighting in, to 2,000,000 men thousands of miles from the United States and, in addition, to encourage these men to fight with smiles and confidence was a fraction of the needs your labors supplied."[107] The paper made haste to comply with its instructions, and the issue of 13 June was indeed the last. This also contained the only pictorial supplement published in the paper's career, featuring photographs depicting the history of the paper.[108] Subsequently, the members of Censor and Press Company No. 1 assembled at Clignancourt Barracks on 17 June, and prepared to depart. After a night journey on the French train, the "Victory Flier," they reached Brest, and on 1 July they saw the shores of France fade from sight from the decks of the U.S. Army Transport *Pretoria*. Twelve days later, the company landed at Hoboken and went immediately to Camp Mills, near New York City. The unit was there broken up into casual companies, and the men were sent to camps nearest their homes and discharged. So, in this usual, prosaic Army fashion, "passed an organization that had made history of an everlasting quality and [which] had materially aided its country in a time of need."[109]

2

Advertising

Every Friday with me is a red-letter day, because your paper comes around as regular as clockwork, and every item is read, from the title down to the advertisement of Wrigley's Chewing Gum.

1st Lieut. J. A. Purcell
(5 July 1918)

The New York Sunday Sun once praised *The Stars and Stripes* for providing "genuinely good reading about the war," further observing that the advertisements, "of which there is a wholesome looking acreage, are as interesting as the columns they adjoin" (3 May 1918). Though *The Stars and Stripes* would have been solvent without any advertising, the money helped, and there were other good reasons for including ads: they seemed to be the kind of reading matter that the doughboys craved and they gave the paper an air of success.

The paper's advertising policy was early set forth by the Board of Control. There were to be no liquor ads; no advertisements of patent medicines nor "fakes"; nothing obscene; and no political matter. Neither were ads to be keyed to special spots in the paper.[1] The paper soon obtained the services of two competent advertising agencies. Of these, the A. W. Erickson Advertising Agency of New York City efficiently handled the paper's advertising in the United States and Canada. The firm solicited copy, collected the fees, distributed *The Stars and Stripes* to agents and advertisers, attended to the billing, kept the books, sent out promotion materials, and in general ran the American end, all without pay. Though not contributing its services gratis, the advertising representative for Great Britain was the Dorland Agency, Ltd., 16 Regent Street, London. However, its connection with the paper was ended in late November of 1918, and Peggy Quainton, who had been in charge of the paper's account at the agency, took on these affairs on her own.[2] At the paper, the first advertising manager was 1st Lieut. William K. Michael, of the 101st Machine Gun Battalion, who worked in that capacity until 6 February 1919, when 2d Lieut. Raymond S. Fendrick, a cavalry officer attached to the Air Service, replaced him for some weeks. Sgts. George E. Mulvaney and Harold Sigmund, and Cpl. Saul Goldberg assisted the officers.[3]

A. W. Erickson was apprised of the planned paper a month or so before it began publication; in fact, Viskniskki put Erickson on the spot, informing him that he had "told [the] General Staff they can surely depend on you to get advertisements for [the] paper, which must be self-sustaining, from firms [that] America [is] doing [a] large army business [with] and whose products [are] greatly in demand by soldiers." He needed five hundred linear inches per issue, to be sold initially at one dollar per inch. He told Erickson that if he were interested, to sign up firms for three-month advertising contracts.[4]

In this way was launched a sometimes stormy but workable relationship. Erickson seemed more than pleased to cooperate, concluding that it was his patriotic duty to serve as the paper's agent without charge, though at some inconvenience, and as it proved, vexation, to himself.

One of the disturbing things was that when Erickson lined up the advertising as instructed so little of it appeared in print. This was naturally a matter of considerable concern, especially to the advertisers involved. As Erickson rather sourly wrote to Viskniskki on one occasion, noting that in many letters he had been informed of how the boys like to see "good old American advertising," it seemed to him that "they are not seeing as much as they could." He did not desire to continue hustling ads that were not going to appear. In fact, "this is creating an unsatisfactory situation," because, as he chided, "you asked for 500 inches; you are inserting only 100." Surely, Viskniskki "could make a better showing than you are doing." Another sore spot was that the paper looked "like a foreign paper at the present time," and "all the advertisers are getting hot under the collar and we are getting howls of dissatisfaction."[5]

A cable emphasized the same message: "American Tobacco Company greatly disturbed you are not running Bull Durham advertising. Get it in immediately. Can't you run more American advertising [?] Everybody [is] kicking."[6]

And they continued to kick. In mid-October of 1918, Erickson once more wrote that advertisers were "frightfully sore at us because they get so little advertising and the foreigners get so much." He noted, for example, that in the 20 September 1918 issue American advertising totalled only 138 inches, while foreign advertising reached 329 inches.[7]

Other tensions resulted from errors that appeared; on one occasion the Arrow Collar ad appeared twice in the same issue—that of 4 April 1919.[8] Furthermore, advertisers were often not pleased with their ad's placement. Hart Schaffner and Marx, for instance, complained that their presentation was "not receiving due prominence," and asked for a better positioning of their advertisements.[9]

These matters no doubt contributed to the firm, even enthusiastic, support that Erickson accorded Viskniskki's proposed American Edition. He not only obtained permission of the War Industries Board to print it, he also lined up the financing of the venture if required. A Mr. Knapp, who controlled the lighting industry in Chicago, as well as being the owner of the Acetylene Products Industry of America, had agreed to underwrite the planned edition.[10] Though Viskniskki intended to make the American paper identical to the Paris Edition, and strictly controlled from that office, no doubt Erickson had other ideas.

Another sore spot was the steadily increasing advertising rates. The paper's business people were not entirely ignorant of methods of computing charges and were never loath to implement raises. They were aware that every substantial increase in circulation justified a rate increase and acted accordingly. For example, by the 4 October 1918 issue, the original one dollar per inch had risen to $7.50 per inch, as the paper's circulation had by then reached 260,000.[11] As of the first of January 1919, when circulation reached 500,000, the American advertising rate was set at $11.50 per inch; by 4 April 1919, when the paper was scheduled to exceed 600,000—though it never reached this figure—the cost was to be $14.00 per inch.[12]

These increases caused Erickson some embarrassments, and he noted on one occasion that the Ivory Soap people did not wish to continue their ads if the rate went up, since "this order was sent up purely as a matter of sentiment as the goods are not on sale in France," though they later became available.[13]

Still, Erickson was able to obtain more than enough advertising, though he admitted that it was much more difficult to procure after the Armistice, because "the edge of enthusiasm has been dulled and the war fever is past."[14] Then, too, the failures to print ads continued to irritate. As late as the end of April of 1919, Erickson once more observed that "as you know, we have been after [advertisers] very hard for contracts, and it is very embarrassing sometimes to try to explain the omission of [their ads]."[15]

But business was still sufficiently good for Erickson to open a separate little office and hire two people to run it at fifty dollars per week. This was rent free to the paper and Erickson also reminded the Paris office that "of course, there is no charge for the work which Mr. Bennett, myself, and some of the other men in the Agency are giving *The Stars and Stripes*. That is our little bit and we are willing to keep it up."[16]

Erickson's helpfulness made it extremely difficult for him to comprehend a scathing letter that he received quite unexpectedly from 2nd Lieut. Raymond S. Fendrick, in April of 1919, in which he stated that "an opinion that prevails, locally, in this office, that it would not be a real newspaper without some advertising in it, is rot." Fendrick went on to say that "advertising revenue has never been vital to the paper." Erickson, when he received the letter, "felt like resigning and cussing besides." For over a year, he complained, he had been "giving a tremendous amount of valuable time . . . trying to secure advertising for a publication which [now] writes me that it is so profitable that it doesn't need any advertising and is so proud that it doesn't want any." Erickson could only say that "in all my experience I have never been handed anything just like this and I am afraid the Lieutenant has had very little experience not only in publishing but in ordinary business affairs.'' In fact, he decided that ''we are too busy trying to make a living to give a lot of time to things that are not essential,'' and resigned. But Watson and Ayers, apprised of the damage that Fendrick had done, in separate cablegrams, hastily asked him to reconsider. Mollified, he did so, assured by Watson that his work was indeed greatly appreciated and he should not be nonplussed by ''the exasperating letter sent you by a boy, who . . . has left to seek other employment.'' Subsequently, Erickson continued to represent the paper's advertising interests for the remaining few weeks of its life.[17]

The British connection with the Dorland Agency was initiated by H. P. Somner of that firm. In a flattering letter he described the paper's almost instantaneous success, and ''I found everyone in London talking about it, although until this morning, I was not able to secure a copy.'' He went on to say that ''at lunch today, instead of using my meat card, I had a light lunch and '[The] Stars and Stripes,' and found the latter very 'meaty' indeed.'' His professional eye was ''particularly struck by the very fine advertising copy that you are carrying, and . . . you have evidently a real live man on the job,'' as far as Paris was concerned. But he could also see a great need: ''so far, this great big city of London which is just hungry for an opportunity of making known its facilities for taking care of the requirements of the U.S. Forces is not yet represented.'' There was no reason why it could not be represented and he immediately offered his services.[18] An arrangement was speedily worked out, with a 20 percent commission being paid for services rendered, and the Dorland Agency was soon actively engaging advertisers for the paper, the paper's account having been turned over in the office to Peggy Quainton.[19]

Some of the same matters arose as with the Erickson firm, however, especially regarding the placement of ads, the British advertisers being even more sensitive on that point than were Americans. Quainton made every effort to please the customers, on one occasion writing that ''they are making a big stretch in advertising in a paper that depends largely on its French circulation, and the majority of adv.'s we have sent you are for the very best firms in London, so please, your nicest and best attention.''[20]

Lieutenant Michael readily agreed, and replied, ''you may rest assured that we will co-operate in every way to please our advertisers and will give them the best possible position in the paper at all times.''[21] However, these assurances were sometimes honored in the breach and tensions continued to surface from time to time on that score.

Another matter that had to be watched concerned censorship rules. An advertisement sent over to Paris for Gieve Waistcoats could not be used in its original form because, while the product was worthy, the leading display line focused on the numbers of men who had been shipwrecked since August 1914 and this information was not permitted to be published. Were the text altered, the ad could be run.[22]

Somner replied that he did understand the paper's position and "you simply mustn't think of me at all. I'll have to take the little unpleasant things with the pleasant and just keep smiling. That's my nature anyhow." In any case, he continued, "I have put myself heart and soul into the business of giving you a good representation, and we have only just begun to skim the field and have only approached the very best advertisers."[23] Peggy Quainton likewise noted that she was becoming acquainted with "your strict and rigid rules, and quite understand that they can not be departed from." She promised to carefully censor all material in the future.[24]

In another instance, one prominent British advertiser, the music dealer Darewski's, used the expression, "Nigger Stories" in an ad. Quainton persuaded those concerned to delete it in the interest of the sensibilities of certain Americans.[25]

But these amicable exchanges ended abruptly on 29 November 1918, when Viskniskki, for reasons not clear, but apparently involving some misunderstanding about advertising rates, cavalierly terminated the Dorland contract. The company was "astounded," and sent a representative, George Kettle, to Paris in an effort to resolve the difficulties. In this he was not successful.[26]

But the Dorland Agency's loss seemed to be a golden opportunity for Peggy Quainton who quickly entered into an agreement to represent the paper in London. Severing her relations with the company, she soon had her own contract.[27] She journeyed to Paris in late December to work out details of operations and was shortly fully engaged in her new position.[28] She did cause the London office some momentary consternation, claiming that she had the right to use its facilities, but Regimental Sgt. Maj. Alfred L. Prosser, on duty there, told her "that her position in the eyes of the A.E.F. was that of a civilian privately engaged in the advertising business and that while I am ready to co-operate with her in any reasonable way, she must be laboring under a false impression with regard to this." He plaintively asked the Paris office to "please disillusion her."[29]

This Mulvaney made haste to do and she was pointedly informed to hire her own office. While the London office would take care of mailing her correspondence on behalf of the paper, nothing else could be done. However, Captain McClatchy did say that she might use the office if Prosser was not in but this was a matter "left up to you both to settle as I can do nothing further from this end."[30] One gets the impression that Quainton was a formidable character.

Subsequently, a few documents crossed the channel between the Dorland Agency and the paper's Paris office. On 10 January 1919, Somner requested the return of advertising cuts as they had to pay for many of them. A pencilled notation on the letter, perhaps by Mulvaney, simply stated: "Unless they have personal ownership kiss them off."[31]

However, in the meantime, someone with a conscience, either at the paper or G.H.Q., undertook to resolve the differences between the agency and *The Stars and Stripes*. Accordingly, Capt. P. G. Mumford, the G-2 inspector for the paper, and a Major Swan, of the Judge Advocate's office, G.H.Q., AEF, went to London to sign an agreement that had been negotiated. It was recognized by the American officers that Viskniskki's action had been "without due cause," and the agency had, as a consequence, sustained losses. The agreement stipulated that the Dorland firm was to pay the paper for advertisements that had been sold, and *The Stars and Stripes*, in turn, would allow the firm to recover 11,200 francs in damages. All mutual claims were thereby renounced, and the matter ended "in an entirely amicable manner."[32]

Following this, at the agency's request, Watson returned their advertising mats and agreed to cease delivering copies of *The Stars and Stripes* to the agency's office. They had apparently seen all they wanted to see of the American paper.[33] Peggy Quainton continued to represent the paper's interest in London for the time remaining.

Unquestionably, the paper received much more advertising than it could use, not that it desired to use all of it. As the 7 February 1919 anniversary issue expressed it, one curious feature of the business department was that it served "for once, . . . a newspaper that did not care two sous about making money and . . . could look any damned advertiser in the face and tell him to go to hell." This point of view was nurtured by Viskniskki, among others. As he expressed it on one occasion, "the aim of *The Stars and Stripes* is morale, not money; patriotism, not profit. We labor to promote the things of the spirit, not the fullness of the pocketbook. The heart, not the dollar, controls the policy of the paper." To Viskniskki, "therein lies the secret of the paper's great hold on the affections and the morale of the Army. Deviate from this policy one iota, and the power of the paper wanes, a great morale-building-and-maintaining agency is dissipated and destroyed. The A.E.F. is the greatest heart adventure on record. *The Stars and Stripes'* sole mission is to reflect and stimulate and refresh that heart, and when heart and business clash, business (for the first time in the history of modern newspaperdom) must give way to heart." As he put it in Biblical terms: "What would it profit the A.E.F. if through *The Stars and Stripes* it gained all the francs in France and lost even a fraction of its high faith and hopes of the spirit?" Though the two gods of efficiency and system had a place at the paper, they were necessarily minor gods. The main god was that "of the Heart and Soul of the A.E.F." He had deliberately run the paper along these lines from the start, and vowed that he would so "insist on its being run as long as I am the Officer-in-Charge." He enjoined all members on the staff to keep these ideas constantly in mind as they performed their daily tasks.[34] Of course, when Lieutenant Fendrick later attempted to apply those truths literally, he ran afoul of Erickson and Watson.

The paper naturally encouraged its readers to patronize advertisers, and to "give them first call on your trade, . . . whenever you can. A firm that advertises in *The Stars and Stripes* proves by so doing that it has your interest at heart" (1 March 1918). The readers also obviously found some entertainment in the ads, and perhaps a comforting, familiar sight in a foreign, often hostile, environment, and they were at least something to read. As one doughboy, Pvt. Peter M. Walsh, of the field artillery put it, he was pleased to get newspapers from

his hometown, which were better than packages, because "even the advertisements [furnish] enjoyment" (5 July 1918). To some advertisers, then, the war
was an unusually good opportunity to make a good impression or to cash in on
a boom—a rapidly expanded market had suddenly appeared, as far as some
products were concerned; it remained only to exploit it. While a patriotic desire
to help along *The Stars and Stripes* and the AEF was not altogether absent, it
was clear that the paper's circulation, which reached over 526,000, more than
70,000 of which was in the United States, provided a sales opportunity which
should not be ignored.[35]

Some of the advertisers presented their ads in a straightforward fashion; other
presentations were cloying and saccharine; yet others were ludicrous, sometimes
resulting in considerable scorn from the doughboys, newly initiated into the
mysteries and habits of military life and ways.

Typical of the latter was a lengthy letter to the editor in the 21 February 1919
issue of the paper. Signed by "A.E.F. Grouch," it referred to an advertisement
by Hart Schaffner and Marx, appearing in the 7 February 1919 issue of the
paper. "If this firm, which expects to do a land office business when the boys
return to the U.S.A., really wants to realize this expectation, it had better get a
doughboy to illustrate its advertisements," he advised. Attention was called to
the fact that in one ad illustration "the three squads pictured have eight men to
the rank; it looks more like a crowd of hungry stevedores charging the mess
line. . . . [Furthermore], the artist, or perhaps cartoonist, who drew this evidently
has never been to the small towns of France, or he would know that it would
be an impossibility to march a column of eight files through the streets."

Some of the ads struck the men's fancy. In a short column, "Trench-Way
Ads," in the 21 June 1918 issue, an ad that appeared regularly in the paper was
parodied. "Under shell fire—Wear Paris Garters. No metal can touch you," a
reference to that advertiser's famous slogan.[36]

Though no mention was made of it, a Valentine's Valspar Varnish ad was no
doubt ridiculed, at least by men in the Air Service. That company announced
its pleasure in having "Valsparred" the Berkman Scout Aircraft—claimed to be
the "first American-built camouflaged airplane . . . [which could] climb higher
than the Woolworth Building and also return to earth in a single minute" (30
August 1918). This ludicrous piece was obviously written by someone intrigued
by the concept of camouflage—as many people seemed to be during this period—
and possessing little knowledge of aircraft.

Other advertisements affected the language of the trench and the cantonment.
Lowney's Chocolates, for instance, employed such slogans as: "Lowney's Chocolates—'Dig In' "; "Not a 'dud' in the box!'"; "A rational ration"; "Get some
before they Argonne! Ouch!"; and "That Victorious Taste."

No doubt many doughboys laughed loud and long over another notice that
appeared in the 17 May 1918 *Stars and Stripes*: "To Let or Sell in Perigord.
Beautiful Historical Chateau." Sited on 150 acres of arable land, it was nine
hours from Paris. Day trains with dining cars and night trains with sleeping cars

provided comfortable means of getting to the property. It was richly furnished, with linen and silverware, and possessed thirty rooms, two autos, and six carriages, all for 15,000 francs for the summer season or for sale at $100,000. The interested soldier could contact A. Libois, at 14 Rue Duphot in Paris.

Various hotels, restaurants, and theaters were included in the columns, launching a type of advertisement that continued from first to last. The Elysée Restaurant on Coventry Street, Piccadilly Circus, made a strong bid for Yank business: "American Officers and Men Greetings! May you have the best of luck in France. The Allies cannot thank you sufficiently for coming over. To posterity must be left the full appreciation of your glorious and victorious sacrifices." Since this particular advertisement appeared in the 17 May 1918 issue of *The Stars and Stripes*, the "glorious and victorious sacrifices" were mainly in the future, but when they did come later in the summer, the restaurant was among the first to extend "Congrats" to the AEF, "on your recent achievements. Glorious! May your luck and your pluck continue. Of the latter we have no doubts. Of the former, it is in the lap of the gods. Come along and see us when in town."

The London theaters avidly sought American business. For example, the Stoll Theater chain, which numbered four houses, frequently announced its show bills in the paper. The Stoll Picture Theater styled itself "The Most Palatial Picture Theatre in Europe." It may well have been, with its thousands of luxurious stalls, its fifty private boxes and its tearooms. In early June 1918, it was presenting Douglas Fairbanks in "Wild and Woolly" and Pauline Frederick in "The Hungry Heart." The London Coliseum, another Stoll establishment, at Charing Cross, facing Trafalgar Square, was "Europe's Principal Variety Theatre," with a weekly change of programs. The summer of 1918 saw on its boards, Beatie and Babs, Phyllis Dare, and Alfred Lester, among others. Tearooms and cafes were part of business. In addition to the programs featured at the Stoll theaters, a serial film, calculated to appeal to Americans was being screened at all four: "My Four Years in Germany," by the recent American ambassador to Berlin, James Watson Gerard.

Though he could only anticipate later business from members of the AEF, Charles Dillingham, by means of a brief ad that appeared for many months in the paper, sent "Greetings to the Boys 'Over There' from the New York Hippodrome 'Over Here.' "

Goods, services, accoutrements, clothing and accessories relating to the soldier and the trade of war predominated in the advertising. Solid silver identity bracelets and discs were popular, as was other jewelry. Tiffany and Company of New York placed frequent small ads. Several firms in London offered expensive badge brooches, encrusted with diamonds, representing the Great Seal of the United States, for £30 or $145.50 each and up. Numerous ads for the now highly popular wristwatch—such as the Longines line—appeared. The National Portable Typewriter Company sold "The War Time Typewriter," which was a real soldier's machine. It was small, light and extra strong and would give splendid service, "under trying conditions."

The soldier's comfort and appearance were uppermost in the minds of some manufacturers if their ads were to be believed. Razor advertisements appeared often and throughout the paper's existence. The most emphatic was the Auto Strop Razor, pushing a selection of military shaving kits, featuring the "only razor that sharpens its own blades," which it accomplished by means of a strap arrangement. Somewhat less persistent were the Gillette and the American Razor Companies, the latter of which simply hoped that its "Ever-Ready" Safety Razor would be as commonly used "Over There," as "Over Here." All razor companies offered shaving kits, most featuring distinctive "trench mirrors." To assist in the chore of shaving, Mennen's shaving cream seemed ideal for use in the field since it lathered just as well with cold water as with hot, apparently.

As to the shave, the obtaining of one in a French barber shop was regarded as a peril closely akin to combat, worthy of war decorations, not to mention the fact that the men were horrified when doused with the strongly scented perfumes and powders upon the completion of the ordeal. Seeking to alleviate the anxieties, The English and American Barber Shop, at 5 Edouard VII Street, urged members of the AEF who wished to feel at home to go to "the only American style barber shop in Paris."

Soaps were obviously needed and "brave Ivory"—"99 44/100% Pure—so pure it floats"—proudly asserted that "Ivory always follows the Colors," and observed that "Over here, no less than back home with 'the folks,' there is joy in a bath with Ivory." Indeed, Ivory was available on all battle fronts, "wherever Gen. Pershing's brave boys [were] fighting." It was doing its share "in bringing cleanliness and health to Uncle Sam's lads in Khaki."[37] Perhaps beyond the pale, however, were certain soaps from England. The dirty doughboy seeking the best could buy "Morny Bath Soaps de Luxe," which were of unusual quality and "exquisitely and originally perfumed." The troops could choose "Chaminade," "June Roses," or "Mystérieuse."

There was more to army life than to be smartly clipped, shaved and bathed. The rather new, bewildering existence, featuring seemingly endless hikes and sentry duty, placed an inordinate strain on the legs and feet. Shoes and stockings were therefore widely advertised in the paper. Walk-Over shoes welcomed all soldiers to their numerous stores in France, "where they [could] apply for any information and where all possible services of any kind [would] be rendered free of charge." The company also provided a free French conversation book. Boston Garters could hold up one's socks, desirable since "Wrinkled Socks Make Sore Feet, Sore Feet Make Poor Hikers, [and] Poor Hikers Never Get There." Interwoven Socks, "Leader of the Foot-Guards," could also help "Win Your Fight For Foot Comfort," and Fastep Foot Powder was unsurpassed for burning, swollen, tired or aching feet.

Other fatigues and discomforts could be alleviated by such items as the "Army-Navy Ear-Drum Protector," a scientifically-constructed device, far superior to cotton, to be inserted in the ear to avoid damage from gunfire and other battlefield noises. It sold for one dollar per pair. Another enticing creation was the "Amex-

Kit,'' a combination property bag and air pillow, sold by the John Wanamaker firm of Paris and New York. However, since it sought to capitalize on the word ''Amex,'' sales were no doubt few, since the American troops did not like the term's being applied to the AEF.

Sellers of underwear and pajamas saw an excellent opportunity in the rapidly growing numbers of Americans in Europe. A certain luxury was promised by several firms in the form of chamois leather underwear, which were easily washed and kept clean, and were helpful in keeping out the cold and damp of the trenches. If these were no doubt practical, one wonders what the average doughboy thought of such ads as the one for ''Best Quality Cotton Pyjamas for Summer Wear,'' by Robinson and Cleaver of London, or the offerings of Swan and Edgar, a high-class gentlemen's outfitters, which featured the ''Swan-Stripe pyjamas,'' and whose claim was ''We Pyjama the World.''

Prestigious clothing firms in England, long accustomed to the trade of British officers, hoped to add their American cousins to their clientele. Many of these featured twenty-four-hour service on custom-made uniforms. Among these were Burberry's, which also had a Paris branch; Gamage's of London; and Barker's, ''The Great Military Outfitters.'' There was also Bernard Wetherill, the firm founded by the man who had ''Filled the Breach'' in the breeches world. One of the items most advertised was the trench coat, among which was the Thresher Trench Coat, claiming to be the original ''Cute Coat'' recommended by the War Office the first winter of the war. Barker's pushed its widely-advertised ''Kenbar'' creation.

But by far the most aggressive British store seeking the business of the AEF was the Junior Army and Navy Stores, located near Piccadilly Circus at 16 Regent Street, London. It ran the first of its many elaborate and lively ads in the 31 May 1918 issue of the paper. The firm's initial greetings read in part: ''As the foremost Military Store in Britain we extend you hearty greetings and good wishes. You come well-equipped, your requirements will be small—we know that, but our welcome bears none of the coldness of commerce.'' The stores had already welcomed Canadians, Australians, and South Africans. Americans were now received, though ''British Soldiers [were] As Welcome As Ever.''

A later ad invited all members of the AEF, ''quite apart from rank and fortune,'' to visit and make use of the services offered, even if they only desired the time of day. ''Let us smooth the way for you—let us help you to see and enjoy this Old Country of ours—let us help Britain to overcome her national bashfulness and show you the true warmth of her kindred feelings.'' Indeed, ''Britain must be your 'Blighty' Land,'' and Junior's must be ''America's Blighty Store.''

The store once loudly proclaimed that it was first in the war and first ever since. ''Our Managing Director was in France FOUR DAYS BEFORE WAR WAS DECLARED by Germany. It wasn't his holiday, he left hurriedly to contract for military supplies because our organization *sensed* that the war clouds were about to break." Nor was that all. The peripatetic Managing Director also journeyed to America, taking his "Military Expert" with him, to study the requirements and desires of America's sons. Their visits to the cantonments and meetings with high administrative officials in Washington gave them, as they claimed, a sure knowledge that would assist the company in serving American soldiers and sailors in Europe. Thus "There's No Can To Our Tail."

Junior's soon found it necessary to lease a new store across from its main establishment. Styled "The American Rendezvous," it was a "happy combination" of shop and club, to which Americans were invited to "come and take [free] tea with us as soon as you get a chance to visit London—come and browse through your home[town] paper and all the American Magazines—write your letters here—smoke and gossip." Those members of the AEF who could not visit London were invited to drop a postcard indicating their hometown and the store would send them copies of their hometown newspaper.

The intense advertising barrage was obviously successful. The store's ad, published in *The Stars and Stripes* issue of 29 November 1918, included a letter, perhaps authentic, purportedly sent by an American doughboy who asserted: "I have watched with extreme interest your advertising space in *The Stars and Stripes* and must tell you how much I enjoy your advertisements. Your copy is refreshingly original and if any of us American soldiers ever get to London—it is a safe bet that one of the places we will look up will be the Junior Army and Navy Stores." The store's comment: "So we may say quite frankly that this mode of advertising adopted . . . has business as its basis and it is succeeding more and more because it is backed up by the thousands of Americans who can and do recommend the . . . STORES from personal experience."[38]

However, a Mr. Richards of the stores at first had complained to Dorland's regarding the placement of his firm's ads, insisting that they be discontinued "until you let me see exactly what position my advertisement is to occupy in the future. I am just as discontented with the second advertisement as I was with the first."[39] This message was relayed to *The Stars and Stripes* for action. But the British firms had apparently never encountered anyone like Viskniskki and *The Stars and Stripes*. In no uncertain terms, he reminded Somner that "one of the conditions under which advertising would be acceptable would be no guarantee of position whatsoever to any advertiser." While Lieutenant Michael attempted to be fair in the matter of placement, no guarantees were made and no exceptions would be allowed. The matter of where the ads would appear would remain solely in the paper's hands. Hence, the advertisements for the store should be discontinued. Viskniskki then proceeded to enlighten Somner further regarding the paper's modus operandi, calling attention to the fact, which "you may care to pass . . . on to the Junior Army and Navy Stores—that this advertising proposition is not the cold, cut and dried business affair of civil life." He insisted that "there should be something more back of the spirit that prompts putting an advertisement in *The Stars and Stripes* than the mere thought of self in connection with shillings and dollars." Furthermore, Viskniskki asserted, all present and prospective advertisers must also agree "to abide cheerfully, faithfully, and whole-heartedly by the other rules governing advertising which we have already sent you." In short, he had no intention of deviating from any of the paper's policies.[40]

Better advised, if not convinced, the British knuckled under, and the Junior Army and Navy Stores' advertisements continued for many weeks subsequently. Later, however, Mulvaney hoped to keep the store's advertising when Peggy Quainton took over, writing her that "the Junior Army and Navy have been running a very desirable ad and we would like to do further business with them." One of the reasons, no doubt, was that the ads were huge ones and brought in a pretty shilling. Still, it was to be on the paper's terms. But the 20 December 1918 issue saw the last ad.[41]

Well aware of the competition from abroad, some American clothiers hoped to keep the business of Americans even while they were in Europe. Kahn-Tailoring Company, of Indianapolis, for one, insisted that its tailored uniforms were "made to fit the inches, ideals and indomitable spirit of America, with its fighting crest up." It offered uniforms made to order by mail if the men knew their exact measurements.[42]

Other American clothing firms sought to jolly and josh the men along until they returned and then perhaps they could cash in. Typical was the Truly Warner hat firm of New York. It recognized that "Crowns Are Going Out of Style in Europe. They'll All Be Wearing Truly Warner Hats, When You Get Through." Another observed that "I've Got Your T. W. Laid Aside For You When You Shed O. D." Again: "Way Back on Broadway We're Waving Our Warners To You," and finally: "May You Knock 'Em Into A Cocked Hat."

The House of Kuppenheimer preferred to send homilies: "Keep your smile pinned on; it may give another cheer; it may soothe another's fear; it may help another fight if your smile's on tight."

Alex. Taylor Company, military and athletic outfitters, was similarly disposed. A long series of ads pushed its athletic equipment, observing that "Athletes Make [The] Best Fighters," featuring the picture of a wildly leaping doughboy, rifle in hand, and a somewhat idiotic smile on his face. Alex. Taylor, the proprietor, stated in one of his presentations: "here's the glad hand, boys, and I wish with all my heart I were there with you. If I can do anything for you let me know."

He may well have been sincere. He kept up the barrage in several ads, in any case. The one in the 29 November 1918 issue of the paper included a poem by Taylor himself, though obviously written prior to the Armistice:

The Yankee Rattler

The Yankee Rattler's biting hard,
   His teeth are sinking deep,
He's strafing Huns by day and night,
   They see him in their sleep.

He's got a breed of courage
    The Germans can't produce,
And when they reach the Rhine ''Good Night,''
    They'll wonder what's got loose.

We're just the tail behind the head,
    That aids the mighty force,
We're turning out the wherewithal,
    We're fighters at the source,
I wish that I were with you,
    For here's the honest truth,
Instead of just a rattle,
    I'd rather be a tooth.

One of the more persistent of the encouraging, josh and jolly group was the Minute Tapioca Company, of Orange, Massachusetts, which began in the 23 August 1918 issue of the paper a long series of open letters to the members of the AEF, ''From the Minute Men of '76 to the Minute Men of 1918 in France.'' Affecting a rather light, supercilious tone, the first missive reads in part:

When we Continental Minute Men went out to fight at Paul Revere's summons, one thing they didn't tell us was that we were going to learn a lot from this thing and come back better educated and with broader minds. I suppose you fellows are pretty fed up on that sort of talk, even though you know it's true. . . . [But] New York boys are learning that there is a whole United States on the other side of the Hudson River, and Boston boys are finding other foods besides codfish and beans. Here's hoping all of you take a look at Berlin.

The company accentuated the positive: ''Think of the tremendous adventure you boys are having. Think of the thrill, that will last your whole lifetime, of having been at the front and in the thick of the greatest war in the world's history!'' When the men return think of the salutary changes: ''What men you will be after the long hard battles, the discipline, the physical training and the confidence of tried and successful courage.'' It would have great effects for future generations—a sally toward a somewhat dubious Darwinism took this turn: ''Your children will inherit a strength of body and of mind that will be worth all the hard work and grind you are going through now. Every struggle today is an investment in health for your children and for the future greatness of your country.'' When your children are asked, '' 'What did your papa do in the war?' they can throw out their chests and say 'He fought in the front line with the 108th.' '' Consequently, each soldier would be ''prouder and prouder all [of his] life.''[43]

But four enterprising American stores were determined to do more for the men in the AEF than send greetings and merely hope for their future business. In May 1918, William Filene's Sons Company of Boston; Joseph Horne Company of Pittsburgh; L. Bamberger and Company of Newark; and Scruggs, Vandervoort, Barney of St. Louis, engaged a Miss Evans and a Miss Chipperfield, two American women who had lived in Paris for a number of years, to establish at 208 Rue de Rivoli a Paris shopping service for soldiers. These women had been buyers for American stores in France for some time prior to the war and knew their way around. The soldiers were assured indeed that the two women were not simply "Americans who speak English in thin slices and can't remember whether Boston is the capital of Illinois or a district out West—but real honest-to-goodness American women who have made a trip to Boston and New York since the war was declared." They were now giving their time to buying for the soldiers in France, who were urged to "write to these women . . . even if you have nothing to say," or if they desired to receive copies of American comics, cut from American papers, such as "Mutt and Jeff." The members of the AEF were encouraged to order by mail the things that they wanted and could not get in camp, such as jam, honey, freshly-roasted chickens, potted ham, or tongue. The women also promised to see to watch and fountain pen repairs. Gifts and money from home could be sent through the stores in America; in fact, orders could be filled more easily in Paris if family and friends would take advantage of the service, since shipping space for packages from home was at a premium. The sponsoring stores made no charge for the service, good will alone being the motive, and the fact that "Filene's," "Horne's," "Bamberger's," and "Scruggs" for a time could boast of a Paris branch (31 May 1918).[44]

The pleasures of tobacco and chewing gum were persistently extolled. Pipes of various descriptions were advertised, and the Wyse Pipe, "The Famous Trench Pipe," seemed especially well suited to the military profession. Its roofed-in top enabled the smoker to smoke contentedly away in the wind and rain. A British invention, the pipe drew in air from the bottom, the use of ridges preventing ashes from falling out.

As to other forms of smoking, Fatima (called "Fat Emmas" by the men), "A Sensible Cigarette" produced by Liggett-Myers Tobacco Company, in numerous issues of the paper simply presented a one-word ad: "Greetings!" Another favored brand, emphasizing a chivalric theme, insisted that "The Knight of the White Horse Prefers Murad at any cost."[45] The P. Lorillard Company, makers of "Climax Plug, The Grand Old Chew," was not only following the flag in 1917–1918, supplying chewing tobacco "to the soldiers fighting for the Liberty of the World," it had supplied tobacco to the soldiers of all of America's struggles since the Revolutionary War. Owl and White Owl Cigars made their pitch as follows: "Fine chap, Frère Poilu! But nix on his *tobac*." What was needed naturally were dependable American cigars.

Army Club Cigarettes, a British product, presented several rather fanciful sketches featuring selected military professions, as the one in the 15 November 1918 issue dedicated to the "Bombing Officer": "We are the real 'Bang Boys' and you should see Fritz bolt when we start our trench raid chorus of 'Here we are, here we are, here we are again.' It's a pretty lively game with any amount of 'good hits,' 'runs,' and 'catches.' Latterly we have begun to fill the German 'pillboxes' with our Blighty Pills for Boche People.'' Of course, it was "no joke . . . looking Fritz's machine-gun in the face time after time.'' After a raid, the bomber enjoyed nothing so much as a Cavander's Army Club cigarette.

In the 26 April 1918 issue of *The Stars and Stripes* an ad for Lucky Strike cigarettes put in an appearance. The cigarette had been launched in January of 1917, and by December of that year, its producer, The American Tobacco Company, was turning out 15,000,000 cigarettes per day. Its advertising emphasized the toasted Burley tobacco which accounted for its great success, "never duplicated in the history of cigarette making.'' Thus, Lucky Strikes appeared on the battlefront in World War I, if not with quite the same panache as in World War II with its famous slogan, "Lucky Strike Green has gone to war.''

But the most flamboyant tobacco ads were produced by the "Bull" Durham Company. That concern's chief product was tobacco for "rolling your own,'' referred to grandly as "The 'Makings' of a Nation.'' Some thirty-six million sacks—one hundred train-car loads, weighing two million pounds—of "Bull" Durham was transported to Europe each month, every single one of which "is chuck full of real American sentiment and love for you.'' This quantity was the company's entire output, which, as it was proudly asserted, was sent entirely to the men overseas. Though "Bull" Durham would be missed at home, it would be given up gladly because it was an even greater necessity for the men "who had gone to fight for *us*—to *win* this war for *us*.'' But the folks at home would not forget the little muslin sack, "gone for the present on its mission of hope and inspiration to you boys in the trenches.'' These men were exhorted, therefore, to "Go to it! Smoke Out the Kaiser! Roll your own into Berlin! When you light up the Huns will light out! Good old 'Bull' is the one bull the Kaiser Can't throw.'' It was also hoped that "there's enough yellow cord about the top of the 'Bull' sacks to hang every man in the German Army with a double twist in the cord for Willie and Hindenburg.'' Rather far-fetched, grandiloquent, and imaginative was one of the company's ads: "Every Hun U-Boat in the Hun Navy is looking for the big shipment of . . . 'Bull' Durham. Sections of the War Zone Sea, they say, look like an asparagus bed after a rain. But they won't get [the ship]. She will pass them in the night. Besides, she is convoyed. A squadron of destroyers guard her, and every gunner at every gun knows she's carrying inspiration and hope for you boys in the trenches.'' Thus, "the smoke that follows the flag is always good old 'Bull.' '' In fact, "The Makings of a Nation,'' would be "the *leavings* for the Kaiser,'' and the men could "light up with 'Bull,' and blow right into Berlin.''

Chewing gum was a favorite item featured in much *Stars and Stripes*' advertising. It certainly enticed French children—as did the tobacco, for that matter. But the doughboy was an avid customer in his own right. The American Chicle Company manufactured the Adams Pure Chewing Gum line, which could relieve the thirst and prevent fatigue—though perhaps not all of it—and hence was beneficial on the march. It is interesting that an article appeared in the Sunday edition of *The New York Times* for 15 September 1918 by one Gertrude Atherton begging Herbert Hoover to put an embargo on chewing gum "because our soldiers might teach the French the American habit of chewing gum." Hoover, apprised of the request, "merely smiled," so it was reported. Captain Waldo, when informed of the article by J. F. Bresnahan, vice-president of the American Chicle Company, merely noted that it was "too silly to be even amusing this side of the water."[46]

Wrigley's billed itself as "The Universal Military Service Gum," which had been adopted by French, Canadian, and British soldiers, even before Uncle Sam's "stalwart boys" began hitting the line. The company's Spearmint or Doublemint chewing gums were a "little bit of the U.S.A.," and could lighten and brighten any weary day, and, especially when one could not smoke, and there were such times in the military, "Wrigley's will solace you."

The paper did not publish alcoholic drink ads, but the first issue did include a welcome from a well-known French potable: "Standard-Bearers of America!", it began. "You have come to the Home of Perrier, the Champagne of Table Waters, delicious with lemon, sirops, . . . and a perfect combination with the light wines of France."

Other sundry blandishments appeared in the paper. Roberts and Company wanted Americans to be informed of their "real" American drugstore in Paris; the IXE Tearooms also proudly announced that genuine American Ice Cream Sodas were being featured in its numerous Paris locations.[47] Many opportunities appeared for obtaining one's portrait, either photographed or painted. The 3-In-One Oil Company, makers of "The Greatest Gun Oil in the World," saw a natural market suddenly spring up. The product, which could "eat up rust faster than it could spread," could also shine up a rifle sling, "so the captain can see his face in the leather." In fact, 3-In-One users were "conspicuous by their absence from the delinquency book."

Banking houses and financial institutions saw an opportunity for rendering service. Among others, Lloyds of London, the Wells Fargo Company, and the ubiquitous American Express Company placed themselves at the service of the AEF. The latter offered to serve as the safe repository for regiment and company funds, and would handle gifts and flower deliveries in the United States.[48]

The paper was the medium informing the men of the AEF of many educational opportunities and newspapers, maps, guides, books, and magazines frequented the paper's pages. A "Professor P. H. H.," who lived at 15 Rue Victor Cousin, hoped to teach conversational French to "American Gentlemen." He promised to help them lay a practical base in the French language which would enable them to "find their way," and later to perfect their skills. Their *séjour* in France would be made more pleasant as a result, and the knowledge would also "during all your life . . . help you in business and sciences." His proposal was typical of many such schemes. Numerous French books and manuals were also offered. When, following the Armistice, Headquarters of the AEF instituted a grandiose educational program, the paper featured this in several notices.

The Pelman Institute of London, sellers of "the little grey books" of Pelmanism, wanted to place the soldiers' feet on the road to success. Pelmanism was no secret, the institute claimed, but was primarily a means of developing the faculties of the mind by "regular and scientific exercise," just as an athlete develops muscles by exercise. Great things were promised those who would but "Pelmanise."

Brentano's, the famous bookseller, located in New York, Washington, Paris, and elsewhere, sold books of all sorts, stationery, periodicals, copies of U.S. Army regulations, and war posters. Campbell's Map Store in Paris provided maps of all the fronts, and "plans, guides, [and] aeronautic maps for American officers and soldiers." The Michelin Tire Company widely sold the *Michelin Illustrated Guide To The Battlefields*. Among other books advertised was Lieut. Edward Streeter's popular *Dere Mable. Love Letters of a Rookie*, which was illustrated by Corp. Bill Breck. It had sold 550,000 copies in the United States and then proceeded to take Europe by storm.

Popular American magazines advertised in *The Stars and Stripes*, such as *The Literary Digest*, and *McClure's* *"Win-the-War" Magazine* saluted the Yank newspaper: "You have the livest and most virile paper published today by Americans and we are proud to back it up." In fact, *McClure's* desired to do for the ninety-nine million Americans at home what *The Stars and Stripes* was doing for the men in Europe. It was pleased also to be able to offer the newspaper the free use of any American illustrations or articles published in it.

The Stars and Stripes presented its own first thirteen issues, sold as a package, wrapped for mailing, perhaps to the home folks, "who will treasure and preserve them as a personal letter from their own part of the A.E.F." Libraries, historical associations, and schools would no doubt want the collection as well, especially at the low cost of five francs or one dollar.

The American Daily Mail featured its low price of fifteen centimes, as did the Army Edition of *The Chicago Tribune*, "The World's Greatest Newspaper." It was pushed as *The Chicago Tribune's* "individual contribution to the war against Germany." The special edition was not published for profit; all of its earnings to the end of the war were to go to whatever Army funds that Pershing directed, and the paper promised to reveal its accounts at any time to AEF Headquarters. It encouraged soldiers to handle and distribute the Army Edition to make extra money for themselves.

Music dealers cashed in on the fact that the Great War was a singing war. Hawkes and Sons of London kept current sheet music available, and its ads provide a running commentary on the most popular song of the day, such as "John and Sam"; "The Dream Girl"; "On the Quarter Deck," a march; "Nelson's Call," a march; "The Land of the Maple and Beaver," a Canadian patrol, as it was called; "Top Hole," a fox-trot; "The Call of the Khan," a Chinese selection; "Colonel Bogey," a famous march; "Handel Wakes," a one-step; "The Voice of the Guns," a march; "Gallant Serbia," a march; "Humoreske"; "The Machine Gun Guards," a march; and "God Send You Back to Me."

Chappell and Company, also of London, proudly announced that it had available Haydn Wood's great success, "Roses of Picardy."

Herman Darewski of London sold not only sheet music, but collections of comic songs, books of ballads, "grease paints," sketches, and patter, and for vaudeville teams and thespians comic story books, recitations, and provided them with wigs, bones, makeup, and much else.

Many agencies, which established headquarters in Paris, used *The Stars and Stripes* as a bulletin board to inform the men of their services. The Knights of Columbus and the YMCA were frequent users of the paper and the Christian Science War Relief Committee announced the opening of reading and writing rooms at 3 Avenue de l'Opéra. The Moose Lodge established a Paris branch and urged the members to get in touch. A notice in the 7 June 1918 issue of the paper asked all members of the Fly Club to contact W. G. Wendall at 3 Rue des Italiens, Paris. The D.K.E.—Delta Kappa Epsilon Fraternity—set up an overseas bureau and club in Paris at the Grand Hotel, Place de l'Opéra, and London at 5 Paper Building, the Inner Temple. The American Red Cross established a home service for soldiers at 4 Place de la Concorde in Paris, seeking to ease the minds of worried soldiers, informing and advising them as to family or business matters at home, and allotments and allowances.[49]

One of the most ambitious service programs was that of the American University Union, located at 8 Rue de Richelieu. It functioned as a club with the general object of meeting the needs of American university and college men and their friends in Europe while on military or other service in the cause of the Allies. On 20 October 1917, it had taken over the Royal Palace Hotel, which was to provide a home, for modest cost, for use of members finding themselves in Paris. It served as a clearing house for information of its members. Since the Union was supported by annual fees paid by various colleges and universities in America, students and alumni of these institutions enjoyed membership privileges without cost; these might "call upon the Union in person or by mail to render them any reasonable service."

The Royal Palace Hotel, of which the Union had exclusive use, was located only one block from the Louvre and the Palais Royal station of the Metro. It could accommodate one hundred guests and possessed an excellent restaurant. A lounge room was provided with leading American newspapers, magazines and college publications; a writing room, a canteen, an information desk, a library and other facilities were on the premises as well. Frequent entertainments and concerts were given and afternoon teas were served every Saturday.

Numerous universities and colleges used the Union's offices in keeping touch with their alumni and former students. *The Stars and Stripes* often announced specific functions such as the University of Virginia's alumni dinner held in Paris on 5 October 1918. A Yale meeting was scheduled for 7 December 1918 at the Hotel Palais d'Orsay, and the same establishment was the site of a Harvard victory dinner on 14 December. A Wisconsin varsity Christmas celebration was held on 26 December 1918, at the Union's own facilities.[50]

Prominent in the newspaper was a certain type of advertising the purpose of which was only to place a firm's name before the public. The rank and file would surely not be customers in the normal course of events. For example, for many months the firm of Bessonneau's, the creator of a line of aircraft hangars, and other types of sheds, tents, and shelters, advertised in the paper. The Barrett Company, an American firm making roofing materials, proudly announced that it provided "Roofings for Buildings of Every Kind that Man or Beast Lives in," and that millions of square feet of their roofs now covered Uncle Sam's buildings in America and Europe. Since the name of Barrett stood for the best in roofings, readers were urged to "See That You Get It Also," though how the average doughboy was to accomplish this was not stated. The machine tools company, the Butterosi Syndicate, in numerous ads, featured its high-speed and carbon steel taps, dies, drills, drill presses, and lathes. Dickson, Walrave and Cie. promised in an ad that ran for many months that "Under the 'DW' tent-shelter you defy Rain, Wind, Mud and Snow."

Several ads appeared appealing to British-American friendship. The 5 July 1918 issue of *The Stars and Stripes*, for instance, included a lengthy presentation from the Junior Army and Navy Stores in celebration of 4 July. Choosing to call 4 July "Liberty Day" instead of "Independence Day," Americans were reminded that the day was a good occasion for the great English-Speaking Peoples to celebrate "their union against the fiendish opponents of democratic freedom." It was hoped that the Union Jack and the Stars and Stripes might long fly side by side, "for we are all of one kith and kin, one heart, one honor, as we are one in voice."

The issue of 27 December 1918 presented a large notice beginning "We Fought Together—Now Let's Keep Together." Thus was announced the English-Speaking Union, founded on 4 July 1918. The first men to hold the joint presidency were ex-president William Howard Taft, and former British prime minister Arthur James Balfour. Vice-presidents were numerous and included Winston Churchill; Vice-Adm. William Sowden Sims, U.S.N.; William Ferguson Massey, premier of New Zealand; William Morris Hughes, Australia's prime minister; the Archbishop of York; Franklin D. Roosevelt; and Viscount Northcliffe. Dedicated to promoting a good understanding between the United States and the British Commonwealth, its joint headquarters were Philadelphia and London. But at five dollars or one pound, the membership dues were high.

Junior's also observed that Saturday, 7 December 1918, was being celebrated in America as "British Day." The firm was gratified, being confident that the deepening of Anglo-American relations would go far in rebuilding the prosperity and harmony of the world.

The advertisements reflecting solicitous concern for the men of the AEF became, if anything, more numerous after the Armistice than before. This was partly the result of the sure knowledge that the men would soon be coming home and their business could then be anticipated. Along the same lines, various firms desired to keep in touch with the men who had been associated with them before marching off to war. In others, good men were sought to fill new positions that a return to normal business operations would require.

Alex. Taylor instituted a series of quaint ads addressed to specific individuals whom he knew:

Hello, Corp. Arthur Haab!
Hands Across The Sea
Keep the dirty Huns a-dustin'
Keep the hand grenades a-bustin'
Keep the bayonets a-thrustin'
Keep the home folks keen and trustin'
          At a Boy![51]

Less bloodthirsty was another appearing in the 13 December 1918 issue:

Hello, Platt Adams
How's the big game going
Hands across the sea?
Sorry I'm not with you
Sad to a degree
Never mind, old skipper,
When the peace bell tolls
We'll go back to Healy's
And the toasted rolls.

The Locomobile Company, manufacturers of Locomobile cars and Riker trucks, sent its New Year's greetings to the Locomobile men in the service. The Aluminum Cooking Utensil Company, makers of "Wear-Ever" cookware, likewise sent its salutations to the men who had been with the company previously, expressing pride in their achievements and promising that "your jobs are waiting for you—every one!" There would be some new jobs as well. The Gillette Safety Razor Company promised that "A Hearty Welcome For All Gillette Men and Gillette Friends in France Will be Extended to Them at Our PARIS OFFICE," at 17 bis Rue La Boëtie. Goodyear Rubber Company likewise opened an information bureau in Paris, at 17 Rue Saint-Florentin, to serve men who left the company's employ to enter the service.

Local governments wanted to be remembered. The mayor and members of the Milwaukee County Council of Defense, on behalf of the people of the county, sent holiday greetings to "Milwaukee County Soldiers and Sailors in Service."

Much more exuberant was Toledo, Ohio, which placed a large ad in the paper's 8 November 1918 issue. The city loudly proclaimed that it led all U.S. cities in the Fourth Liberty Loan, recently completed, by being the first to reach its quota. It had done this in the Third Liberty Loan as well, and was ready for the next call. The Toledo boys in France were urged to "keep up your good work. We follow your record with thrilling pride. . . . We're with you heart and soul.'' The ad went on to say:

"Now All Together, Everybody, OUT LOUD!''

We're strong for Toledo,
    T-O-L-E-D-O.
        The girls are the fairest,
        The boys are the squarest
Of any old town that we know.
We're strong for Toledo,
    T-O-L-E-D-O.
        In any old weather
        We'll all stick together
In T-O-L-E-D-O.

The message concluded: "You'll Do Better in Toledo, After You Lick The Kaiser.''

An interesting half-page presentation appeared in the 20 December 1918 issue. It was by "The Franco-American Manufacturers' Association,'' a group of French manufacturers and American Army officers, most of whom were engineers and chiefs of purchasing departments, now awaiting discharge. The appeal was to American manufacturers, rather curiously, through the AEF. The pitch was that American soldiers knew from first-hand experience what France now needed. Devastated France must be rebuilt. The association desired to buy the rights to make American-owned devices in France. The American manufacturer could benefit by selling their rights and licenses, avoiding the helter-skelter scramble for European business. They could in effect virtually establish a branch of their factories in France. The individual soldier stood to benefit by putting the association in direct touch with any American firm from which rights to produce and market his device in France might be obtained. A finder's fee of 2,500 francs would be paid to the doughboy when deals were completed.

However, this ad caused no end of trouble. Certain objectionable features were immediately apparent to many readers, particularly in the high command. To some, it seemed questionable for the paper to appear to be supporting French industry, perhaps at the expense of American. But more glaring was the apparent case that serving American officers were lending their names and using their positions for business purposes. A certain Lieut. Col. F. E. Drake decided to call the attention of Brig. Gen. Charles Gates Dawes, the general purchasing agent, AEF, to the ad, since there had been reference to army officers in purchasing departments. Dawes in turn informed Harbord, who, observing that "the impropriety of this advertisement needs no argument,'' recommended its discontinuance.[52] This order was soon forthcoming as were instructions for an investigation. Watson soon found himself in some hot water. Fortunately for him, perhaps having some initial misgivings, he had cleared the ad before its publication with the Judge Advocate's office in Paris.[53]

The investigation, conducted by Maj. Gen. A. W. Brewster, the inspector general of the AEF, centered on a certain Capt. H. G. Waite of the Quartermaster Corps at Tours, engaged in gas and oil purchases, who was determined to be most directly involved, as well as on *The Stars and Stripes*. The Inspector General's final report concluded that Waite had acted in ignorance and not with any intent to use his official position for private gain. *The Stars and Stripes* had thought it had cleared itself by consulting the Judge Advocate's office. It was furthermore determined that the Franco-American Association was a legitimate organization with substantial backing and it was in no way fraudulent; it would also stand behind the offer to pay the 2,500 francs as advertised. The advertisement, however, was to be permanently withdrawn and the IG recommended that a general order be promulgated cautioning officers with reference to forming business relations while still in the service. He also recommended that Captain Waite should be officially admonished, which was subsequently done.[54]

As far as *The Stars and Stripes* was concerned, the matter was dropped as Watson indicated to the paper's business manager in early March: "The contract is dead, [the] claim will be cancelled, and this office will decline to discuss it. If brought forward by the Manufacturers' Association reference will be made to G.H.Q."[55]

In the meantime, the home-coming soldiers were appealed to by numerous firms and organizations. For one thing, *The Red Cross Magazine* wanted letters or articles recounting soldiers' personal experiences, and would pay fifty francs for any which were published. The publication also planned a book tentatively entitled: "The Soldier's Story of the War," and wanted contributions for this as well. Michelin Tires hoped that "when you get back to the good old U.S.A. remember the fighting help you have had from the good old Michelin Tires."

Mallory Hats presented a skit emphasizing that when Private Brown got home one of the first things he did was to stroll downtown and buy himself a new hat: " 'Oh boy,' said he, 'you've no idea how fed-up a fellow gets of a hat that's been stamped out of a bit of Bethlehem steel, with no more individuality than a spoke in a wagon wheel.' " So he walked out of the store "with a blithe new Mallory tilted ever so slightly to one side—just to show how he felt toward the world." Another firm had just the thing for the returnees, a song billed as "The Great Home Coming March Song Classic," which went in part: "Out where the hills and valleys meet, Out where the flowers grow wild and sweet, in My Mid-West Yankee Home." This was certainly "the song to sing as long as you are in the service of Uncle Sam. [Also] the song to sing on your triumphant return to your 'Yankee Homes,' [and] The Song To Sing Forever Thereafter." The Equitable Life Assurance Company had many jobs available for the right persons: "*Mr. Soldier Man!* If you have made good in the Army WHY NOT MAKE GOOD WITH US?" The Colorado School of Mines had scholarships available for the ambitious. Truly Warner hats had instructions for the men returning: "When You Get Back Home, Report at Once to Head-Quarters." Tapioca hoped that its faithful expressions of solicitous concern would now pay off: "After brave adventure into the wilds of Army cooking, no matter how good it is, man alive, won't home dishes taste fine when you get back? How about a big, luscious apple tapioca pudding made of Minute Tapioca?"

Finally, atop the New Amsterdam Theater, the "Ziegfeld 9 O'Clock Revue and New Midnight Frolic" awaited the men's return. It promised to always stage "A night of Beauty, such as even Paris has never seen." This surely would convince the AEF, if it needed it, that it was home at last.

Advertising was important to *The Stars and Stripes* though it was not crucial as to an average newspaper requiring its revenues. Indeed, the paper on occasion affected a cavalier attitude toward it as some businesses discovered to their shock. Certainly Viskniskki desired to emphasize *The Stars and Stripes'* more idealistic side rather than the grubby aspects of trade. Yet because many of its readers obviously enjoyed reading the ads and since the familiar displays gave the paper an air of success, advertising was tolerated it not avidly sought.

The historian, in particular, can be grateful that ads were published in *The Stars and Stripes*. One can ascertain therein the state of the art regarding many products, at least those hawked, for whatever reasons, to soldiers of the AEF. Advertising methods of the day can be studied, providing some insight into the cognitive level of Americans of the time. What the doughboys were reading, eating, and viewing on stage and screen, what music filled the air, and numerous other things, are revealed in the advertising columns of the paper. Since *The Stars and Stripes* served as a bulletin board, all sorts of interests can be discovered. In addition, certain attitudes and activities of the home folks can be determined and certain aspects of the relations between the Allies can likewise be detected. In short, a study of the paper's advertising adds dimension to our view of life in the AEF and of its times, reason enough to consider it.

3

Army Mess and Uniforms

An army cook is known by the mess he makes.
(15 March 1918)

" 'I asked for bread and ye gave me a stone,' quoted the
drafted deacon as he tackled his first hardtack."
(6 June 1919)

"Things we hear of but never see: Spiral puttees that will
not come down."
"Messkit Maxims"
(2 May 1919)

Of course, the men did think a great deal about what they ate and wore and *The
Stars and Stripes* did not neglect such matters, publishing numerous poems,
articles and comments on the subjects of army cuisine and dress which reveal
some interesting insights relating to soldier life in the AEF.

Having already encountered army chow in the training camps, a particular
trial for the men was eating it on board the transports on the journey to Europe.
Any soldier who has made the journey could sympathize with an infantryman
who remembered it distinctly:

Transport Chow

The boy sat on the greasy deck
    A-eatin' of his chow;
They'd run him off the forward hatch,
    And chased him out the bow.

The wind had blown his bread away,
    He'd slipped and spilled his beans,

And now his neighbor's coffee
Was a-soakin' up his jeans.
....

S. D. Boyer, Co. E, Infantry
(26 April 1918)

But whether on board the transports or in the camp, the mess sergeant was regarded as the perpetual enemy and was unceasingly abused in the paper in poetry and in prose. But the editors could be fair about it. When Cook Harry C. Ricket of the infantry won a Distinguished Service Cross for bravery he was warmly praised. He had been decorated for keeping his kitchen in action at Château-de-la-Forêt, near Villes-sur-Fère on 28–29 July 1918, though under intense German bombardment, which had driven all other kitchens from the area. He also conducted a first-aid station, and throughout the action aided, as well as fed, hundreds of wounded, exhausted, and hungry men (13 September 1918).

In addition, *The Stars and Stripes* gave equal space for rebuttals from the cooks, as the following "Chant of Army Cooks" reveals:

We never were made to be seen on
parade
When sweethearts and such line the
streets,
When the band starts to blare, look
for us—we ain't there,
We're mussing around with the eats.
....

Anon.
(15 February 1918)

However, the edge went to the complainers and even the officers weighed in with the usual sassy comments common to the enlisted men when it came to their food. The "Ballad of Officers' Mess" attempted to guess what the cooks had hidden " 'midst all the juice," but gave it up, deciding that "they had a zoo" (5 April 1918).

The food items that were most objectionable to the average doughboy were corned beef in its various manifestations, referred to as "corned Willie," "corned Bill," or "monkey meat"; "slum," short for "slumgullion," a term which was applied to a wide variety of dishes, and which because virtually synonymous with meals in general, the stoves even being called "slum-guns"; salmon, invariably called "goldfish"; the lowly army bean; and the execrable hardtack. If the volume of letters and poems is any indication of the degree of hatred of these various foods, corned Willie wins hands down. An interesting article in the 28 June 1918 issue of the paper elaborated. "Corned Willie," the author explained,

6. "Corned Willy and Aleck." Sgt. Alexander Woollcott eating his army fare. *Courtesy of the Library of Congress.*

was sometimes called "monkey meat," especially when it was canned Argentine beef. The French seemed to have had an unending supply of the delicacy, which they willingly shared with the AEF. Some of the boys called it "gassed mule"; others believed it to be "either boiled llama or some other South American animal which the natives coax from its lair and drive into the can. The can is then sealed up and stored for 30 years." The Yanks did not eat it at all unless absolutely necessary to keep from starving. It was normally issued as part of emergency rations. It was supposed to be heated by a can of condensed alcohol, with which the men were also provided, but the alcohol was more often than not used to boil water for coffee. In its various forms, of course, corned Willie was apt to appear any place, any time.

The burning question, then, was how to avoid a meal of monkey meat, and to these ends the ingenuity of the men was taxed to the limits. The story was told of one infantry battalion which was carefully guarding an old French wicker cradle in which sixty four-week-old chicks were growing up—rather too slowly to suit the men, of course. A company of engineers was tenderly caring for a cow which issued them milk daily. They had to keep an eye on her for fear that the artillery roughnecks in the next wood would steal her and obtain a "once and for all" issue of four fine quarters of fresh beef. Another cow was caught by some Marines. They wanted to kill her, but no one had the heart. So they staked her out in No Man's Land, hoping that a German gun would do their dirty work. But the gentle bovine lived a charmed life and "the rising sun of the third day disclosed her still browsing, contented and intact. Whereupon the hungry Marines rose and went forth and slew her. And that night there was great feasting and rejoicing in the camp of the Marines" (28 June 1918).

As someone observed regarding the almost equally hated "goldfish," "the greatest drawback to living on the Pacific Coast is that it is the home of the salmon industry" (13 June 1919). "Tip" Bliss of the paper's staff, excoriated it in a poem:

> Pensive, piscatory, pink 'un,
>   Tantalizer of my hunger,
> Animal I hate to think on,
>   Basest sold by any monger.
> ....

(25 April 1919)

Though not as distasteful as the foregoing, the bean was not universally regarded as gourmet food either, and no matter how wise or foolish a company's cook might be, the two things that all-too-often appeared were "bosom of sow," and "beans-beans-beans," as Cpl. Vance C. Criss lamented (21 June 1918).

But if bad, the men of the AEF were frequently reminded that their food was gotten to them at great sacrifice, and *The Stars and Stripes* sometimes replaced the light-hearted banter about food with more serious injunctions. The troops were not always careful to conserve food. They were accordingly reminded that they were able to eat whole wheat bread and meat, whereas the "people at home have had to put up with corn pone and rye bread in order that it might be spared us. . . . People at home have instituted meatless days in order that we might have it. . . . In any case, our gain has come through careful saving by the people at home. We owe it to them . . . to see that it is not wasted or thrown away" (12 April 1918).[1]

In an attempt to improve the men's food the Congress also took a hand as one of the paper's articles revealed: "That ancient and venerable and highly profitable body which votes the money to buy us our grub has, out of the kindness of its large and collective heart, extended its privileges of free seed distribution to the United States Quartermaster Corps. So, it you haven't received your little package . . . trot right up to the supply sergeant's diggings and ask him when it's coming in." Indeed, Headquarters at Chaumont soon issued General Order No. 34 directing that a garden service unit be established by each division attached to the Quartermaster Corps.[2]

The paper was impressed with the progress made by the units that, in carrying out the order, created productive gardens. These were most impressive at permanent establishments such as hospitals, S.O.S. units, and Air Service bases. The latter often bought pigs for fattening on mess scraps as well as on garden produce. One unit called its swine "Willie," "Hindenburg," "Tirpitz," "Ludendorff," and when the Germans began to shell Paris with the famous long-range gun, saw no reason why another should not be called "Big Bertha" (31 May 1918). Nevertheless, nothing was more welcome to the men after the Armistice than the improved menus made possible by the easing of shipping restrictions, and the arrival of canned chickens, soups, and large quantities of fresh apples was warmly applauded (31 January 1919). They were further heartened when the U.S. Army sold millions of cans of salmon to the French, Belgians, Poles and Russians (4 April 1919).

If eats were important to the average doughboy, what he wore was hardly less so. Matters sartorial came in for their share of comment in *The Stars and Stripes*. An inordinate emphasis was placed on headgear. No doubt many a would-be and soon-to-be soldier had visions of wearing the jaunty, durable campaign hat, for so long identified with the Army's career and martial accomplishments. However, as Albert Jay Cook observed in his "The Ol' Campaign Hat," it would soon be a thing of the past; its peaked top would no longer be a familiar silhouette. But the hat evoked memories:

. . . .
Yet still I dream of other times and what I
    used to be.
The Mauser crackles once again—the smoky
    Springfield roar

Avenges those who manned the Maine upon
    the Cuban shore.
Fedora-style I did my bit in jungle sun and
    dirt,
And now I've got a mortal hit, just like the
    old blue shirt!
I hear the tingling 'Frisco cheers, the squat
    "Kilpatrick" sway,
As boldly swung we from the piers—Manila
    months away.
Luzon, Panay—I saw them all, Pekin was not
    the least—
O I have felt the siren call that sweeps from
    out the East
Below the line of Capricorn in divers times
    and places;
I've heard retreating yowls of scorn from
    herds of Spiggot races.
The Rio Grande and Vera Cruz—I knew them
    like a map,
And now it looks as though I lose—the jackpot
    to a cap![3]

For all of its virtues, however, the campaign hat was clearly impractical and unwieldly since in combat the steel helmet, variously referred to as the "steel Stetson," "Carnegie derby," or "charleyschwab bowler," had to be at the ready and in a twinkling must replace what other headgear was being worn.[4] The old fedora would only get in the way. So, the "good old honest-to-God bonnet," was replaced with something practical, flexible, and "pocketable," which turned out to be the almost universally hated "overseas" or "rain-in-the-face" cap. It was a sad day, then, when the old, time-honored hat, which was expensive, and got "perversely out of shape the day before inspection," was replaced. The old article would at least keep the sun and rain out of a man's face, and "kept him from looking like a German prisoner." He could also go out in the daylight without feeling that all the "good people of France were humming under their breaths that popular ditty of a generation ago: 'Where did you get that hat?' " Wearers of the old hat could also avoid the experience of one soldier who, dressed in his overseas cap, was thus identified: "I would say you're some kind of a sailor" (21 June 1918).

To Ralph J. Hutchinson of the Quartermasters, the replacement for the "old Army lid," a thing of beauty, was simple proof that all of the tailors had died, the new cap having been devised by "a ragman from the remnants he gathered in trade," after a dope-fiend or a cubist had "concocted [its] shade." The new creation ruins the soldier's appearance, he asserted, and, "we resemble an army of tramps, or a nut-factory out for an airing.'' Hutchinson plaintively asked General Pershing to show some mercy and order the designing of a new cap (22 March 1918).

Those who suffered did shortly see a new, somewhat more acceptable version, the most important thing about it being that ''the New Overseas Cap . . . differs from the old overseas cap'' (24 May 1918). Still, it was never regarded as the final answer. One writer to the paper later advised the Army that a desirable recognition of what had been accomplished in winning the war would be the return of the old campaign hat, which would ''make us look and feel again like real Americans.''[5]

Two other clothing items also excited considerable comment, at least early in the career of the AEF. Later, they seem to have gone out of style. These were knitted ''wristlets,'' used to close the gap between sleeve and glove, and the unusual, rather comical, ''belly-band.'' This was a scarf-like piece which, wound around the torso, transformed its wearer into a living, semi-mummy. This innovation was described in a poem by an unknown convert to its effectiveness in which he strongly urged his readers to ''Wear a belly-band in France!'' Among other things, this marvel was not only proof against a weak stomach and the ''wracking, fearsome gripe,'' it guaranteed sleep, security and comfort, and the Red Cross knitters who produced it would surely win ''all the favors Heaven grants!'' (22 February 1918).[6]

The feet were a perennial concern to doughboys. While the Army perhaps travelled on its stomach, the running gear had its own problems: ''So, when our grandchildren ask even the least of us what we did in the Great War, we can say, almost to a man, 'I went in with 6 1/2 B's and came out with 8 D's.' And we can add, in all solemnness and truth, 'Feet won the war.' '' (21 February 1919).

Those abominable wrapped leggins, also called ''putts'' or ''spirals,'' came in for their share of bitter castigation. The men could not understand why the U.S. Army adopted something that the British had employed principally in India to protect soldiers against snakebite. ''A Doughboy's Dictionary,'' though, was of the opinion that the answer might be that they were ''part of a scheme to increase the size of fatigue squads by making a larger number of men late to reveille'' (15 February 1918). To be sure, the canvas leggin was available, tried and true, and so much easier to use. But the same column, in another issue, defined that item as ''a venerable mud collector possessed of a solitary virtue; namely, speed in adjusting to the human form. Now classed as belonging to the early flintlock and pitchfork period of American warfare'' (22 February 1918).[7]

Even at that, those items of the uniform so deplored were often not available, at least in the early days of France, until supply caught up with demand, and the supply sergeant came in for his share of abuse. He always seemed to be out of overcoats, belts, blouses, and underwear, though for some reason, he seemed to possess an ample supply of ''that awfullest of headgear—yes, the cap called 'Overseas!' ''[8]

But whatever the difficulties, the men were enjoined to make every effort to look like soldiers. *The Stars and Stripes*, which was only occasionally given to badgering the men, in the 3 May 1918 issue printed an article by "A Private," entitled "Spick-And-Span-ness," focusing on clean and proper dress. The German and British emphasis on spit-and-polish were extolled as models for all the men to emulate. There was a psychological dimension to it: "If a man knows he looks like a soldier, the chances are decidedly in favor of his acting like one. That, of course, is the way all of us want to act. It's the way all of us have got to act if we're going to see this job through as it ought to be seen through."

To be sure, "there have been great soldiers who were also 'sloppy' soldiers, but they have been few and far between." Those who might point to the celebrated slovenliness of Grant, "caught in an unguarded moment by one Civil War historian while he was clad in his old slouch hat, muddy hip boots, and even muddier jacket, with the inevitable cigar tucked securely between those iron jaws," had to understand that this was exceptional. Or those suggesting that General Frederick Funston, having been observed in such a state of *déshabille* at Vera Cruz that a military observer of a friendly country asked, "and who, pray tell, is the little Chinaman in the slicker up at the head of the column?", was looking at another exception excusable in the circumstances. And though there was admittedly "Napoleon's weather-buffeted old greatcoat," which was notoriously at variance with the brilliant uniform of his famous Guards, these exceptions only proved the rule: "It takes a pretty big soldier to be able to get away with it, and certainly not all of us can aspire to the titles of Grant, of Funston, of Bonaparte."

There was the better example of George Washington, since no one ever heard of *his* not being spick and span, even at Valley Forge. Others worth emulating were Henry of Navarre, with his "well groomed horse and that waving plume," not to mention Richard Coeur de Lion and "his inimitable kingly 'just-so-ness.' " The moral was clear: "The innate neatness and cleanliness and orderliness of the soldier is as old as the profession of arms itself." The football trainer knew the value of sending his charges onto the field at the second half with clean uniforms—it bucked up the team. "What works in the game of football will work in the game of war," (another truism of the period). If cleanliness was next to Godliness, even more so, spick-and-spanness was "the very essence of soldierliness."

There is good reason to suppose that one of the targets of this lecture was the Air Service. If not lacking in "spick-and-spanness," the most notorious of nonconformists regarding dress were the aviators. Even their commanding officer had to order them at last to "cut the comedy stuff," and *The Stars and Stripes* likewise chided them: "The man who goes up and down through the Army looking like a second-hand jewel chest or a misappropriated tailor's dummy is the same person who, sometime previous to April 6, 1917, used to parade up and down past Washburn's Drug Store with his trousers at high tide so that he could show one black and one white sock" (29 November 1918). Well known in World War II for their studied attempts to set themselves off from mere groundlings by dash and flair and a certain flamboyance in dress, these proclivities of airmen were already apparent in World War I.[9]

Another matter attracted some attention in the paper's pages. The high, hard collar on the officer's uniform was far from popular. Many American officers felt that the British officers' roll collar made much more sense; it was sufficiently dressy and far more comfortable. But appeals to change the American uniform met with unexpected opposition even among officer members of the paper's staff. An editorial explained why the "chaste and modest high collared blouse" must be retained, and the roll collar rejected. "Such a coat would be comfortable no doubt, but, really, haven't we got a lot more important things to do over here than crane our necks at ease? What if our blouse is a bit close? . . . [It was a case of] spare the high collar and spoil the soldier. Whatever may be said against the present regulation blouse, its top surely does keep a man's head up and his chin in. And when a man has his head up, his chin in and his eyes front, on the alert for anything that may come along—look out for him!" (1 March 1918). Besides, the French had certainly fought well for four years in a similar collar, it was pointed out (28 June 1918).

One confusing item of dress was the Sam Browne belt, reserved only for officers, made especially so since war correspondents, members of the Salvation Army, Red Cross and the YMCA persisted in wearing it.[10] This led to a great deal of embarrassment. The enlisted men, in particular, hated to be caught in the act of saluting nonmilitary men. Orders were issued to correct the matter, however, and things smoothed out eventually.

If the Sam Browne belt was an item of controversy, the ignorance of proper military dress manifested among the civilians at home was a persistent irritant. Artists depicting men in battle elicited considerable scorn. The column, "Gas-Alert!" elaborated: "Artists back home who draw pictures of us . . . are doing rather better these days. The last portrait . . . to come into *The Stars and Stripes* office had every detail of the uniform right except the buttons, the pockets, the collar ornaments, the belt, the putts, and the hat. The trousers, at least, were correct. That is some improvement" (15 February 1918).

The drabness and sameness of olive drab and the strong individualism present in Americans naturally led to their coveting distinctions that denoted their excelling in the new arena of competition as so recently on the athletic field and in the business world. In the military, as Napoleon had once remarked, it was by baubles that men are led, and though many Americans felt that undue bragging was bad form, the pressure to obtain something to indicate exceptional performance was great. French awards, particularly the *Croix de Guerre*, were among the first to attract attention, and the paper was soon publishing accounts of American medal winners. Other articles discussed American awards, such as the Congressional Medal of Honor, the Distinguished Service Medal (DSM), and the Distinguished Service Cross (DSC), and what sort of feats were apt to win them.[11]

But if medals were difficult to win, another distinction was more easily obtained: the six-month service chevron. This consisted of a V-shaped bar of gold lace an inch wide worn on the lower left sleeve, one inch above the cuff band on officers' uniforms, and four inches above the cuff edge for enlisted men, with the point down. A blue chevron denoted less than six months' service in a theater of operations. A gold stripe, similar to the six-month chevron, was awarded for wounds, only worn on the right sleeve. Any member of the AEF could wear the service stripe who had served continuously in the area known as the Zone of the Advance (23 May 1919). But difficulties arose as to how the time required was computed. Did time enroute from the United States count? Could one begin counting the days from the receipt of orders to sail? The answer to such questions was no, but many letters to the editor revealed much confusion on that score and complaints of men fudging when computing the time they had been in the zone (22 March 1918). Further arguments arose when men outside of the Zone of Advance wondered about their service time; would it be recognized? What about the men in the United States? Many there burned to get to France to no avail. Must their ardor and patriotism go unrecognized? They fervently hoped not and were eventually granted silver service chevrons to denote service in the United States (17 January 1919). But this did not please them altogether, and one poet deplored the silver stripes instead of gold that adorned his sleeve, " 'Cause I couldn't sail away." But hopefully his lady love understood:

> . . . .
> But, my darling, don't you bleat.
> No one thinks you had cold feet;
> You had to do as you were told—
> Silver stripes instead of gold.
>
> Chaplain David M. MacQuarrie
> Camp Merritt, New Jersey
> (21 February 1919)

In fact, a bitter battle was waged between the veterans and the stay-at-homes, the latter having certain political advantages in being able to lobby Washington, and obtained the ear of Congressmen who, in the Army Bill of 1919, originally included provisions for the abolition of all service chevrons. This seems to have been proposed by the House Committee on Military Affairs, chaired by Hubert S. Dent, Jr. Response was immediate from the veterans, and *The Stars and Stripes* received an outpouring of mail, many of the letters being published in the 28 February 1919 issue. One began: "I notice that Congress wants to abolish our service stripes because they would make painful distinctions between the lucky men who came to France and those condemned to service at home." The writer facetiously supported the measure, and further suggested that all should also be put under bond "not to mention our service in France." Furthermore, wound stripes should be abolished, "because doubtless many of the Home Guards would have been wounded if they had only had the chance." It should be made a misdemeanor for winners of decorations to wear these "unfeeling reminders before soldiers who never had a chance to show how brave they were." Even General Pershing must not be allowed to sport his decorations so as not to hurt the feelings of other generals who had not been made commander-in-chief. Cpl. Raymond Kukuck, of the 51st Pioneer Infantry, continuing the attack, asserted that "if the lace-drawered boys at home are going to be jealous, and the country is going to stand for it, we can only say that some of our ideals are going to hit the toboggan." He concluded: "If the soldiers and the people at home begrudge us our honors and distinctions, after we have earned them—well, they are not the sort of soldiers and people we thought them," and since "we are only human, and we have had a great sufficiency of flapdoodle and bunk, . . . we do not want our honors and distinctions taken away through meanness and jealousy— after we have earned them."

No announcement or contemplated action so aroused the wrath of the AEF. It demonstrated to the men that the wartime alliance between the combat zone and the home front was temporary and tenuous and it "proved to them stronger than words that those at home are forgetting, even while the homeward stream of wounded still flows on, what the A.E.F. has done for them." Whether such attacks as these in *The Stars and Stripes* were responsible or not, Congress hastily withdrew further consideration of the measure.

There was another problem with rank chevrons. Orders were issued that non-coms' chevrons would in the future be worn only on the right arm, which meant, one soldier observed, that "you have, therefore, only half the reason for wanting to be a non-com that you had before." This was done to bring American practice in line with that of other Allied armies, though just why this was deemed necessary was not clear (7 June 1918). In any event, as one observer commented on the "dis-ornamenting" of non-coms, they are now "non-com on one side and a buck private on the other" (21 June 1918).

No doubt one of the reasons that distinctions were suspect was that considerable abuse was often apparent in their wearing. The men persisted in seeking medals even if not earned or if somehow they could convince themselves that they had earned them. A letter in the 20 December 1918 issue invited *The Stars and Stripes* to attack "the atrocities now seen wherever there is a leave center or hospital, *though never on the line*." Many so-called "decorations" had appeared, such as the "Marne ribbon," the "Château-Thierry ribbon," the "Argonne ribbon," the "St. Mihiel ribbon," and others (7 March 1919). Also unauthorized was a red, white and blue ribbon for service on French soil; a red-yellow-black decoration for service in Belgium; a gold star for being among the first 50,000 men in Europe; and a silver one denoting that the wearer had volunteered rather than await the draft (23 May 1919). The men especially abused the wearing of the colorful, and hence highly desirable, *fourragère*. These abuses were dealt with at length in General Order 31, G.H.Q., AEF, of series 1919, which forbade the wearing of the spurious battle ribbons and the unauthorized use of the *four-ragère*, setting forth what was allowed. Only four AEF units, which had served with the French Army, could wear the *fourragère*, and then only the members who had been present at the time of the award. These were U.S. Army Ambulance Unit 646, formerly Sanitary Service Unit No. 5, which for its four citations in French Orders of the Army, could wear the yellow and green *fourragère* of the *Médaille Militaire*. The 103rd Aero Squadron—formerly the Lafayette Escadrille—and the U.S. Army Ambulance Units 539 and 625 could wear the red and green *fourragère* of the *Croix de Guerre*.[12]

Other distinctions had been developed during World War I. Among those which especially pleased the officers was the colored piping which was attached to the overseas caps indicating the arm to which the wearer belonged. For example, light blue stood for the infantry, scarlet for the artillery, and yellow with scarlet threads for the cavalry. The Air Service was assigned green piping with black threads (13 and 20 September 1918).

Both officers and men could also wear the new organizational shoulder patches which were rapidly gaining favor (7 February 1919). There also grew up some controversy as to which patch took precedence when a wearer was transferred and whether or not the patch could be worn in the United States.[13] To get around the difficulties, one member of the AEF suggested, in a letter to the editor, that the men who were sufficiently proud of their organizations should have the patches tattooed on their left arm corresponding to the place where it would appear on the sleeve, so that no one could ever take it away (14 March 1919).

Another change came rather late regarding the uniform: breeches were replaced with full-length trousers. "It has been officially decided that the A.E.F. has grown up and must put on long pants," one article began. "Old Papa Quartermaster has announced that the knee breeches of its childhood days are to be cast aside forever." General Order 28, G.H.Q., AEF, series 1919, indicated that leggins would still be used, however, "but the Marines wore 'em that way in Belleau Wood, so it can be done." Mounted organizations would continue to use breeches. The reason for the switch was that, despite an additional cost of about nineteen cents per leg, the trousers were more comfortable and the breeches, especially when wet, impeded blood circulation which compounded feet problems. The absence of the swagger flare and the flap and tongue also simplified production (21 February 1919).[14]

Finally, another fashion note is of interest. This concerns the coming of age of the wrist watch, yet another consequence of the Great War. An interesting, lengthy article in the 15 February 1918 issue discussed this newly-useful adornment, noting its new respectability. Somewhat earlier, indeed, the wrist watch, "bejeweled and fragile," was worn by women, or by "lounge-lizards," i.e., "the boys who had their handkerchiefs tucked up their sleeves," or "who tried to sport monocles and endeavored in vain to grow mustaches and to cultivate un-American accents." Thus, it was rather "the mark of the woman and the she-man." As such, it "was ridiculed by stage comedians, by cartoonists of the press, by haberdashers and men's outfitters of all sorts.'' To buy one was ''to buy social ostracism at the hands of one's fellow-creatures,'' and to wear one in public, especially ''in the allegedly more rugged portions of the Middle West, was to invite physical violence,'' not to mention the possible consequences were the watch flaunted in the face of an Arizona cowboy. But the watch had been wonderfully transformed, revivified and reglorified as ''part and parcel of the practical equipment for the most practical of wars!''

The Stars and Stripes, then, serves as a mirror reflecting the changes in army styles and assists the historian of military history in this regard. During World War I changes came in U.S. Army dress and styles. The overseas cap arrived, for a time replacing the campaign hat. Though the latter would reappear, in World War II it was again superceded in general use by the overseas cap once more redesigned. Trousers arrived in place of breeches; a more colorful uniform was likewise forthcoming, better tailored and enhanced by piping and patches. New decorations also arrived. Similarly with army cuisine, *The Stars and Stripes* faithfully recorded details of the common fare, what the men thought of it, observing as well changes therein. The latter came when authorities could transport a greater variety of food to Europe. When shipping space was at a premium, however, foodstuffs that could be readily maintained in an unrefrigerated state, such as dried beans, hardtack, canned meats, and both ''corned Willie'' and canned salmon, were far too common. Yet the men were kept in a rather good state of health, and for all of their grousing, appeared to the underfed European troops as veritable giants from the New World. They seem to have had enough nourishment and energy to have played an appreciable role in the defeat of the Central Powers, the object, after all, of their arrival in Europe.

4

Rank, File, and Brass

Oh, the General with his epaulets, lead-
    in' a parade,
The Colonel and the Adjutant a-sportin'
    of their braid,
The Major and the Skipper—none of
    'em look so fine
As a newly minted corp'ral, comin' down
    the line!

Anon.
(22 February 1918)

I don't care who writes the songs of an army so long
as I can write its guard rosters.

"Phatigue-Squad Philosophy"
(9 August 1918)

Buck: Say, these here . . . kings of France weren't much
on rank, was they?
    Corporal: How's that, buddie?
    Buck: Why, they was most of them Louis's.

(21 March 1919)

Eve must have been a Major
    In the doughty days of yore,
Because the Bible tells us
    About the leaves she wore.

"Star Shells"
(19 April 1918)

One of the complicated dilemmas that confronted the editorial staff of *The Stars and Stripes* was how to keep the relationship between rank and brass—frequently apt to be a touchy one—in the proper perspective within the content of the paper, which was largely published for the benefit of the enlisted men. Furthermore, the majority of the readership consisted of volunteers or draftees, men of distinct democratic tendencies, who normally looked askance at leaders, would-be rulers, and gold braid. Unfortunately, the army was hierarchical in structure and placed a premium on discipline. The paper approached these matters with some caution, clearly not desiring to destroy the unity of the AEF. Accordingly, a sort of standoff existed, tacitly recognized: respect for brass, up to a point, would be maintained, in exchange for some freedom of expression. There were boundaries over which the paper would not step. But then the High Command would refrain from intervention to squelch expression if it were kept in certain limits. Just where those limits were was sometimes a matter of debate.

One way out of the matter would be to accord freer expression vis-à-vis the non-coms who, to a considerable extent, were regarded as fair game, and these became the butts of much discontent. The paper also sought to persuade the men, particularly at the buck private level, that theirs was an honored position, and they should be content with their lot. The fact that so many of the paper's staff were in that lowly state must have been of considerable comfort to the majority of the AEF similarly situated.

A series of poems in several of the early issues of the paper set the tone of respect for high-ranking commanders, with a general relaxing tendency noted as the ranks were treated in turn from top to bottom. Presented under the general heading, "As We Know Them," the first was concerned with "The General."

> He wears a cord of shining gold, a collar
>   decked with stars
> To show he is the fav'rite son of Mister J. H.
>   Mars;
> We tumble out the guard for him, and snap up
>   to salute;
> Because he's been a Dad to us, we all swear
>   he's a beaut!
>
> . . . .

To be sure, he "rolls around the country in a big, high-powered car," but this was not an idle occupation. He had to "chin with other Generals," planning "how he's going to make his fight." True, he did not have to walk a post or scrub the pots and pans, nor did he "tote a pack," or wallow in the muck, "but if his plans go woozy, why we are all out o' luck!" In short, "his life is not one grand, long dress parade," and since he often lay awake at night, and fusses with maps all day, his "thatch [was] prematurely gray." Still, "since he knows

his game / We'll follow him through hell and back, and / never mind the flame!''
(15 February 1918).

In another "As We Know Them" poem, the "Colonel on the Staff" was
scrutinized:

> He doesn't warm up easy chairs as much as you might think;
> He does a lot of planning, and he wastes a lot of ink,
> But all the same he's right up front 'most every day to call,
> And the tricky German snipers love to plug him most of
> all.
>
> . . . .

Indeed, "he has won no cushy job, the Colonel on the Staff"; he had "little
time to eat and sleep, and never time to laugh," and in fact, had one of the
world's toughest jobs, "the givin' of advice!" Then too, if he did not produce,
he was "hauled before the General and gets the very deuce!" Those who might
covet his place should perhaps reconsider. Was his position all that desirable?
Maybe one's own lot was not so bad after all (22 February 1918).

Along the same lines, the rank and file were informed, as in one article, that
the "Lamps Burn Late Down At G.H.Q.," at Chaumont: "A chance visitor to
G.H.Q. who tiptoed along the echoed corridors of the big caserne the other night
and caught glimpses through each half open door of high and mighty officers
toiling like bank clerks at the end of the month realized suddenly that he was
looking upon the light of the A.E.F., which shines for all. And the light of the
A.E.F. is midnight oil" (7 June 1918). So as further to make the point, Pershing
and his staff were said to inhabit an "old barnlike French caserne," implying
that even the top brass lived in less-than-desirable digs, perhaps a comfort to
the doughboy billeted in a smelly French barn somewhere.[1]

Other articles extolled the virtues of heroic military commanders of old, with
an eye, no doubt, to instructing officers and men alike, and providing them with
eminent models. The second issue of the paper, appearing on 15 February 1918,
gave the editor the perfect occasion to rhapsodize on "Our First 'C.O.' " Washington was no doubt with the AEF in spirit, the piece suggested, since the latter
was "fighting the self-same fight that he fought, defending human liberty against
military tyranny, helping to make the world sweeter and fairer to live in and
work in." In fact, the editor asserted, "we are his army just as much as was
that tattered band of Continentals, clad in motley uniforms, carrying motley
weapons, which he transformed from a mob into an instrument of victory."
Since the United States Army, like the Senate, was a body of continuous existence, members of the AEF were members of the same army, "in spirit and
purpose and continuity, as that which Washington commanded." It had never
gone to war except on behalf of human liberty; it had never been defeated in
this venture. "It has therefore the proudest heritage—and cleanest record—of

any army in the world.'' Washington must look down ''from the abode of all good and clean fighting-men who have departed from this world,'' with favor upon what his infant nation had become. He had other reasons for pride: ''He sees that nation lined up in battle array side by side with his ancient ally, France, endeavoring to its utmost to repay France for the precious aid which La Fayette [sic] and the Comte de Rochambeau rendered him in his struggle.'' He could but be gratified that his ancient foe transformed as ''the new England, the democratized England, the liberty-loving England which we may now hail with pride and affection as our Mother-Country,'' had seen the error of its ways. It was no doubt obvious to him that as he was fighting America's fight, ''he was also fighting the battle for English liberalism,'' and hence ''beholds with joy the reunion of the race.'' Time and mutual understanding had healed old wounds, and ''he exults in every fibre of his fine old liberty-loving soul,'' to see the new concert.

To be sure, Washington had to contend with pacifists in his day, as America had in 1918, but as the editor clearly emphasized, ''as we have not,'' Washington also had to contend ''with traitors in high military places.'' Perhaps more to the point, the editor also observed that ''he was a stern man, a cold man in his military dealings, [and] a strict disciplinarian.''[2]

Indeed, those men who were strict disciplinarians were singled out by the paper as those who, in the last analysis, more often than not, did the best job in preparing the men for the ordeal of battle. As the men were bloodied, this became increasingly clear: ''The men swear now by a captain they had all cursed for his severity in the tedious days of training,'' one article recounted, ''and a captain who, in those days, was a genial, easy-going favorite, is a favorite no longer.'' Similarly, ''one grim sergeant whose name used to be a hissing and a byword among the privates he afflicted is the hero of his company today'' (28 June 1918).

> Hey-diddle-diddle! The Loot, in the
>   middle
> Of night, waked the whole platoon;
> The bunch got sore at the false alarm
> And got even by cussing the moon.
>
>   Anon.
>   (22 March 1918)

This rendition from an infrequently appearing column, ''Mother Goose for Doughboys,'' clearly reveals that even lower-ranking officers had to be accorded respect but not quite as that manifested toward those higher up the ladder. But officers of lower rank, being closer to the men, were naturally better known, both as to their positive and negative attributes. The lieutenant could be the object of light fun, especially the ''shavetail,'' or ever-present ''2d Loot.'' But if the butt of comments and jokes, the editors felt that he had his place. "Where he really shines," one editorial has it, "is between and on the covers of magazines printed and distributed in the States." Indeed, "no self-respecting heroine, brain-daughter of a self-respecting short story writer, ever thinks of clinching in the last three paragraphs with anyone but a second-lieutenant." Certainly, "no fiction editor will consider a story which does not have for its hero the much-aggrieved, much-put-upon, but none the less dapper—that's the word—and handsome shav-etail." To be sure, his lot was a bit hard in France; "with mere majors and captains ranking him out of his bed or girl at every turn, it could hardly help being so." But once he returned home, "preceded by the all compelling fiction barrage now being laid down in front of him, his conquest will be easy. And gosh. How he will enjoy it!" (18 April 1919).

The "2d Loot" was in fact sometimes put upon. *The Stars and Stripes* could occasionally join in the fun. Sgt. Maj. Lewis L. Curyea, of the 147th Machine Gun Battalion, expressed poetically what was no doubt a recurring fantasy of the rank and file, the day when, after the war, a former officer or non-com found it necessary to apply to *him* for a job:

> . . . .
> He says, "all right; don't rub it sore."
> So I took 'im in m' groc'ry store.
> . . . .
> [And] I'm jus' 's happy 's I kin be;
> I gotta Lieut—ee workin' for me.

(3 January 1919)

But these abused officers of lower rank were often admired. At least one was by the men of his particular platoon, who collectively wrote a poem about him:

The Prayer of the Third Platoon

The Third Platoon is a good one,
    And we thanked our lucky stars
That we had the best little lieutenant
    Who ever put on the bars.

The bars were of gold when he joined us,
    But he was so game and so bold
That the high command saw he earned it,
    And traded him silver for gold.

He was smaller than most of the small
        ones,
    And 'tis true he looked pretty young,
But he showed his worth and his valor,
    Wherefore his praises are sung.

He was with us when we were rookies,
    He trained us to do squads right,
And later, in this strange country,
    He led us into the fight.

He was with us on post in the trenches,
    He led the battalion patrol;
Charged with us across the Ourcq
    When we made the Boche hunt his hole.
. . . .

But, as the poem continues, he came the "first Sunday in August," to bid the platoon goodbye, with "something like a tear in his eye." As for the men, they were plunged into despair and were, in fact, downhearted, "for we loved our Jonesie well." Indeed, when he was with them, they "would have chased the Boche through hell." They pleaded with their colonel, therefore, to "send us our Teddy Jones." The exigencies of war being what they were, they probably never saw him again.[3]

Still, no matter how officers were viewed, they were officers. Central to military courtesy and discipline attendant thereupon was the salute. This unnatural act was among the more difficult to teach a thoroughly democratic rank and file. *The Stars and Stripes*, on several occasions, therefore, sought to instruct its readers on "this business of saluting—this very necessary business of saluting." Lieut. Col. Andrew J. Dougherty, of the 357th Infantry, was called upon to inform the paper's readers on saluting's finer points and essential meanings. "When an enlisted man, a lieutenant, a captain, a colonel, a general salutes his superior, he says by this act, 'I will obey you'; and the smartness with which the salute is made is an exact measure of the way we will obey." But it was no one-way street: "When an officer returns the salute of an inferior in rank, he says: 'I will strive to the limit to prepare myself to lead you to victory.' " In the last analysis, in fact, "a soldier will fight as he salutes." This was food for thought, the editor asserted, and the act of saluting scores of times daily formed a habit which "neither fear nor sickness, nor physical weakness can break" (15 February 1918).

"Bran Mash," the author of an article, "Etiquette Talks For Doughboys," put it a bit lighter: "The oldest and best families in the A.E.F., . . . still adhere to the quaint, graceful and altogether pretty custom of saluting all commissioned officers. . . . The same custom is prevalent in the Army of France, the British Expeditionary Forces, and the other social organizations now spending the season in Europe." Certainly, there were details about saluting that were worthy of closer attention: "In all cases, care should be taken, when elevating the hand to the face, that the thumb is tucked carefully in. If the thumb hangs loose . . . it is apt to come into too close proximity to the nose." This had the effect of robbing the salute of its original meaning, and what was worse was that "the poor cheese'' who did not practice thumb control usually got no credit for good intentions (15 March 1918).

Since saluting was so highly regarded, *The Stars and Stripes* subsequently featured several articles on the matter. ''A Private'' wrote a lengthy article on the subject, ''Why I Am Proud To Salute,'' which closely followed official pronouncements. The private recognized that saluting was all part of the game, and he rather enjoyed it. Saluting proved that he belonged to the organization, and he was puzzled when he saw soldiers suddenly becoming ''absorbed in the landscape'' just as an officer came by. There was nothing denigrating about the courtesy, he insisted; it was in fact the ''high sign'' of the ''oldest and most honorable fraternity in the world.'' Furthermore, the salute was not to a particular officer, but ultimately to the President as commander-in-chief of the Army. The officer returning the salute was likewise ''saluting the whole rank and file of the American Army and, beyond it, the great people from whom it was recruited.'' Commissioned officers were, after all, only designated representatives of the President, who could not be everywhere, thus when an officer was saluted, ''it is just as if I were saluting the duly elected head of my nation, in the choosing of whom I had a hand.'' Now: ''What could be more democratic, or more simple, than that?'' In light of these considerations, any man who ''slops through'' a salute ''is by that act proclaiming himself no true champion of democracy; for he belies the very democracy that sent him forth. And where, pray tell, shall we get off if we neglect to respect the principle which we have sworn to defend?'' (26 April 1918).[4]

The Stars and Stripes also felt constrained to close ranks around the brass against German ridicule. A German army officer, writing in the *Bremerzeitung*, commented on a statement by the American Secretary of War, Newton D. Baker, that within a year's time the American Army had expanded its officer corps from 9,000 to 110,000 men. ''That is truly an American masterpiece of accomplishment,'' he snorted, ''to sew epaulettes on a hundred thousand men and call them officers!'' This was too much for the columnist of ''Gas-Alert!'' It was perfectly conceivable, he retorted, that America indeed had 110,000 men fit to be officers, and reminded his German antagonist what Napoleon had said about Marshal's batons in knapsacks (15 February 1918).[5]

As far as *The Stars and Stripes* was concerned, there was one category of men standing between the commissioned ranks and the enlisted men, i.e., the so-called ''Third Lieutenants.'' This term humorously referred to the ''un-commissioned officers.'' These unfortunates had completed officers' training school after the order came down that no more men were to be commissioned. And since they obviously fit somewhere between a second lieutenant and a buck private, it seemed natural to refer to them as ''dovetails.'' Most of these men also wore a black stripe on their sleeves, no doubt ''as a delicate tribute to the memory of the too-late Sam Browne'' (10 January 1919).[6]

Below the magic line separating the rank and file from the brass, the non-coms had to be obeyed by lower ranks, but were, for all that, regarded in a different light. Good non-commissioned officers, like their officer counterparts, were respected. They were often viewed as the backbone of the army and veterans of long Regular Army service were advanced as ideals for younger soldiers. Many of the former had served in Cuba, Puerto Rico, the Canal Zone, China and Mexico. The old regular was a paragon of sorts; he was only rarely guilty of the "senseless grumbling" that "some of the more recent recruits were apt to affect." When the latter complained because they did not "get grapefruit and cinnamon toast for breakfast, porterhouse steak and mushrooms for dinner, and lobster à la Newburgh for supper," the old hand did not kick. "He's been in places where wormy hardtack was a luxury, and where canned Willy of the vintage of Andrew Jackson was a feast." He did not complain about trench life either. He had "campaigned for days in the swampy rice fields of the Philippines, without rubber boots, without hot food, [and] without the prospect of a relief coming up before long." When others worried about long hikes, he remembered harder times when his nostrils had been filled with alkali dust, "galloping fifty miles a day / upon a diet of beans and hay." Those prone to grumble were advised to drop around to the old sergeant's billet. They would come away "convinced that this business of soldiering in the year of grace 1918 is a picnic, an office outing, a club field day, . . . compared to what it might be." In fact, "the old boy has forgotten more about real roughing it than you ever read about, and still he isn't soured on the proposition. In fact, he is the most persistent optimist in the Army of which he is the backbone. More power to him!" (1 March 1918).

Another view of "The Top" appeared in the series, "As We Know Them":

Some kids was born with golden spoons, our Top was born
    with nails
A-sandwiched in between his lips—or maybe 'twas third
    rails!
For verbal lightin' he can wield as can no other guy,
And if you have a button off, you'll know the when and
    why!

He's served his sev'ral hitches and has hiked it on the plains;
He thinks it's too darn lady-like for us to ride in trains
Or open trucks or camions; and if he had his way,
We'd all get fallen arches from a-walkin' 'round all day.

He bawls at us at dawning and he bawls at us at night—
The only thing he lives for is to give recruits a fright;
He's harder than the Skipper and the first and second loots,
And six foot men, when facin' him, just shiver in their
    boots!

. . . .

However, the poet did recognize that if the "Top" didn't make such demands, "we'd get it from the Skipper," and "one such guy's enough!" (19 April 1918).

"The Army's Poets" column was the means used by men of Company D, 306th Infantry, to commemorate their own "Top-Kicker," 1st Sgt. Ben Goold, killed in September 1918, near Vauxerre, by the River Aisne. He was, they remembered,

> As strict as iron, as tough as rust,
> A bulging bean, a hard-boiled crust,
> He growled like hell, he cussed like smoke,
>
> . . . .
>
> Some woof
> Was our top-kicker.
>
> . . . .

(24 January 1919)

Being much closer to the buck private, the corporal was a logical butt of jokes from the lowliest ranks. One query asked: "Were there corporals in Shakespeare's day?" So it would seem, for what other possible rank was the Bard referring to when he described the soldier, "full of strange oaths, and bearded like the pard / Seeking the bubble reputation / Even at the cannon's mouth"? (27 December 1918).

More devastating was the poem, "Corporal's Call":

> When first we came to foreign lands
>   The native jackass yodeled for us,
> So like the bugles and the bands
>   We learned to love his daily chorus.
> More keenly pitched than reveille,
>   It shook the rafters of his stall
> Or cross the sward rolled heavily—
>   We knew it as the "corporal's call."
>
> . . . .

Anon.
(7 February 1919)

There were several means whereby the privates, some restive in their lowly status, were placated. Some of that propaganda that the paper's Board of Control felt should be insinuated into the paper was of this sort. Bucks were sometimes lectured to, as an anonymous letter writer did on one occasion. He pleaded with the men, for example, to work for the good of the country and not to seek "selfish promotion." They were enjoined to remember that "the essence of self is one of the noblest things a man can give to his country." The key, therefore, was "not what we are worth to ourselves, but what we are worth to our country, whose servants we are" (5 July 1918).

In fact, the desire to obtain promotion could be regarded as downright un-patriotic. As an editorial expressed it: "The Kaiser has no great cause to fear the major who, on the first day of his majority, says to himself, 'now, how soon can I become a lieutenant colonel?' instead of 'O Lord, help me to shoulder this new responsibility.' " The real patriot had no time to think of promotion. "He does his job for all he is worth and takes what rank comes along." Thus, those who scheme for promotion, even from the buck private rank, are not good at any rank. The moral was clear: "Don't 'better yourself.' Better the Army" (12 April 1918).

To be sure, some would be promoted, and if it came, well and good, but these would remain relatively few. Accordingly, the paper often exalted the buck private as the foundation stone of the army and the epitome of the ideals of the democratic nation at arms. The omnipresent poet addressed this subject, a typical example of which was entitled, "John Doe—Buck Private," by Sgt. Allan R. Thomson:

> Who was it, picked from civil life
> And plunged in deadly, frenzied strife
> Against a Devil's dreadful might?
>   Just plain "John Doe—Buck Private."
>
> Who jumped the counter for the trench,
> And left fair shores for all the stench
> And mud, and death, and bloody drench?
>   Your simple, plain "Buck Private."
>
> Who, when his nerves were on the hop,
> With courage scaled the bloody top?
> Who was it made the Hun swine stop?
>   "J. Doe (no stripes) Buck Private."
>
> Who, underneath his training tan
> Is, every single inch, a man!
> And, best of all, American?
>   "John Doe, just plain Buck Private."
> . . . .

And, it was only "Doe—Buck Private," who "rang again the Freedom bell"; and it was "John Doe (God's kind) Buck Private," who also heeded not "the laurel pile / That scheming other men beguile," and who stood "modestly aside the while," an admirable creature withal (3 January 1919).

Finally, as an editor in the final issue of the paper expressed it, in his "The Bucks," "The man in olive drab perhaps does not realize the prestige of having been a private all through the war,'' he began. Yet, ''he knows just what he did . . . for the keystone of the Army arch has been and always will be the lowly buck. . . . '' But this lowly rank must not be considered as representing a failure, because bucks ''were [the Army's] hewers of wood and its drawers of water. They suffered the most. They gave the most. And there are many who think that, despite stripes and francs, they got the most out of it.'' When the buck returns to his nation ''as a free citizen in a free country,'' he will be content to let others argue over the Army's promotion system, of how some men were placed over others, how others took advantage of favoritism. There were more important things closer at hand. Indeed, ''there await the great ranks of all of us who work, a future where there are no bars and stripes, and where, in the words of President Wilson, 'there is no uniform except the uniform of the heart.' ''

5

Hospital, Chapel, and Morgue

Keep a clean heart in a clean body, and may God be with you.

J. Cardinal Gibbons
(1 November 1918)

Only those who fought with them can ever know the height of religious devotion and patriotism to which they arose.

General Pershing

Among the numerous topics discussed in *The Stars and Stripes* were those regarding medical matters, what the men believed regarding faith, and how they considered their dead. The paper published suprisingly little on medical topics when one considers that the number of wounded men in the AEF reached over 200,000, a ratio of one in ten.[1] Given the paper's role as morale booster, it was no doubt thought improper to dwell upon the sufferings of the wounded. Accentuating the positive, the paper preferred to emphasize the efficient, expert medical care the men could expect, even at the front. The 17 May 1918 issue, for example, published a piece on a typical American hospital train, billing it as "one of the world's finest," a deluxe affair, in fact. On board every provision was made to meet any emergency; the wounded were not forgotten in this war— such was the message.

There were other assurances. When the men were wounded experience revealed that they could be expected to bear up courageously. Medical staffs often marvelled, so it was often asserted, at the courage of the wounded Americans and at their grit and ability to bear pain and suffering with fortitude. One article recorded that there was "only one outcry in [a] busy week in four dressing rooms" (14 June 1918). Another case was recorded of an infantryman shot through both arms and both legs, with his thighs broken. In addition, he was shot in the abdomen and the hip. Despite this, the paragon, while his wounds were being dressed, enthusiastically discussed the battle then raging at Château-Thierry. " 'What's this fellow got, lieutenant?' asked someone peering over the surgeon's shoulder. 'Guts,' said the lieutenant respectfully'' (14 June 1918). Another officer, observing the wounded returning from battle as they went in: cheerful, nervy, without a whimper or complaint, was driven to exclaim: "God! There's no living man too good to be a private in the American Army!'' (9 August 1918).[2] Likewise typical was the *bon mot* which went: " 'Well, after all,' said the buck who had just lost a leg in the Argonne, 'there's one advantage in having a wooden leg. I can hold up my sock with a tack' '' (15 November 1918).

Less serious topics were trenchfoot and venereal disease, though no laughing matters, to be sure. As to the former, several articles focused on this bothersome fungus and how to prevent it, often emphasizing proper footwear and clean, dry socks.[3] As to VD, one interesting article, addressed to "*the fathers and mothers, sisters and brothers, wives, sweethearts, and friends of the men in the American Expeditionary Forces,*" was aimed at mitigating certain alarms apparent at home as to the AEF's amorous conduct. Readers were assured that "the percentage of venereal disease in this army of yours is three-tenths of one per cent.—the smallest percentage on record for any army, or any civil population, in the world's history" (8 February 1918). Nevertheless, especially after the Armistice, a concerted effort was made to cope with the problem no matter of what magnitude. The men who became infected were segregated into labor battalions located at the bases at Le Mans, St. Aignan, St. Nazaire, Nantes and Bourdeaux. They would not be returned to the United States until well, the average quarantine being forty days or so. This was provided for by General Order 32, G.H.Q., AEF, of series 1919, and emphasized that the pride in the AEF "must not be marred by the return of anyone to civil life who, by his misconduct, has rendered himself incompetent to maintain that high standard of citizenship which America rightfully expects of her returning soldiers." Another consideration was the future health and welfare of American citizens, which demands "that the soldiers of the A.E.F. return to their homes as clean in person as they have been brave in battle." Court martial regulations in such matters were to be rigorously applied and men going on leave "shall be advised of the necessity of preserving the Army's standard of morality" (7 March 1919).

One of the difficulties surrounding the labor battalions was that regular construction and stevedore outfits were often confused with those with the VD men, causing chagrin and embarrassment if not worse. This resulted in a spate of letters to the editor insisting that some distinction be drawn between those who were being disciplined and quarantined and those pursuing their normal duties. Furthermore, it became known in the United States that some of the men were being held in France pending cures, giving rise to rumors that units which were not being immediately shipped home were infected with VD.[4]

More to the paper's style as to medical subjects were articles of a much lighter tone. For instance in one, Capt. W. H. Mook, of the Medical Corps, perhaps half seriously, hoped to see the name of German measles changed to "Liberty Measles," and suggested that all Allied medical officers go along, though there is no evidence that they did (18 October 1918). Likewise, several accounts appeared poking fun at the medical staff's propensity to prescribe "CC" pills on every conceivable occasion or else liberally applying iodine to wounds of whatever seriousness (24 May 1918 and 7 March 1919).

Also as a matter of considerable concern to medical staffs, the omnipresent, cordially hated, infamous louse or "cootie," sometimes called a "grayback," "seam squirrel," or "Bolshevik flea," received an inordinate amount of attention. It was a well-known fact that the louse was a common carrier of several diseases such as trench fever and typhus. This necessitated massive delousing operations. To be sure, if there were need for smiles and bearing up, it was in connection with this pest, and it was the lighthearted side that was stressed in *The Stars and Stripes*.[5] Typical of the things reported to the paper was the information that a certain military unit amused itself by developing a number of cootie mottoes: "One Good Coot Deserves Another," "It's A Long Coot That Has No Turning," "All That Itches Is Not Coot," and "None But The Brave Deserve The Coot" (26 April 1918). And Jimmy Murrin of Headquarters Company 112th Infantry, in a letter to the editor observed: "I have not seen a single cootie in France. They are all married and have large families" (29 November 1918). A poem on the perennial subject, by Sgt. A. P. Bowen, went like this:

If I Were A Cootie

If I were a cootie (pro-Ally, of course),
I'd hie me away on a Potsdam-bound horse,
And I'd seek out the Kaiser (the war-maddened
    cuss),
And I'd be a bum cootie if I didn't muss
His Imperial hide from his head to his toe!
. . . .

The cootie would then similarly treat the Prince of Bavaria, and spend a few days with "that Austrian crew," as well as old "Hinden," perhaps "under the Linden" (1 November 1918).

Pvt. Arthur Mann of the 12th Field Artillery had heard that a poet had won a prize for the world's shortest poem:

Adam
Had 'em.

His own suggestion was,

dam [*sic*]
'em.

(7 February 1919)

The artists got into the act; Rube Goldberg invented a complicated "cootie separater" (13 September 1918), and Wallgren devoted one of his "Helpful Hints" cartoons to the subject of "How To Get Rid Of Cooties," with several outlandish suggestions (31 May 1918).

The object, obviously, was how to become free of the hateful pests. Suggestions wry, humorous and serious came into the paper. One suffering soldier proposed that about three monkeys should be issued to each company of infantry, serving not only as pets, but for delousing the men (31 May 1918). More serious was an old-timer, an ex-lieutenant of the 10th New York Artillery, J. Sumner Welch, who reported that at the siege of Petersburg, where the whole earth seemed alive with nits or "greybacks," he had employed a white-hot running wire eight inches or so in length, dragged along the seams of clothing where the nits tended to shelter. This had worked like a charm and he felt that similar relief could be expected were this expedient employed in France (16 August 1918). "Itch and Scratch," in a letter to the paper, informed the men that "Sag," a salve used to counteract poison gas, worked wonders on cooties (29 November 1918). This may have been the inspiration for the chemically treated shirt, which rumors indicated would soon be issued. However, conventional delousing methods, at last successful in ridding most of the AEF of lice, obviated its introduction (8 November 1918).

The normal delousing procedures continued to the very end, though, pursuing the men on shipboard, where "the cootie drill" was as common as the lifeboat drill. Every soldier was ordered to spend fifteen minutes each day searching his clothing for lice. The ship's medical staff was to hold frequent inspections and the men found with head lice were to have their hair clipped and were then to bathe with anti-cootie soap. Civilian passengers, including women, were to be subjected to hair clippings if they could not rid their heads of lice by soaking their hair in a carbolic solution (31 January 1919).

All in all, the medical department personnel of the AEF worked diligently in the discharge of their duties. They indeed often boasted that they were destined, with their ever-present needles, to fire "the last shot of the war," a responsibility which would "be borne with the same modest demeanor with which the department in other days wore the privilege of firing the first shots" (21 February 1919).[6]

As to religion, to the men of the AEF matters of faith were closely bound up with how they lived, how they faced battle, and the touching respect they paid their dead. However, the faith that the men professed—at least that reflected in *The Stars and Stripes*—was not that brand dear to the hearts of many clergymen and overly-pious people, the latter of whom sometimes attempted to intrude. They were usually firmly rebuffed. The men also wanted to pay their own respects to their dead buddies and were not overly inclined to leave these matters to certain clergymen for whom they had little respect. They were capable of a deep faith, but on their own terms. Those formally charged with ministering to the men's spiritual needs were the chaplains whose place was formalized in early 1918. Chaplains were commissioned officers, ranging in rank from first lieutenant to lieutenant colonel. But regulations issued in 1918 no longer permitted the chaplain to wear his rank insignia. "Why should he?" the Headquarters Chaplain of the AEF, Bishop H. C. Brent asked, "His functions remain unaltered whether he be lieutenant or colonel; but he is to be distinguished by the cross on his collar which signifies the unchangeable commission of his unchangeable office." There was to be, as soon as they could be commissioned, one chaplain for each 12,000 men. Among their duties was that of cooperating with the AEF's auxiliary organizations, such as the YMCA, the Red Cross, and the Knights of Columbus in spiritual and relief matters concerning the troops.[7]

But the men had their own ideas as to the ideal chaplain who was often portrayed in the paper. Typical was one of the "As We Know Them" series devoted to "The Chaplain":

He doesn't wear a Sunday suit nor yet a Sunday face;
He wears khaki the same as we, and goes from place to place
A-visitin' the hospitals and cheerin' up each lad
That for any sort o' reason is laid up and feelin' bad.

He doesn't pull no highbrow stuff, or talk of Kingdom Come,
But any "cits' clothes" parson he can sure make out a bum;
He doesn't mind mild cussin', and he'll smoke a cigarette,
And doesn't say you'll go to hell for swiggin' somethin' wet.

Still, if you *ask* him for it, he will tell you, 'bout the Lord,
The First and bravest Christian, Who would never sheathe the sword
Until all wrongs were righted; how He set His people free
Although the Romans nailed Him to the Cross o' Calvary.

In short, "he doesn't force his preachin' down a helpless feller's trap," though, "if a feller wants it, he has got it right on tap." He would write letters home "if your arm's too sore to write," and if a soldier felt like praying, "he'll sit up with you all night." He stood in for the homefolks and did the things for the men that they would do were they only with them. Perhaps most importantly, the chaplain would "jolly you and brace you up and tell you not to fear / 'Bout gettin' by the sentry, old Saint Peter, 'way up there / If you only do your duty" (8 March 1918).

To one editor, it was plain that "one of the benefits to arise from this war is going to be the knowledge that the average parson (meaning the lucky parson in khaki) will gain about the average soldier (meaning the average man).'' For instance, the parson would learn that the average man has ''an awful lot more good in him than the whole brood of parsons (and those who train parsons) ever suspected.'' Furthermore, they would learn that the average man is ''a lot more responsive to the things of the spirit—though in his own way— than the average parson could have deemed possible.'' The parson would learn that it is not always the man ''who cusses the worst who is bound for perdition.'' He will have seen gruff, rough men comfort children frightened by bombardment or go out and save a wounded buddy. He may see a common soldier pay the supreme sacrifice without a whimper, and ''having seen all that, the parson will be mighty lenient in judging that man on little scores,'' such as cussing, perhaps. While this was not condoned, ''the point is that the parson will get down to bed rock in his appraisal of men, and not spend too much time fussing about their exterior embellishments. When he gets down there, the doughboy can understand the dominie. The former will lose his distrust for the latter and the latter will lose his skepticism about the former'' (5 April 1918).

The average doughboy, then, preferred his own kind of ''Sky Pilot,'' one who could overlook at least the pecadillos, if not sins of greater weight. No doubt about it, among the ''Things One Learns In This Man's Army,'' was that ''a chaplain is a human guy'' (8 March 1918).

If acceptable chaplains were clearly identified and described in *The Stars and Stripes*, what the men did not like in the religious sphere was even more graphically portrayed. In reference to a ''Pharisee'' coming to France ''to save the souls of our boys,'' the paper was emphatic: ''For this man, and for every one of like breed, this newspaper has no words sufficiently strong in which to express its contempt.'' These men, ''so filled with their own smug self-righteousness . . .have not the faintest conception of the ever-recurring miracle of the Allied battle line.'' Because they had ''never really comprehended the teachings of the Master they profess,'' the complaint continued, ''they cannot know that the smiling, cursing, battle-stained doughboy needs no help in saving his soul.'' They could not be expected to know ''that in offering and spending his life in a righteous cause the American soldier finds it. They can never comprehend that in saving the soul of the world the soldier saves his own'' (25 October 1918).[8]

What the editor was getting at was often affirmed, as in the 27 September 1918 issue, in which he assailed a preacher who, at a combined entertainment and religious service asked the men to stand up if they wanted ''to come to God.'' The editor's bitter comments were that ''there are a good many men in this Army who hold the belief that a man who, with a gun in his hand and a smile on his face, takes his chance in the battle line in this war, who faces death for the principles for which we are fighting, is working out his own salvation, and that he doesn't have to stand up in an entertainment hall in a back area to accomplish that salvation, either.'' Furthermore, the Army chaplains, men clad in Army khaki, and carrying steel helmets and gas masks, were alongside the men and no other preachers were needed or desired.

However, this rough and ready theology did not go unchallenged. Chaplain James C. Peterson asserted that "the religious belief that every soldier who goes over the top thereby redeems his soul is not American, but Turkish-German." The editor, unconvinced and unshakable, retorted: "He that loseth his life in a righteous cause shall find it, good chaplain. Jesus Christ Himself has promised it" (22 November 1918). As far as the paper was concerned, this was and remained the last word.

If many doughboys detested the religious "do-gooders," such organizations as the YMCA and the Red Cross came in for their share of knocks. When the Y launched a drive for funds at home, the paper editorially hoped that zealous speakers would not seek to "pry open pious purses by means of alarming stories about the iniquities of Army life, which—in matters of clean-living—is, after all, rather more decent than civilian life." There were still fresh memories of former campaigns of the YMCA which featured the hymn intoning:

> Lift up the Red Triangle
> > against the things that maim—
> It conquers booze, the wrecker,
> > It shuts the house of shame.

The editor "most devoutly hoped that no old ladies of either sex" would be beguiled in contributing a single cent in the delusion "that, without our brothers of the Red Triangle, the A.E.F. would relapse into a riotous group of venereal drunkards" (28 June 1918).[9]

The Stars and Stripes devoted considerable space to pieces, both in prose and poetry, that probed the fact of death and its meaning within the context of the Great War.[10] The spectre was accordingly viewed from many aspects. A group of chaplains who had buried the dead, killed while storming the slope above the Ourcq, were described in the paper: "They were . . . much uplifted men, and their eyes were shining as they made their brief but eloquent report. 'In all that battlefield,' they said, 'we found, without a single exception, that every one of those boys died crouching forward, died with his face toward Germany' " (16 August 1918).[11]

A doughboy editor of the paper remembered a dead buddy as follows: "I shall forget him in the morning light; and while we gallop on he will not speak; but at the stable door he'll say good-night." Indeed, he felt that this illustrated the fact that the experience of the army in France had resulted in "a new feeling toward death, a better understanding. It is no longer strange and mysterious; it has moved among us; it has struck [often] suddenly." The buddy who died had left perhaps casually, maybe "without a handshake when he piled into a camion and rolled away, or when we crawled out of the fox-hole he was just gone; or maybe we didn't hear about it at all until long afterward because, Armywise, he had been transferred and we hadn't." At the time, things were happening "mercifully fast and furious and we couldn't think at all." Now that there was time to think on these things, and when the victory for justice and right had been won, "it all seems a part of the plan, loss as well as victory, death as sure as discharge." But no matter what the circumstances were, the buddy would still be with his friends, "not in the busy rush of the life we'll take up again, but quietly at the day's end—living and real; for his going from us was unmarred by the harsh convention of civilian death, and quite cheerily, across the golden shadows, we'll answer his goodnight" (30 May 1919).

But one bereaved young woman saw her sacrifice in more personal terms and questioned the cant, romanticism, and idealism so often manifested, more realistically assessing the hard fact of separation:

The End of Youth

In northern France my soldier lover lies,
My soldier lover, with his clear boy's eyes,
And with his smile, so brave, so sweet, so wise.

He heard the call of Death on Honor's field,
And answered: "Here!" his soul to service sealed,
High-hearted at the pledge Truth had revealed.

I glory that he lived and had his share
Of that great glory, given those who dare
Give all for Freedom—but I care! I care!

What of the promise of his youth and mine?
What of our home and hopes of love's design?
What of the lonely years in long, long line?[12]

The romantically-inclined crusaders seemed to have had the edge, however. Perhaps this feeling was strongest among the home folks. In any event, it is surprising how many Americans agreed with an unknown girl who submitted "A Sister's Prayer," which the paper saw fit to print:

Dear God, if I were but a boy,
    I would enlist at once and fight
For liberty. Oh, what a joy
    To give my life for Thee and Right!

My hand, O God, I shall not give
    To one who has not taken part
In this great war that Freedom live!
    A soldier, Lord, shall have my heart!

(14 June 1918)

Along similar lines, Chaplain Thomas F. Coakley, himself a veteran, found it hard "to only watch and pray," but he was solaced in that,

....

I have sent my son to France,
   My flesh and blood to fight for me.
O happy son! This is your chance
   To die for God and Liberty!

                              (14 June 1918)

The dead, then, were sacred, and *The Stars and Stripes* could be harsh on those seeking to capitalize on the war dead in any way. One incident greatly incensed the editor. A newspaper trade journal—unnamed—featured comments by Frank S. Newell, circulation manager of *The Cincinnati Post*, who was quoted as saying that as the casualty list "has a certain news value which in turn produces a certain circulation . . . value, I think every circulation manager should insist upon having a definite place for the list every day." The editor was indignant, insisting that the casualty list was the nation's roll of honor—it was not merely a "feature" to boom newspaper circulation. Such callousness was beyond the pale, he continued. While as a part of its duty to the reading public such news would be printed as a matter of course, "any newspaper which looks at the casualty list merely as a revenue-getter had better shut up shop, for it is not American, nor human, but merely sordid to the point of shamelessness" (13 September 1918).[13]

If the dead were commemorated, there were also serious attempts to ascribe some definitive meaning to their sacrifice. The Easter season of 1918 caused some to reflect on this aspect of death. The real significance seemed to lie in that the Prince of Peace and the Allies fought as one; indeed, Christ was to come to judge the living, and the dead, who had championed His cause, the cause of justice and freedom. In truth, no man who lives or dies striving to bring about His peace need fear His judgment. The Christ loved and preached peace; but He loved justice and freedom more, and for them He laid down his life. Our fight is His fight; His peace, when it comes, will be ours" (29 March 1918).[14]

God must be in the Allied war effort, then, and perhaps the war was truly a war to end all wars. Were this only true, then the dead surely would not have died in vain. Sgt. John Fletcher Hall of the infantry thought that he saw this possibility, and for its realization offered "A Prayer From The Ranks":

....

Grant us this prayer: that the toll that we pay
   Shall not have been levied in vain;

That when it is sheathed, the sword of the world
    May never see sunlight again.
When the roses shall climb o'er the crumbling
            trench
    And the guns are all silenced in rust,
May War find a grave where none shall disturb
    Through the ages his mouldering dust!

                                            (5 July 1918)

To at least one of the paper's editors, the conquest of the Holy Land seemed a sure sign from heaven of the righteousness of the Allied cause and a justification for the great loss of life: "Jerusalem, Bethlehem retaken—and now comes Nazareth! The shades of Godfrey de Bouillon, of Richard Coeur de Lion and of the good St. Louis of France must look down with envy upon the forces of our British Allies who, in this twentieth century, have made the great dream of Christendom come true" (4 October 1918). It all seemed so grand, and the triumph was perhaps in fact the battle of Armageddon which was occasion for hope and a deepening faith, for "Death and hell were cast into the lake of fire," as "the inspired saint wrote," and he also saw a new heaven and a new earth, for the first heaven and the first earth were passed away, and there was no more sea. An official British report seemed to sum it all up nicely and with a fine edge of excitement: "On the north our cavalry traversing the field of Armageddon." Thus, as the editor concluded, "even in this war there are a few thrills left" (4 October 1918).

6

Morale and Esprit

Buck No. 1: The regiment's goin' to attack at dawn
and get those woods east of the village.
Buck No. 2: What they goin' to take the whole regiment for? Why not just send a wood detail?
(21 June 1918)

Goodbye, goodbye, goodbye,
    The decks are deep with men,
We're going out to God knows what,
    We'll be back God knows when.
Old friends are at our side,
    Old songs drift out to sea,
Oh, it is good to go to war
      In such good company.
Pvt. Stewart Mackie Emery
(23 August 1918)

Things One Learns In This Man's Army: That the fellow
who went to so eastern a college that he can't pronounce
his rrs is able to bang the Boche with the best of the
cowpunchers.
(8 March 1918)

Given the nature of *The Stars and Stripes* and its mandate to build morale, pride
figured prominently in its presentations. The first issue set the tone, exulting in
the American Army and observing that taken all in all, it constituted a force
"which is in every way a worthy successor to the first army of liberty, whose
commander was George Washington." It was "proud of its heritage, proud of
[the] people at home who were supporting it . . . proud of . . . the greatest
cause for which any army was ever called upon to champion." Indeed, "it would
rather rot under the soil of France than to do anything which would cast discredit

on the homes it left, which would impugn in any way the good name of the great people from whom it was recruited.'' The AEF promised to come home to America ''clean in body, excellent in mind and heart, and with the record behind us of a man's size job manfully done.''

After some months of apprenticeship, when that Army began to win victories, the pride seemed justified. But such was the temper of the times that the paper, while recognizing the desirable aspects of being proud, cautioned against hubris. ''Let us be confident, but not over-confident,'' one article on the subject of ''Brag'' began. One of the reasons was that the home folks must be encouraged but not misled. ''Let us not claim to more than we can, but to let our performance surpass our claims. Let us leave bragging to the Germans—they're better at it than we are.'' Only in this area, though, was the AEF to concede superiority. Confidence was essential, but ''brag won't win it. Brag doesn't win wars. The things that win wars are ships and steel and leather and lungs and—guts!'' So, the ''bull-artists of Berlin,'' were to have a monopoly on boasting until they have been thoroughly beaten, and ''then, and then only, we may crow, and crow indeed'' (1 March 1918).

If bragging was off limits, pride was not, though it skirted bragging at times. Much of the latter centered on the divisions and many invidious comparisons and heated arguments ensued as to which had played the greatest role in winning the war. The paper's editors were asked to rate the divisions but emphatically declined, averring that ''the editorial staff of this newspaper, though made up of men of almost incredible bravery, does not care to answer this question. We do not feel equal just now to a fight to the death with the entire A.E.F., minus one division.'' Indeed, any division could give ''a clear, concise answer, given without blushes and with overwhelming conviction. For divisional pride, divisional spirit, which lightened packs, shortened roads, stormed heights, killed Germans and confounded prophets, glowed throughout the A.E.F. from the days of the first trench raids.'' None of this was forecast and many would have said, ''who can get worked up over an anonymous outfit? Who can burn with zeal merely by belonging to the Blank Regiment of the Blank Division?'' But ''the divisional spirit of the A.E.F. was one of the seven wonders of the war.'' But one of the consequences was ''that there was nothing in all the A.E.F. quite so colossal as the ignorance of one division about its neighbors.'' If a division was missing from the battle line, and though it might be at some distant battle point, ''its American rivals invariably assumed (and hinted) that it was idly luxuriating in some cushioned rest area.'' As for the proverbial division on the left, ''well, it was notorious for always lagging behind. . . . And a prize of one centime is hereby offered for the detection of any member (cook, corporal, colonel) of any division who ever, in the midst of a battle, admitted for one moment that the division on the left had caught up with it'' (17 January 1919).[1]

However, the paper editorially could accept the interpretation that *all* of the AEF engaged on the firing line was collectively the object of pride. ''The hand of time can never erase from the pages of history what American divisions did at the post of honor in the world war of 1914–1918," one such piece affirmed a few days after the Armistice. "The story of American valor along the Meuse and in the Argonne will shine radiantly through the ages. It will glow in the printed word as long as men read of the deeds of their fathers, as long as the passion of liberty swells in the bosom of mankind." The glory of that story would "be none the less refulgent" because of the knowledge that only a year before they went forth "with boyish smiles and boyish confidence to face the flower of the German hosts," most of the troops were childishly ignorant of the simplest matters of war. They were sneeringly called green troops by the enemy and perhaps by the Allies as well. "But, bringing youth to the war-torn battle hosts, we believed in our youth. We believed in the holiness of our cause and the job given to our hands to do. We knew that in our keeping were the liberties of the Republic. We believed in America unconquerable." That, of course, was "why today the words Marne, Belleau Wood, Château-Thierry, Ourcq, Vesle, St. Mihiel, Argonne," and many other places, "are shining in deathless splendor in Columbia's diadem" (15 November 1918).[2]

Pride in the nation and its great endeavor reflected the warm glow of a sense of belonging to something greater than one's self; of being bound up in one of the engines of history. The poem, "U. S. A.," the "Fighting Carol of Head-quarters Company, 320th Infantry, of the National Army," captured something of the sense of invincibility then so common. It was suggested that it be sung to the tune of "Tammany."

U.S.A., U.S.A.

With bayonet and shot and shell,
We will give the Kaiser hell;
        U.S.A., U.S.A.
Jab 'em, jab 'em,
Shoot and stab 'em;
        U.S.A.
. . . .

Anon.
(15 February 1918)

Another poem, less violent, though reflecting a sense of the grandiose and the grandeur, commented upon America's service flag.

We want a place for our Service Flag,
For the Service Flag of America.
We looked in vain to find a place,
In all the world there wasn't space.

So we borrowed the sky and hung it wide
Over the world from side to side,

And when the world is dark at night
Our stars are shining clear and bright.

....

Anon.

(7 June 1918)

The service flag, so highly hung, could never drag in the dust; plainly, "God made America's Service Flag."

There was also glory in the knowledge that America had had a hand in liberating territory from the oppressor, which was also in the American tradition. The colonists had liberated their country from the British; their descendants helped the young republic of Texas to throw off the Mexican yoke. Again it was American fighting men who emancipated the black man. Later, an American army "brought liberation to the republic of Cuba, now one of our Allies." Thus, the old cry is heard anew:

Hurrah! Hurrah! We bring the jubilee!
Hurrah! Hurrah! The flag that sets
                    you free!

Indeed, "it is the particular business of that flag, and of the men who follow it and love it, to win freedom for themselves and for others. So it has been in the past, so it is now, may it always be" (27 September 1918).[3]

Certain it was that the tide of Yankee power in this war would not cease mounting until the job of defeating Germany was completed, as "The Chant of the A.E.F." suggests:

We've helped to sweep them from the
        Marne,
And send them on the way;
We've helped to nail them at the Ourcq,
And spoil their pleasant day;
We've swung along the open road
And hammered at their line,
And now we're out to bing 'em,
To bing 'em on the Rhine.

....

Anon.

(16 August 1918)

Not only were they proud of the nation; the men were pleased with what they were becoming under the stress of war. One interesting article was addressed to

E. S. Martin, editor of the old *Life* magazine who had complained that the stories about American troops in France sent back to the United States were too sentimental; indeed, were mere "twaddle." He felt that there was very little left to the war except "duty and mud." Also, there was "little promise left in it of glory comfortably endowed for anyone." The editor's reply was a brisk retort: "Duty and mud? Plenty of both, to be sure, but a lot more besides." Martin was advised to "get it out of your head that this war is a dreary, written-out, stale undertaking." It was in fact, "full of life, full of color, full of interest, full of promise, full of hope! Don't pan the war, Mr. Martin. It has helped many of us to find ourselves, has taught us lessons of sacrifice and service. In short, . . . we—over here—are finding it a damned good war, the best we ever attended!" (22 March 1918).[4]

Sgt. Richard C. Colburn focused on one thing that the military life was accomplishing: it was working wonders on the plutocrat, as his poetic rendition, "The Plute," made clear:

> He may be a plute in the circle back home, but it
>   don't get him nothin' out here;
> His belly may ache for a glass of champagne, but
>   he's lucky as Hell to get beer.
> His custom, you know, in the land of the free was
>   to rise from his bed about nine—
> A valet would dress him and button his shoes
>   and bring him his breakfast and wine.
> *But how things have changed since the draft*
>   *sucked him in!—he rises at 6:30 now,*
> *And, drinking black coffee, remarks on the fact*
>   *he's walked half a mile for his chow.*
>
> . . . .

In truth, though he departed as a number, he would be returning to his home and former station as a man (5 April 1918).

Certainly, it was on the training fields where much of the change was coming. In fact, the wonderful spirit soon to be manifested at the front was "merely the result of the spirit shown from the start by the men back home in training camps, [and] by those stationed for further training back of the lines in France." Training life was characterized mainly by "grind and detail and drudgery, day piled upon day and week piled upon week of the hardest sort of work, mental and physical, that knew no glory of the moment, no variety, no thrill." But those who refused to become discouraged through the dreary days of training were proof against discouragements under the trying conditions at the front. Assuredly, there was pride in all of that (16 August 1918).

Then there were the names that the troops took pride in, notably "Yank," and "doughboy." However, considerable controversy surrounded their selection and use. Certain imaginative journalists and songsmiths thought that the name "Sammies," derived from "Uncle Sam," was appropriate for U.S. troops. Rarely has anything met with such a concerted opposition. *The Stars and Stripes*, among others, made no secret of where it stood, as a short column, "So Say All of Us," for example, indicated, concluding that "Satan judges especially harshly the man who wrote a popular song entitled 'When the Sammies Sail Over the Sea' " (10 May 1918). As one of the editors asserted: "Never, so help us, have we nauseated and unnerved a doughboy by calling him a Sammie" (19 April 1918).

The matter seemed worthy of some analysis as an editorial undertook to do in the 29 March 1918 issue. It began by observing that "a Sammie may be defined as an American soldier as he appears in an English newspaper or a French cinema flash. It is a name he did not invent, does not like, never uses and will not recognize." Indeed, "when he sees it in the papers from home, it makes him sick." The name was simply a name that "was ineffectually wished on our troops the day of their arrival in France." Though the American soldier had had his baptism of fire, he had still not been christened, at least not to his satisfaction. The paper surmised that this would come in time. When it did, it might "be the inspiration of some ambulance driver . . . or the outburst of some eloquent cook." Therefore, while the American soldier did not yet know what his name would be, one thing was certain: "He simply knows it won't be 'Sammie.' "[5]

The plaintive poem, "From One of 'Em," set the matter even more forthrightly:

> Dey're goin' to call me "Sammy"—
> My Gawd, what have I did?
> Why don't they make it "Ferdin-
>   and,"
> Or "Cutie dear" or "Kid?"
> . . . .

Anon.
(17 May 1918)

Far more desirable was a good, loud-bellowed YANK, a name strong, big, and frank, of which no one need be ashamed. Even the Southern boys now seemed willing to accept this "rugged, man-sized sound" (31 May 1918), admitting that "yes, we've got a country now," concluding that "we're all YANKS, everyone of us today." And such newspapers as the influential *Arkansas Gazette* used "that formerly hated word in the headlines, adopts it, glories in it.'"[6]

If apparently no one in the AEF could tolerate "Sammie," some did accept the first officially-inspired term, *Amex*, short for American Expeditionary Forces. But they were decidedly in the minority and again *The Stars and Stripes* diligently put it down. One writer felt that it was appropriate since it was very close to the French word for friends, *amis*. While Yank was virile enough, he agreed, in France there was a common expression, "Rough as a Yankee," which suggested negative connotations. But the editor protested that Amex was so obviously a contrived word that it scarcely filled the bill (13 September 1918).

The troops at length saw their fervent wishes realized and the paper breathed a sigh of relief:

That nickname is Yanks. Nothing more, nothing less, nothing else. It means Dixie and Yankee Doodle rolled into one. It means that 1861 to 1865 is forgotten, demolished, blotted out against the mighty epoch of 1917—to a finish.

"Sammy" was a joke, and a painful one. "Buddy" failed to land. The others hit the soapy chute with equal éclat.

You can't manufacture a nickname in a century, but one can be hooked to you in a day. Yanks it is (2 August 1918).

That matter being settled, there remained, however, difficulties surrounding the use of the term *doughboy*. There is little doubt that it was originally intended to refer to an infantryman, though the exact origins of it were debated in the letters column from time to time. One letter writer, signing himself "Grandpa," was typical. He insisted that the term doughboy, "as applied to a gravel agitator," had not originated in the Philippines, as some alleged, but earlier, in the Indian campaigns following the Civil War. As proof, he referred to Frederick Remington's painting, "The Doughboy," which depicted a plains infantryman in full kit (16 May 1919).[7]

Be that as it may, it still meant an infantryman. Accordingly, many readers deplored the fact that even *The Stars and Stripes* often lapsed into the support of those who called all U.S. soldiers by that name, which was simply not accurate. In the process, the "Queen of Battles" was deprived of her full credit. It was a shame to have the name denoting her troops sullied by its being indiscriminately applied to all who wore the same uniform, sometimes even the Marines![8] In defense of its position, one of the paper's editors insisted that "the dictionary known as 'General Usage,' " had sanctioned the use of the term's being attached "to every living man who wears the olive drab." He also noted that the term originally carried with it a good-natured derision, but that of late, "the name appears insensibly to have taken on a new accent of respect." Nevertheless, he was adamant on the point of usage, and from the spring of 1918 or so, doughboy was used to refer to American troops whatever their branch of service.[9]

If the infantry could not obtain exclusive use of the term doughboy, there is little doubt of the pride exuded by the so-called "Queen of Battles." It was one of the most praised and celebrated arms in the AEF. The poetic salutes to it in the paper were numerous. One good example was entitled, "Tribute":

. . . .

Oh, they've met the Hun at the length
    of a gun,

And they know what he is and they
        mind what he's done,
So that's why they sing as they slog to
        more fun!
You doughboys, you slowboys,
Here's luck, an' let her go boys—
We like you, Infantry.

....

                                        Anon.
                                (7 June 1918)

Another poem, taking the form of an air, must have been sung on marches, or if not, it certainly should have been:

"Yes, There Is Rest"

Of all the animals alive
I'd rather be the bear;
He gets a full meal once a year,
And never cuts his hair—(I tell you).

Chorus: Yes, there is rest, yes, there
                is rest;
        In the Infantree—
        In the Infantree—YOU SAID
            IT!
        Yes, there is rest,
        Yes, there is rest,
        In the Infantree there is rest,
            SWEET REST!

....

                                        Anon.
                                (21 June 1918)

An editorial observed that even in an age when massive strides had been made in the development of armaments, "the greatest instrument of the Army of today, the instrument which stands out conspicuously above all others, is the same instrument which made or broke all armies of history—the infantry." All else in the Army was subservient to that branch. In truth, "plodding their way through rain or dust, fighting through shrapnel or gas, the infantry is the sun of the planetary system of the Army." In short, "the infantry is of that branch of the service which in terms of military science, is defined as 'the arm of accomplishment' " (27 September 1918).

Courage in battle was analyzed by the paper keenly aware of the apprehension felt by many of the men on the eve of battle. The editor sought to reassure them, observing that even in a mechanical war dominated by destructive machines, individual courage still counted; in fact, he noted, "this war will be won by the side which, on high and in the ranks, back home and in the field, can show in greatest numbers the men who never yield. For in war, from the dawn of history . . . only one thing has ever counted. . . . And the name of that thing is courage" (26 April 1918). The first winners of decorations should assure some as well. The first DSCs led the paper to exult that "the doers merit the honor and the congratulations they have received. But it is the A.E.F. that is honored most, in the possession of these men" (29 March 1918).

Not only that, many heroes were simply awaiting an opportunity to shine. In fact, the only test of a hero is the opportunity, another article confidently asserted. "Psychologists never have been able to classify and catalogue the qualities [that] go to the making of a hero. There is no way of telling one in advance" (21 June 1918). The point was often made, then, that "the story that the citations tell is that the valor of the fathers is not dead; that the spirit of service, of sacrifice, of absolute unselfishness in the face of death lives in and moves and permeates the America of today at war" (27 September 1918). The message was clear: American troops need not enter battle hesitantly; they could and would acquit themselves as men of courage, as heroes.

The saga of the "Lost Battalion" was evidence that heroes were simply waiting in the wings. This incident was thoroughly discussed, though the editor was at some pains to separate fact from fiction. One editorial focused on the Battalion's commander, who "is—and always will be—fondly known from Maine to California as 'Go-to-Hell' Whittlesey, under the delusion that he made that ringing reply to the German call for surrender, when, as he has always scrupulously explained, he made no reply whatever, ringing or otherwise." There was no need, the message was, to embellish the facts which were heroic enough as they stood, and there was nothing to demand that heroes necessarily be flamboyant; a becoming modesty could also serve (25 April 1919).

But *The Stars and Stripes* was nothing if not thoroughly democratic, and no branch of the service was ignored. If the "Queen of Battles" was just that, it required a great deal of support. One of the major supporting arms was, of course, the artillery; it therefore came in for its share of praise. For example, much was later made of the firing of the first shell in anger by an American artillery unit. It was generally conceded that that event occurred at 6:05 A.M., 23 October 1917, by Battery C, 6th Field Artillery. The deed was done from a position 400 meters east of Bathlemont, in the Lunéville sector. The gun was a French 75 mm. The crew consisted of Sgt. Alexander Arch, chief of section; Cpl. Robert E. Braley, gunner; Sgts. Edward Warthen, Lonnie Dominick, and Frank Grabowski, cannoneers; Pvts. Louis Varady and John Waderczak, also cannoneers. Lieut. Idus R. McLendon was the battery commanding officer; his executive officer was Lieut. Ralph T. Heard; Lieut. Frank M. Mitchell and 2d

Lieut. Arthur P. Braxton were also attached. Of particular interest was that the gun, being located in Lorraine, was actually firing across the frontier into Germany, this being one of the few spots where this could have been done. The gun continued in action for some months and after firing some 20,000 rounds, was sent to West Point to be placed on display. Various shell casings were sent to Wilson, Pershing and General Sibert, then commanding officer of the 1st Division, commemorating the first round sent in the direction of the Huns (7 March 1919).[10]

That French "75" artillery piece definitely captured the hearts of those who served that splendid weapon. It surely was a fit object to be commemorated by a poet who entitled his offering "Mlle. Soixante-Quinze":

> Oh, mistress fit for a soldier's love
>   Is the graceful 75;
> As neat and slim, and as strong and trim
>   As ever a girl alive.
>
> Where the steel-blue sheen of her mail
>   is seen,
>   As the light of her flashing glance,
> In the broken spray of the roaring fray
>   Is the soul of embattled France.
> . . . .

Anon.
(26 April 1918)

For the moment, of pressing necessity, weapons were foremost in the minds of the combatant arms. Perhaps one should not wonder that they sometimes came to be venerated as the instruments needed to get the job of war done. The machine gun naturally captured the imagination of many and one lively poem was produced by someone who had observed that weapon closely:

> Anywhere and everywhere,
>   It's me the soldier's love,
> Underneath a parapet
>   Or periscoped above;
> Backing up the barrage fire,
>   And always wanting more;
> Chewing up a dozen disks
>   To blast an army corps;
> Crackling, spitting, demon-like,
>   Heat-riven through and through—

Fussy, mussy Lewis gun—
Three heroes for a crew!
....

Of course, there were the Vickers and Browning guns as well which were needed "when men have holy work to do," since peace on earth could not come by pious wishes alone, but by such guns with "three heroes for a crew!"[11]

The machine gun and rapid-fire artillery, such as the 75, caused many men to grouse about the old standby weapon—the rifle. But Pershing insisted that it was still fundamental and demanded its mastery and proper employment by the men. *The Stars and Stripes* accordingly sought to inculcate pride in the rifle in the soldiers. An editorial devoted to the subject asserted that the rifle had not been replaced by more modern weapons; in fact, "the rifle has been reestablished in honor during the historic weeks just passed. It was always the most personal of weapons and a soldier who could not warm up to a cannon nor develop any sentiment whatever for a hand grenade would grow tremendously fond of his Springfield, which lived with him and was a part of him. It was his own. Now it rests with a new confidence and a new pride on every shoulder" (3 May 1918).[12]

Trucks and tanks could be the objects of affection, or at least respect, as well. Sgt. Richard C. Colburn of the Tank Corps praised his charges in his poetic offering, "The Tank":

....

Oh, you tank! tank! tank!
She's a Lulu, she's a cuckoo! She's the
goods!
When the Boches see you comin', they will set
the air to hummin',
A wavin' of their legs to reach the
woods.
....

Colburn hoped above all to drive his tank "through the dirty streets of Berlin," and "watch the goose step change to Yankee double time!" (21 June 1918).[13]

The lowly truck came in for praise in the poem, "As The Trucks Go Rollin' By":

There's a rumble an' a jumble an' a bumpin'
an' a thud,
As I waken from my restless sleep here in
my bed o' mud,

'N' I pull my blankets tighter underneath my
      shelter fly,
An' I listen to the thunder o' the trucks
      rollin' by.

....

Some of the trucks were "a-draggin' cannons," and one could tell by the sound the size of the pieces, as "the rumblin' ones is heavies, an' the rattly / ones is light." However, most of the trucks were "packin' loads o' human Yankee freight," and the listener could hear them singing as they rode to battle. Altogether, the poet, 1st Lieut. L. W. Suckert, liked "the jazz 'n' barber shop o' the trucks / a-rollin' by (11 October 1918).

Other combatant arms included the Navy and the Air Service. Rather strangely, neither was well reported in *The Stars and Stripes*, though there was some occasional mention or discussion of what they were accomplishing. While the pieces about these services were not stinting in praise, the infrequency of the appearance of anything at all about them must have rankled.

The editor did get around on one occasion to praising the "Good Old Navy," as well as it might when one considers its splendid record in shepherding the AEF safely to Europe—and back. The American Navy, he explained, was working with the Allied navies, but doing its work in silence, "shrouded in fog and screened by spray. It [was] done in cold and sleet such as even we have never known. It [was] done, day in and day out, with infinitely more peril and risk than attends our work, day in and day out. But it is done uncomplainingly, it is done manfully, it is done in a workmanlike, thorough, American way. . . . It is living up to its splendid traditions. If John Paul Jones, Stephen Decatur, David Farragut and George Dewey were walking the quarterdecks of the Navy today, we warrant they would be well pleased. Good Old Navy! Our very best salute to it!" (1 March 1918).

On another occasion the men were reminded that one million three hundred thousand American soldiers were then in France by courtesy of the Navy, and that all these lives had been entrusted to "the fellows who flaunt red chevrons . . . who wear their trousers upside down, and call their kitchen the galley." But they had been true to their trust and the editor asserted that "the A.E.F. hasn't forgotten you, brother gobs" (9 August 1918). However, the gobs themselves could be pardoned if they felt that they were the largely forgotten men in the pages of *The Stars and Stripes*.[14]

The far more glamorous aviators were likewise only briefly mentioned and, surprisingly, only a few poems appeared attempting to capture the daring new venture of flight and battle in a new version of the ancient trial by combat by modern knights "grappling in the central blue." One lengthy poem, "The Birdman's Day," somewhat got at the flyer's domain:

. . . .

It must be great to aviate mid storm-clouds
      gayly whisking,
To loop-the-loop with joyous whoop,
      One's epidermis risking:

. . . .

In heat or cold the bird man bold
      each chance for glory seizes,
He madly skips and throws back-flips
Amid the gusty breezes!

Anon.
(22 February 1918)[15]

The engineers, both of the construction and the railway variety, were as apt as anyone in pointing out what their accomplishments were in waging and helping to win the war. The "Song of the Railroad Engineers" emphasized this:

We don't know much about the drill
      The Doughboys have to do,
But we'll make the Kaiser clear the track
      And, boys, we'll shoot her through!
We'll highball down the Aisne and
            Somme,
      And this is what we'll do—
We'll ramble into Germany
      With the old Red, White and Blue.

Anon.
(22 March 1918)

Another railroad engineer seated at his typewriter wondered "If all these From: To: Subjects / Are a-doin' any good," and speculated further as to "How many battles were there / Ever won by pen and ink?" There were thrills in wartime, but he was certain that they would never be found "In the Services of Supplies!" Nevertheless, he knew that his job was of some worth, and the railway engineers were going to aid in doing "something to the Dutch! [sic]" (19 July 1918).

In other respects, though, railroading in France was not essentially different from railroading in Louisiana, as the sergeants in charge of some black engineers discovered. Whenever they wanted a particularly heavy piece of equipment moved, they simply began to croon that old song:

De ole hen duck said to de drake,
Dey ain't no crawfish in dis lake,
Let's—DIVE—to the odder SIDE!

At the word "dive," everybody took hold; at the word "side," everybody heaved
and dropped the rail, or whatever was being lifted, where it belonged. As one
editor concluded: "Mr. Orpheus, who moved rocks with his music, would
probably be interested" (15 November 1918).

One of the more articulate members of the engineers was Cpl. Vance C. Criss
who had published in the 7 June 1918 issue one of his many poetic offerings in
praise of his branch of service.

If it's work you would be doin'
Such as ties in need o' hewin',
Till yer back is jes' one ruin,
Join th' Engineers.

....

Franklin P. Adams, of the paper's staff, remembered the little-known, rather
mysterious, chemical corps:

They get no song to boost 'em along, they get
    no words of cheer;
For what they do is a job so new some of us
    don't know they're here;
But they work away in the lab all day to
    help us win the war;
Let's not forget we owe a debt to the men
        of the Chemical Corps.
    For it's HCL to give em hell, and H_2SO_4
C_2O_3 and TNT—the men of the Chemical
        Corps.

                              (12 April 1918)

The camioneers found their poet as well, in this instance, one David Darrah
of the famous Mallet Reserve. This organization consisted of about 1,200 drivers
or *camionneurs*, as the French called them, who were engaged in driving for
France before the United States entered the war:

....

To hell with the Huns! Speed up the guns!
We're bringing munitions, tons upon tons!

What if we croak? The line has not broke,
Anyway living is only a joke,
So, fill the cup high and never say die,
They sang on their camions thundering by!

. . . .

(25 April 1919)

An unknown poet remembered what the driver of artillery horses went through, while maintaining his pride throughout, in his ode to "The Driver":

I'm a slouch and a slop and a sluffer,
    And my ears they are covered with hair,
And I frequent inhabit the guard house—
    I'll be "priv" until "finie la guerre."
But my off horse, she shines like a countess,
    And my nigh made the general blink,
And they pull like twin bats fresh from Hades,
    And they're quick as a demimonde's wink.

. . . .

And when there's some route that's receiving
    Its tender regards from the Huns,
Then we gallop hell bent for election
    To our duty o' feeding the guns.
The gas, the H. E., and the shrapnel,
    They brighten our path as they burst,
But they've never got me or my chevals—
    They'll have to catch up to us first.

. . . .

(28 June 1918)

One of the sore spots in the AEF was the status of the draftees—the men of the so-called National Army. They had their pride as well, though sometimes it was a hurt pride. They did not take slights without explanation as to their rather invidious position. The editor of *The Stars and Stripes*, in the 26 April 1918 issue, came to their defense. He criticized those at home or abroad who saw the members of the National Army disparagingly; those who saw the draftees as "a reluctant army, an army of hangers-back." Some of those who gave voice to this sentiment, "should be shot at sunrise, for they are without vision." That is, the editor continued, "they are without vision of democracy. For, in a larger sense, the draft army of a democracy is a volunteer army." And, "it is this army which is on its way in numberless battalions, the army for which, in these mighty days, the Allies wait expectant. It is the hope of the world.'' All who criticize should remember that it was a draft army which faced the Germans at Verdun and said: ''They shall not pass.''

An unknown ''N. A. Man'' carried the matter further:

....

We didn't volunteer,
But, God knows, it wasn't fear;
We'd have gone in later, anyhow—
Well, anyhow, we're here!

We hate those Huns, the Germans,
For all the things they've done,
And of the things we hate them for,
Our being here is one.

....

(5 July 1918)

Those who served in the rear areas sent an inordinately large number of poems and letters to the paper advancing some sense of pride as to what they were doing as noncombatants. However, the majority plainly did not prefer to be where they were, and felt that they were being unjustly punished by being denied a crack at the Hun. The bruised pride of some was assuaged when, by early May 1918, the status of Paris was changed. As an article described it, ''Paris has always been in the Zone of Advance-in-Price, but not in the Zone of Advance militariwise.'' It had originally been designated as being in the Lines of Communication, which had hurt ''almost as much as it hurt to get in front of the business end of a shell,'' since this designation clearly marked the rear areas. Indeed, those therein ''felt as though [they had] played in the world's series and then hadn't got a cent of the pennant money.'' Then when ''Big Bertha'' began shelling the city, thanks be ''to Heaven and G.H.Q.—two bodies which are very close akin,'' Paris was redesignated, which altered in a twinkling the status of many troops (10 May 1918).

But Paris was only one area to the rear of the lines; what of the men at Tours, for example, or Bordeaux? They continued to toil far from the action at the front and their frustrations were often manifested. To be sure, the men in the rear could vicariously feel a thrill of what was happening on the lines: ''Even America, with all its care and all its prayers for us,'' one editorial began, ''cannot have felt quite the thrill of that battle as it has coursed through the S.O.S.'' As never before, all who toiled behind the lines ''have felt their shoulders pressing against the wheel, felt the strain of the push which will one day, please God, shove the German army across the Rhine'' (9 August 1918).

But just below the surface the frustrations festered, often to erupt. Ralph Underwood, in a poetic open letter from the "S.O.S. to Doughboy," raised the old refrain:

. . . .

No, we ain't been up in a front line trench, and
    we haven't one D.S.C.,
And we don't pretend one thing, old scout, in
    the line of bravery;
Our job has mostly just been to sweat and
    muddle around in muck,
But 'twas good for you lads in front of us, that
    while you fought—we stuck.

(6 June 1919)

If anything, it seems that the stevedores in particular received more praise than anyone else in the rear areas. A Supply Corps Sergeant, C. C. Shanfelter, was one who praised "Friend Stevedore":

. . . .

We ain't had no dugout movies, nor a Charlie Chaplin laugh;
We ain't got no handsome colonel with his neat and nifty staff,
Nor a brave and fearless captain with a flashing sword and gun
To yell, "Now, up and at 'em, boys! We've got 'em on the run!"
We ain't soaring round in biplanes punching holes in Boche balloons,
Nor corralling frightened Fritzes by battalions and platoons.
But when they yell, "Rush order!" then we get around right spry;
For the boys are up there waitin'—on the Service of Supply.

(27 September 1918)

The stevedores were, in the main, composed of black soldiers. But not all of the blacks in France were in the work battalions. Many were on the line, and *The Stars and Stripes* gave them their just due, though some notices could hardly hide a mixed envy and admiration, coupled with a sense of wonderment and perhaps surprise that blacks could fight. Still, the admiration comes across as genuine, and one editorial, commenting on the winning of the *Croix de Guerre* by several black soldiers, observed that "now the slaves of a century ago are defending their American citizenship on a larger battlefield. Now is their first chance to show themselves before the whole world as good and brave soldiers, all" (31 May 1918). Thus, warm was the praise for "our own '*Soldats Noirs*.'"

Many black leaders saw the matter in a similar light. Dr. Robert R. Morton, successor to Booker T. Washington as head of Tuskegee Institute, journeyed to

France after the war at the instance of President Wilson and Secretary of War Baker as an advisor of African matters to the U.S. Peace Delegation. This gave him an opportunity to address many of the 250,000 blacks in the AEF. He talked with men of the 92nd Division, and the 369th, 370th, 371st, and 372nd Infantry Regiments, the latter brigaded with French troops. He also spoke to the stevedores and their officers at Brest, St. Nazaire, Bordeaux, and Gièvres. He found the men well and in good spirits and complimented them on their record and their willingness to work and assured them that both white and black Americans would cordially welcome them home. He stressed that they should be careful to return in a "manly, yet modest, unassuming manner." They had met the test of war; they now had a far greater test at home where a much more doubtful victory awaited. But it was at once a much more severe but important battle. In his words, "it is a battle not against Germans, but against black Americans. This battle is against the men into whose faces I now look. It is your individual, personal battle—a battle of self-control, against laziness, shiftlessness and wilfulness." He urged the men to begin at once to practice self-control in France so as to leave behind a good reputation so that the black might always be welcomed, "not only because of his courage but because of his character" (3 January 1919).

No doubt, the blacks had raised themselves by their great efforts on the field of battle and behind the lines to new levels of respect and pride. However, the old habits and attitudes died hard and were destined to prevail long into the future. *The Stars and Stripes* was no exception, also printing poems, articles and other features presenting the blacks in a more usual light. The column, "Around The Sibley Stove," on one occasion recounted the following:

One Negro soldier in the Argonne was as pale as circumstances would permit, and visibly shaken.

"It's de tawkin' shells what gits me," he confided to a lieutenant.

"Nonsense, Sam; shells don't talk."

"Don' you tawk that away to me. I kin hear 'em plain as day. Four dese ole G.I. cans jus' whizzed by and I heard 'em say: 'Niggah, you ain't going back to Ala-BAM!' "

(18 April 1919)

Another sally, entitled "Experts Only Wanted," was similarly cast.

After noon mess one day the Negro company fell in in front of their barracks. The company was in charge of a sergeant of their own hue. Evidently he wished his men to make a showing, for he started with his admonition:

"Now all yo' niggahs what don't understand military evolutions fall out, for I'se gwine to gib some mighty peculiar commands."

(14 June 1918)

The issue of 3 May 1918 featured a picture of three black engineers equipped with pick, shovel and sledgehammer. Under the picture was the following account, allegedly from their own mouths:

We's ain't no Saimmies, boss. We's de Saimbos, dat's what we is—de Saimbos.

We's done come awn ovuh yere f'om ovuh yonder awn er laivee, to wukk awn dese yere docks an' sech. Oh, we lahks it all raht, we does,—on'l dey's a lot o' nigguhs ovuh yere wearin' dem li'l raid hats what's been ovuh so long dey done forgot dere own languish.

But we's gettin educatified, somehaow, too. We's learnt haow to say "pullet" fo' chicken, and "jaimbone" fo' haim, but dey ain't no Frainch wo'd fo' watermillion, nohaow. An' dey ain't no sweet co'n, no' no yams, no' no possum, 'sept dese Boche as lie 'raound puttending lahk dey daid.

But we lahks hit; oh, yais'm, bet yo' lahf we does! An' sence we been reading of some Frainch books transmogrified into Geo'rgian, we calls ou'selves "De T'ree Dusketeers!"

The Stars and Stripes, then, was guilty of inconsistency, as some readers saw it. On the one hand it praised the blacks; on the other, it lapsed into what were regarded as less than complimentary dialect stories. These were the considerations leading 1st Lieut. Charles L. Holmes to complain to the editor that his paper, "when speaking of the American Negro Soldier, seems to find space only for ridicule, degrading remarks, and prejudicial propaganda." He went on to state that "the . . . Principle of Americanism is 'Justice' to all. The Negro Soldier has always volontarily [*sic*] and freely placed as much of self-sacrifice, patriotism and blood at the disposal of his Government as any other race of men, in spite of such discouragement and unappreciation." He advised the editor to cease "wasting good type and paper in printing such weak and degrading jokes," and other similar matter. "Why not," he continued, "try to find out really what the Negro is doing and has done, then, give the man who has done a man's work, the credit for being a man." Otherwise, he concluded, "keep him out of a paper purporting to represent Democracy."[16]

Viskniskki's response was immediate and visceral. He insisted that no one was making fun of the Negro, "just in the same spirit that no one is making fun of the white man when we print letters of Henry's Pal to Henry. In these stories Henry and his pal are both made to appear ridiculous, but no one thinks that there is any desire to degrade." In fact, he continued, "the stories of colored soldiers, told in Negro dialect, do not hurt the colored man at all; . . . the one result is to make us have a larger liking for the colored man, and I can assure you that no one is poking fun." His conclusion was even more pointed: "The trouble is that you are altogether too sensitive in the matter. You cannot expect to put the colored man above other Americans, and that is what you are doing when you object to dialect stories. In my opinion your view point is entirely warped and your criticism has no foundation in fact."[17]

However, Holmes was not alone in his criticism of *The Stars and Stripes*. General Harts took exception to a certain story appearing in the 28 February 1919 issue. It seems that a certain Col. Robert Whitfield of the general staff had purchased $3000 in Liberty Bonds from a bank in Arkansas. A considerable time elapsed and he failed to receive them. An inquiry elicited the information that the bonds had been sent to a Pvt. Robert Whitfield, of Company I, 370th Infantry. The private had sent the bonds back twice, but when they were returned once more he concluded that "Ah jes' natchully reckoned de Lawd mus' a meant to be good to me." He proceeded to treat his company to the entire wine stock of the best cafe in Delle, near Belfort, which was greatly appreciated by one and all. But then "the gossips got busy when he started picking up odds and ends of fine laces and a diamond ring or so—which fripperies he posted to a lady in the South." But the climax came when he bought "a handsome, tastefully framed landscape painting for 300 francs and hung it over his bunk in a cow stable." Having been at last found out, he was arrested, but the Judge Advocate was "scratching his head" as to the proper charge, as forgery was clearly not indicated, if any crime was. Nevertheless, as the article concluded, the art exhibit rapidly vanished and "the bank where the bonds were hypothecated has made a grab for Private Whitfield's salary past, present and to come," and speculated that the private's pay for the next twenty years would be required to satisfy the debt.

There is no indication as to how matters turned out, but General Harts was upset by the story's publication, and addressed a Memorandum to Nolan demanding an investigation. However, the latter had found the story "very amusing," and saw no reason to pursue it further, concluding that "it occurs to me that we have something more serious to do than to bother with investigating articles of that kind, published in a newspaper which is written to amuse the men, unless there is something in the article contrary to good order and military discipline. There may be something in this article [of this sort], but from a casual reading of the same I fail to see it."[18]

Hurt ethnic pride sometimes surfaced regarding the Jews. Army Field Clerk Ben Gershon, stationed at Bordeaux, once complained to Watson that an article, "Plans for Passover," appearing in the 14 March 1919 issue, had used the term "the Jews" in the American Army. He sensed that this was the result of carelessness but felt that a similar oversight would not have occurred as, "The Micks in the American Army are preparing to celebrate St. Patrick's Day," or "The Wops in the American Army are completing arrangements for a big Christopher Columbus celebration." What should have been used were such expressions as "American soldiers of Jewish faith," or "Soldiers of Hebrew extraction."[19]

Watson responded first by asking a Jew in the office of *The Stars and Stripes* "whether he objected to being called a Jew. He replied that he was very proud of being called a Jew." Watson then sent a copy of Gershon's letter to Col. Harry Cutler, chairman of the Jewish Welfare Board, who from his Paris office responded that "it seems to me unnecessary to dignify with a reply a hysterical communication such as this is, based on a wrong premise. The word 'Jew,' as applied to members of our race, is perfectly proper and dignified, and I personally consider it a badge of honor.'' This was reason enough, Watson concluded, to "feel that any further comment on your letter is [un]necessary,'' as he wrote Gershon.[20]

Pride was sometimes inculcated or strongly encouraged by the high command for its own purpose. At a time when supplies were badly needed, a contest was launched at the ports among the stevedore companies. *The Stars and Stripes* was used as a means of publicizing the effort and it became front page news, with a running account given with charts indicating the progress of the ports involved which were Brest, Marseilles, Havre, La Pallice, Rochefort, St. Nazaire, Bordeaux, Rouen, and Nantes. Rouen and Nantes were at a disadvantage as being smaller, but the others were highly competitive with Brest, Marseilles and Havre being in the closest races. They were handling about 130,000 tons of supplies weekly. Brest had the edge and of the stevedores there, the 835th Stevedore Company emerged the winners. This gave the unit the right to wear the coveted brassards designed for the occasion and to lead a big parade carrying the ''General Connor Banner'' to work each morning, and to enjoy all the special privileges of the camp for a week. The eventual winners would have leaves and other benefits.[21]

This contest, while officially inspired, was of a piece with seemingly countless others that sprang up, both real and fanciful. As to the former, letters poured in to the editor claiming all manner of ''ests'' as they were called, i.e., the tallest soldier, the shortest soldier, the soldier who had the longest enlistment, and countless others. One favorite was to include pictures of the tallest and shortest soldiers of any unit side by side, as ''Mutt and Jeff,'' naturally. Other letters pointed out such trivial facts as to which unit had sent the most money home in allotments. The possibilities seemed endless, especially when tall tales began to appear in great profusion. Some soldiers poked fun at the ''ests,'' as one letter did: ''In the matter of length of service, I believe Old Man Charlie Cogle of our outfit holds the record. He enlisted in 1860, and served with honor as a machine gunner during the Civil War under General Grant. He accepted his discharge after the close of the war, but immediately reenlisted after several intensive disputes with his wife.'' The same ''outfit'' also proudly announced that it possessed the tallest man in the service, one Tommy Shinn, ''who is 8 feet 4 3/4 inches. . . . The shortest man . . . is Burley Mey, whose actual height is 3 feet 2 1/2 inches. He succeeded in passing the medical examination by exchanging the examining doctor's glasses for a pair that possessed great magnifying power. He and Tommy Shinn are pals, and it is a pretty picture to see them together'' (25 April 1919). There were also numerous yarns told, always with greater exaggeration, via the letters column as to the tons and tons of hot cakes produced by a particular cook using perhaps a huge factory system to accomplish his deeds.[22]

The contest and competitive fever spread and soon the letters column was including challenges for spelling bees and other forms of contests, though these were at last held up to ridicule by some doughboys no doubt tired of the whole thing. Even pride was not limitless.

One of the problems confronting Headquarters was that of welding the AEF into a force exhibiting an esprit de corps of a high order. Given that the excitement of participating on behalf of the Great American Republic in the adventure that the Great War was, was to many a sufficient fillip, still something could be done to intensify the ardor of service when days and lines grew long, the "hurry up and wait" factor interposed itself or when many longed for transfers to other units, branches, to the front, or perhaps to the various officers candidate schools. If all personnel could somehow be convinced of the necessity of willingly being where they were, doing what they were doing, armed or equipped as they were, things could simply run more smoothly. Ethnic groups, or members of various social strata, must likewise be permitted to affirm their role in the scheme of things, holding up their heads in the service of a democratic, just America, at last united after the fissures of the Civil War era, and becoming under the war's pressure even more democratic, engaged upon one of the world's great crusades: helping to free the world of tyranny. For all of that, it must be carried off with a modicum of modesty. *The Stars and Stripes* attempted therefore to appeal to pride, in one's self, one's unit, regarding the machines and weapons employed, and in the nation, all properly hedged about with a becoming humility, in itself a lesson from the New World to the Old. This would demonstrate how an armed republic, dedicated to democratic ideals, can and must act, even under the stress of war.

7

Friends and Foes

Do you mind when we once would remark,
　　Ere days of the zone of advance,
That the classiest play in the park
　　Was "Tinker to Evers to Chance"?

Well, here is another today,
　　So take all your cash from the bank,
And place it on this famous play:
　　"Tommie to Poilu to Yank"!

(31 May 1918)

Things One Learns In This Man's Army: "That people may be able to know a devil of a lot without knowing the English language."

(15 March 1918)

The war was won by all of the Allies fighting as one great Army of Liberty.

"Who Killed Cock Robin?"
(22 November 1918)

The Kaiser has gone to Holland and got in Dutch.
(15 November 1918)

The Stars and Stripes contained numerous features, editorials and poems on the Allies, especially regarding the French, though other nations and peoples were not neglected. An editorial entitled ''Team Mates,'' put the matter forthrightly, observing that the United States was in the war "for good and sufficient reasons of its own. Its aim is to lick Germany. To lick Germany quickly and thoroughly it must work in complete harmony with its Allies. Therefore, any man who, by word or thought or implication, seeks to destroy that harmony is doing his part in messing [up] the job of the United States and therefore in prolonging the war," since the purpose of the Allies was honorable. But certain people would seek to "come amongst us and hint in an underhanded way that such is not the case. They will tell us that we are fighting England's battle, France's battle, Siam's battle, Liberia's battle—any battle but our own. They will ask us, for example, why we, who fought two wars against England, are found on her side today. They will ask us why we are over here in Europe at all butting in on a fight that doesn't concern us." The answer was obvious: "We are over here to fight the battle of the United States, first, last and all the time." Thus, "we are here as members of a team, and it is only by team work with our Allies, the other members of that team, that we shall win out." German propaganda, spies and others are attempting to promote dissension among the Allies, and there was only one ugly word of two syllables which adequately describes any member of that team who does not concur: "Traitor" (15 February 1918).

Regarding the Allies, early in the history of *The Stars and Stripes*, much was made of the Australians. The Americans seemed to have established an instant rapport with them, and the paper defined a "Digger" as "a friend, pal, or comrade, snonymous [sic] with Cobblers; a white man who runs straight" (8 February 1918). The Australian soldiers also had their own publication, the magazine *Aussie*, which *The Stars and Stripes* sometimes borrowed from.[1]

The British were featured more often, however. *The Stars and Stripes* naturally turned to a reconsideration of some of America's past traditions regarding the hated "Redcoats" of days past. One editorial observed, along these lines, that the men who had fought at Lexington and Concord were naturally fighting for freedom from tyranny; nothing could alter that fact. But things had changed, and now the descendants of those "embattled farmers today stand side by side with the descendants of the men who opposed them. These are now united." Doubtless, "the Minute Men would have had it so. The Liberals of England of 1775 would have had it so." The famous action of 1775, that of " 'chasing the red-coats down the road, and only pausing to fire and load,' blazed the trail for liberty in England [as well], and by their vigorous resistance opened the eyes of England to the iniquities into which her Teutonic King and his Tory servant[s] had led her. Today the new, the freed England, honors their memory." The men of 1775, "good stand-up-and-go-to-it scrappers. . . made it possible for us to be here today, under this flag, embarked on this glorious enterprize, backed by the great people that sent us forth." The doughboy readers were therefore encouraged "to see to it that we prove ourselves, in the tests to come, worthy descendants of such as they!'', on both sides of the battleline in the Revolutionary War (19 April 1918).

The British, in turn, could on occasion recognize America's wartime accomplishments. Much was made of an article by Lieutenant Colonel Repington, the well-known military critic of the London *Morning Post,* which warmly praised the American effort. This piece was reproduced in the *New York World,* and, after some controversy as has been noted above, in *The Stars and Stripes* (3 January 1919). Repington was especially impressed with the rapid American buildup and the effective use of American troops in battle. Indeed, as he expressed it, "to all soldiers capable of understanding the true quality of troops, the American divisions had taken their degree in war and had passed with honors." He especially praised the American action in the Argonne, where the doughboys "found themselves up against a proposition calculated to appal [*sic*] the stoutest hearts." But the Yanks did not shrink. "They fought silently but grimly, doggedly and fiercely," he recounted. They overcame supply and communication difficulties and persevered. In truth, he concluded, "the sight of fresh American divisions continually thrown into the fight at a time when the British Armies were hammering him mercilessly in the north broke Ludendorff's nerve and filled the enemy's mind with foreboding of inevitable disaster."

The doughboys were perceptive enough to differentiate between the Scots and the English, partly, perhaps, because of the conspicuousness of the former. One anonymous poet explained in his poem, "The Free Ballade of the Naked Knee: A Tribute to a Hardy Race." His offering was dedicated to Field Marshal Sir Douglas Haig, the Scots commander-in-chief of the British forces in France.

. . . .

Sir Douglas Haig, this song to you
    I dedicate—accept it please;
I know how Britain "sees it through"
    When I view Scots with naked knees!
                                    (15 February 1918)

Belgium was quite another matter; that is, it was not viewed with a sense of humor. *The Stars and Stripes* once enjoined Americans "not [to] forget for a moment that we . . . owe to Belgium, who braved extinction that we might be warned and saved. And, recalling that, let us plunge into our task with renewed zeal—for the victorious completion of that task means the restoration of Belgium, the righting of the hideous wrong that was done her, the securing to her forever of the place among nations that is hers. . . . The heirs of those who fought for freedom at Lexington value those who fought for freedom at Liège. Their cause is the same!" (29 March 1918).

There were Yanks in Italy and *The Stars and Stripes* occasionally nodded in their direction, recognizing that the Italians were allies too. Herbert Henry Darling, Jr., of the American Red Cross Ambulance Service in Milan, developed an admiration for the *Arditi,* the shock-troops who were later to be closely associated with Mussolini's Fascists. He admitted that he was neither a poet nor a soldier, but he could not refrain from lauding this illustrious body of Italian troops. Darling recognized that they were not "the nobles of great renown," but were rather "the guys from the roughest part of town," that is, "if a feller can judge from looks." Still, this was their virtue, since when the Austrians saw the *Arditi* attacking, "they run like hell for their lives," fearing their "three devilish knives." With one knife in his mouth and one in each hand, the *Arditi* "jumps over the top," and there was not "a Boche in all Deutschland, who ain't scared stiff o' this wop" (13 September 1918).

Other peoples were recognized in the great struggle against Kaiserdom and its minions such as the Czecho-Slovaks, who, one editor reminded his readers, had been deprived of their independence since 1620, "the very year when the Pilgrim Fathers landed at Plymouth," and had, since that time, been oppressed by Austrians and Magyars, though always yearning to be free. They had John Huss to look to in their history as the great champion of religious and political freedom, and they were also inspired by "Golden Prague," with its famed university, "the shining light of middle Europe." They were paying further dues now in the struggle against Germans and Austrians, and in Siberia, against the Bolsheviks. As such, they too qualified as full-fledged allies and must not be forgotten (13 September 1918).

Among the Allies, however, there is little doubt that France made the greatest impression on the men of the AEF; it could scarcely have been otherwise. One of the first areas of contact involved the beautiful and appealing, but vexing, French language. This led the author of the column, "Phatigue-Squad Philosophy," to observe that "the French soldier may not get paid as much as the American, but he has a lot less trouble with the language of the country." And the same column further noted that "lots of guys write home that they are making rapid progress in French when the truth is that the only words they are really sure of are *oui, non,* and *bière*" (9 August 1919). Regarding the latter, an unknown poet, in his offering, *"Cela Ne Fait Rien,"* commented further:

> My French is a sorry affair,
>   And the words I may happen to use
> Would make a prof. pull at his hair—
>   'Twould give him the bluest of blues;
> Yet one thing I've mastered, I think,
>   Though difficult, quite, was the feat—
> To say when I'm needin' a drink:
>   *Un bock, s'il vous plait, ma petite.*

....

(15 March 1918)

Pvt. Charles Divine, in his "When Private Mugrums Parley Voos," composed other thoughts on the French language:

. . . .

In your pretty little garden
    I could always say "juh tame,"
But it ain't so very subtle,
    An' it ain't not quite the same
As "You've got some dandy earrings,"
    Or "your eyes are nice and brown"—
But my adjectives get manly
    Right before a lady noun.

. . . .

In your pretty little garden
    Darn the idioms that dance
On your tongue so sweet and rapid,
    Ah, they hold me in a trance!
Though I stutter an' I stammer,
    In your garden, on the bench,
Yet my heart is writin' poems
    When I talk to you in French.

                    (25 October 1918)

Alfred J. Fritchey was another who was fascinated by the sound of the French language:

. . . .

The maiden ripples French to me;
    But I am like some argonaut
    In some mute agony of thought,
Lost in sound's sweet tranquility.

                    (20 September 1918)

Withal, one of the "Few Horrors of War That Writers Don't Mention" was "the amateur French conversationalist" (5 April 1918).[2]

Many others in the AEF were incensed, rather than intrigued or pleased, by their first contacts with the French: many shopkeepers were blatantly guilty of overcharging the Americans, though evidences of genuine concern and generosity were not lacking. The paper sought to explain matters, observing that the French officials were endeavoring to curb the practice which threatened harm to the Franco-American alliance. But, the paper went on, "for the sake of France, it is only fair to say that it is a condition that is not peculiar to any one country.'' There were evidences of considerable overcharging of American troops in towns and cities in the United States near cantonments. In short, ''the great god Greed is not a national divinity,'' the article concluded (13 September 1918).

More graphic was an item published in the paper containing an excerpt from a letter written home to his father by a member of an Expeditionary Force, dwelling upon the money-grabbing natives among whom the troops had to make their way:

> They fleece us pitilessly; the price of everything is exorbitant; in all the dealings that we have with them they treat us more like enemies than friends. Their cupidity is unequaled; money is their god; virtue, honor seem nothing to them compared to the precious metal. I do not mean that there are not estimable people whose character is equally noble and generous—there are many, But I speak of the nation in general. . . .
>
> Money is the prime mover of all their actions; they think only of means to gain it; each is for himself, and none is for the public good.

This letter was purportedly written in 1782, and the writer was a Frenchman, the Comte de Ferson, an officer attached to the French Expeditionary Forces helping the American colonists. ''The 'they' were the first Yanks'' (11 April 1919).

Many men of the AEF first significantly encountered the French through the children. A common query was ''Ching gum,'' which was a child's request for chewing gum *americaine*. Thus, the American soldiers were guilty of transplanting the ''Great American Vice'' in France, and it, in truth, had ''corrupted whole French towns,'' which was almost as serious as the similar tobacco problem (22 March 1918).

But there were more meaningful contacts between the Yanks and the French children, which *The Stars and Stripes* was instrumental in. Central to these was a remarkable program to benefit war orphans. It was generally recognized that Pvt. Harold W. Ross conceived, developed, nurtured, and supervised the war orphan's program, thereby, as Watson later recognized, contributing ''enormously not only to the A.E.F., but to the future relations between America and France.'' His endeavors in this connection brought ''happiness to the soldiers adopting these fatherless children, . . . [and] brought relief and a promise of a happier life, not only to the children but to their families.'' Furthermore, the program had ''laid the foundation for a better feeling toward the United States on the part of all these children during their childhood and during their adult life alike.'' Watson was of the opinion, indeed, that Ross had thereby contributed, ''more than almost any individual in the A.E.F. to the cordial relations between the U.S. and the French republic.'' Certainly, he asserted, ''nothing else which *The Stars and Stripes* has performed has brought such high eulogies from leading figures in French affairs.'' *Le Journal* typically asserted, in this regard, that the idea ''was very American,'' as well as ''very touching'' (31 May 1918). This success was, as Watson concluded, "in large measure the personal work of Pvt. Ross," which was carried on in addition to his regular duties at the paper.[3]

The campaign was launched in the 29 March 1918 issue of the paper. The scheme provided that for the yearly cost of 500 francs an orphan would be "adopted," the funds being administered by the Red Cross, which was also responsible for screening the orphans. At the exchange rate then prevailing, this sum amounted to almost eighty-eight dollars. The paper figured that for a typical 200-man unit, each man could chip in two-and-a-half francs, or at the rate of about four cents per month. The paper hoped that some "live wire" in each unit would promptly get busy and raise the funds, sending them in to the paper's headquarters. The Red Cross would absorb all of the administrative costs. Furthermore, the Red Cross would send each child's picture and a biographical sketch to the adopting unit or individual, together with a monthly report on its progress. The Red Cross reserved the right to decide the immediate fate of each child, as to whether it would be placed in a foster home or, if old enough, sent to a trade or agricultural school. The Red Cross would also regularly visit each home or school to see if the funds were in fact being expended on the child's care (29 March 1918).[4]

The paper made haste to adopt the first orphan as an example to others. She was Marie Louise Patriarche who, since she had a mother living, was not, strictly speaking, an orphan, but the latter was seriously ill. The black-haired, black-eyed, dimpled lass was the daughter of a barrel maker who had been drafted into the French Army. He died in battle in 1915 (5 April 1918).

One of the branches that responded earliest and most enthusiastically was the Air Service. A letter from the 10th Aero Squadron stated it clearly: 'We desire to congratulate you upon this idea because it is in entire accord with the principles for which we are fighting, the preservation of the home. . . . Some of us have children at home, others have little brothers and sisters. We desire, in their names, to contribute our mite toward making the life of some little orphan at least a bit happier" (12 April 1918).

Other adoption requests began to pour in, one of which caused considerable interest. An intelligence section strongly desired to adopt a red-headed, freckled-faced youngster. This proved to be a major challenge to the paper and the Red Cross. The latter finally threw up its hands: "They finally found that there had been a red-headed, freckled-faced boy in France once, but that his father had taken him back to Ireland." The group had to settle for a blond (19 April 1918).

However, that was not the last word on that issue, since many other requests for such an orphan were received. But the *"Cherchez La Tête Rouge"* continued without avail (28 June 1918). The paper at last admitted that three freckled-faced, red-headed chldren had been found, but "there was one rub—not one of them was a war orphan" (30 August 1918).

Subsequently, the orphan campaign grew by leaps and bounds, and nearly every issue of the paper reported its progress. Especially satisfying was the fact that many people and organizations in the United States eagerly participated.

Typical of these was the "Carry On Club," of a Portland, Oregon firm, The Foundation Company, a ship-building firm which adopted twenty orphans, one each for the twenty wooden steam auxiliary ships then being built there for the French government. The club consisted of fifteen women employees of the shipyard. *The Stars and Stripes'* adoption program had been featured in the yard's weekly magazine, *Do Your Bit*. This resulted in a "tag day" campaign which raised the required 10,000-franc equivalent.

Also gratifying was a certain letter received enclosing 1,000 francs for the care of two orphans which indicated further that it was "being sent just on the eve of our entrance into battle; we will write more in detail later." The editor could only say that, "hundreds of writers are writing millions of words trying to describe the spirit of the A.E.F., but we doubt if any genius of the pen will ever convey to paper the spirit of the A.E.F. so strikingly and completely as it is set down in those two simple sentences" (26 July 1918).

Christmas 1918 seemed a spendid time to redouble efforts to fete all the children of France—not only the orphans—and many were the celebrations on their behalf (22 November 1918). As to the orphans, the paper launched a "Christmas Gift Orphan Campaign," which was to run several weeks, ending on 16 December. The response was great, and some 294 were adopted in the last week of November alone (29 November 1918). This brought the total adopted by that date to 1,670. But at this point, the S.O.S. created a sensation, turning in 418,000 francs for the adoption en bloc of 836 orphans, the grand result of an intensive campaign. In response to Maj. Gen. James G. Harbord's request— he was the commander of the S.O.S.—no individuals making contributions were identified, thereby highlighting the cooperative effort of his organization. As he expressed it, "the spirit of self-advertising does not exist among its members." Hence no invidious comparisons were possible (6 December 1918).

When the final tally was made of the program, it was revealed that 3,444 war orphans had been adopted. The campaign had lasted from 29 March to 16 December 1918. Thereafter, far more money was collected, but it was used mainly for further assisting the 3,444 already chosen (20 December 1918). As of the end of December 1918, almost two million francs had been collected, or an average of about one franc—approximately twenty cents—per man in the AEF (27 December 1918).[5]

There was so much in France that impressed the Americans. Perhaps the circumstances of being in a war-torn country brought out their sympathies. The French had truly suffered and many doughboys were deeply touched. One unknown doughboy would always remember:

    When I am home again
        I'll build an open grate,
    And in the joyous paean,
        Of dreams that linger late,

I shall be back in France.
    For I am one that loved her lengthy lanes,
The wanderings of Chance,
    The maidens by her roadsides and the trains
Of camions along her lime-pressed roads
That groaned at lifting hills and leaden loads,
And at my grate with fantasy aglow,
How sweet 'twill be for you to know
    The France I love.

. . . .

(30 May 1919)

    Another unknown writer was saddened yet inspired by the "Street of the Pretty Heart," which existed in a village virtually destroyed by German aircraft. "But, in the middle of that pathetic and ruined apology for a street the children were playing away, as merrily as if nothing at all had happened, shouting to one another in glee. And the name of that street—as the battered and half obliterated sign on the corner of the caved-in house at the end, testified—was 'Rue du Joli Coeur'—'Street of the Pretty Heart!' " The scene was symbolic of the way that France had borne her struggle, her devastation—"with the heart-free, care-free spirit of childhood. One may crush, but not conquer, a race whose children can find happiness amid such surroundings, can abandon themselves to play under the very shadow of disaster." This, in short, "is the secret of triumph of the spirit of France over the malignant and evil genius of her arch enemy" (8 February 1918).

    More reverently, Sgt. James Beveridge, of the Medical Corps, felt that France, for what she had endured, was now "The World's Holy Ground":

Ah, France, thy soil is holy soil,
And old Judea's sacred sod,
That saw the agony and toil
Of Him who was both man and God,
Hath now a kindred holy place,
That too hath seen the Saviour's face.

. . . .

(11 April 1919)

    Not only was there France, there were her soldiers, the stoical, brave, enduring *poilu*, who were also of considerable interest to the Americans. One editor wondered just what the *poilu* thought about, "as he sits back in the corner of his little old smelly cafe listening to the occasional shouts of laughter from the uproarious group of Yanks dining at the center table and keeping silent when the speaker of the moment proclaims to all within a kilometer's range that America saved the world and Americans won the war?'' The French soldier simply smiled and borrowed a light and then, ''saluting in his friendly fashion, goes his way. But what does he think?'' (14 February 1919).

Stewart M. Emery likewise wondered what the *poilu* was all about:

> You're a funny fellow, *poilu* in your dinky little cap
>> And your war worn, faded uniform of blue,
> With your multitude of haversacks abulge from heel to flap
>> And your rifle that is 'most as big as you.
> You were made for love and laughter, for good wine and
>> merry song,
>> Now your sunlit world has sadly gone astray,
> And the road today you travel stretches rough and red and
>> long,
>> Yet you make it, *petit soldat*, brave and gay.
>
> . . . .
>
>   (6 September 1918)

Marshall Foch came in for some attention as well, principally regarding how his name should be pronounced, in an amusing poem, ''It's Pronounced Foch'':

> The French will think it is a joke
>> When bungling Yanks pronounce it
>>> Foch,
> Yet will we make a sadder botch
> If we attempt to call it Foch;
> Nor can we fail to pain and shock
>> Who boldly try to say it Foch.
> In fact, we have to turn to Boche
>> To find the word that rhymes with
>>> Foch.
>
>   (12 April 1918)

Armistice Day was also an opportunity for the French and Americans to exchange congratulations and to reflect on the meaning of their alliance. *The Stars and Stripes* recounted details of the celebrations on *''le jour de gloire,''* which was, certainly, ''the greatest day Paris has known since the fall of the Bastille, marking, as it did, the triumph over the last remaining Bastille in the world, the fortress of Spandau.'' One of the highlights of that evening's celebrations occurred at the Place de l'Opéra. Onto the balcony of the famous building came France's best singers. Over and over they sang ''La Barbanconne,'' ''The Star Spangled Banner,'' ''God Save the King,'' ''La Marseillaise,'' and after countless urgent requests, "Madelon." The affair ended as a great community song festival. Then, "as the last notes of the opera's orchestra died away, a French bugler, armed with a sense of humor as well as with his redoubtable clarion, blew the *berloque*, the all clear signal sounded at the end of the air raids that are now no more" (15 November 1918). It had been a wonderful evening indeed to have been a member of the victorious Allies; to have been an American in Paris. Never had French and American amity been so high.[6]

As to the foes, *The Stars and Stripes* had little to say regarding the Central Powers other than Germany. It was as if they counted for little or nothing at all. Germany was the enemy worthy of consideration, and specifically the Kaiser was the villain most often identified, with considerable attention being given to the Crown Prince as well. Initially, the paper focused on German atrocities but soon took another tack. For instance, the first issue featured a front-page article as to how the "Huns Starve and Ridicule U.S. Captives." Three U.S. prisoners-of-war captured in the autumn of 1917 were badly treated according to the account of a repatriated Frenchman witness to their treatment. The same issue recounted an atrocity story about a 17-year-old girl had been forced into being a German officer's mistress. She was later branded with an iron in the form of a cross.[7]

But Chaumont soon issued Bulletin No. 80, stipulating that stories of atrocities committed by the Germans must be officially verified before personnel were permitted to write home about them. Censors were ordered to cut unsanctioned statements out of letters. Neither were accounts of unverified reports to be printed in the press. The reasons given were that unnecessary fears could be generated by such stories, and exaggerations and falsehoods reduced confidence in official reports of the German atrocities which were authenticated (8 November 1918). *The Stars and Stripes* had already admitted that the widespread reports that dead German gunners had been found near Château-Thierry chained to their machine guns were erroneous, but, nevertheless, got in the last word: "That is only a minor detail. The main fact is that all Germany is chained to Kaiserism, chained to a wild madness without a parallel in the world's history" (9 August 1918).

Outrages that were verifiable were often discussed, as when the "Big Bertha" began shelling Paris. One of the big gun's shells fell on a maternity hospital killing a nurse, two mothers, and a new-born child (19 April 1918).

Such atrocious actions led to the understandable view that since the Germans had no honor, there was really only one satisfactory thing to be done: "We must kill a great many. Our job is long and hard, but it is as plain as a pikestaff." Since the Germans had to be knocked "into Kingdom Come," there seemed no better battle cry than the war whoop of "the great Kentuckian," Col. Henry Watterson, the famous Lousiville journalist, who had said "To Hell with the Hohenzollerns and Hapsburgs." It seemed, to the paper's satisfaction, that "they are on their way" (19 April 1918).[8]

Surprisingly little was published in *The Stars and Stripes* regarding the German front-line soldier. Rather, the object of almost continuous attack in the pages of the paper was the Kaiser. All sorts of things were said about him; all manner of gossip dredged up. And Kaiser Bill was frequently the addressee of "letters." Typical was one presented in "The Listening Post" column in the form of a memo:

> From: The Allies
>   To: W. Hohenzollern, Germany.
> Subject: Travel order.
> 1. Proceed plumb to hell.
> 2. The travel directed is necessary in the military service.
>
>   By direction of
>   General Good
>   (3 May 1918)

There was also appreciation of the fact that Kaiser Wilhelm was truly "William The Coward," as one editorial was entitled. Indeed, while the rearguards of his army were frantically battling to cover his retreat, Wilhelm, the commander-in-chief, fled to a neutral country "to gain respite from the wrath of the world," thereby deserting the German Army in its hour of greatest need. In that flight over the Dutch border, "we have at last the full measure of the self-styled War Lord. We see now of what stuff he was made who exhorted his soldiers to be 'as terrible as Attila's Huns,' who boasted of his shining sword, who proudly traced his lineage back to Frederick the Great." For all of his deeds he has been called "William the Damned," with justice, "but in the eyes of all soldiers, his own included, he will go down in history as William the Coward" (15 November 1918).

The Crown Prince was perhaps even more despicable, if possible. A witticism in the 11 October 1918 issue of the paper suggests this:

> I know the Kaiser's a hellion, and all that, but I could
> almost forgive him if it wasn't for one thing.
>   What's the one?
>   He's the Crown Prince's father.

As another article asserted, the "Slipper of Civilization" wielded by the Allies, might make a fairly decent boy of the Crown Price "by spanking him at every opportunity." He had first been laid across their knee at the opening Battle of the Marne and was at that time "administered one of the soundest spankings of all time." Later, at Verdun, "the Slipper of Civilization descended again with telling physical effect. In his last Marne drive, the Allies again let the slipper play a busy tattoo for the good of the world." But, unfortunately, "in spite of all this personal and extensive chastisement, the Crown Prince is one of those bad boys beyond reform. The Allies, by proper and constant application of the slipper, have done their best to make him fit to live with. But he is apparently beyond all reformation." There seemed to be only one thing to be done and that was to take him by the scruff of the neck and drop him in his cell (23 August 1918).

The coming defeat of Germany was closely followed by *The Stars and Stripes* which was gratified by the evidence of an impending genuine German revolution. This seemed a wonderful possibility, and were it to occur, could "it be called defeat if a people rises up, throws off its dynastic shackles, exterminates its junkers [*sic*] or reduces them to 'a virtual impotency'?" It was time to "let Germany hear, as she must hear, the great call of the free democracies of the world, and not one of her two million dead shall have died in vain" (25 October 1918).

Yet, why had Germany been defeated? There was no lack of theories and possible answers. One clever, perceptive piece, appearing as an editorial, suggested a novel approach. Entitled "Germany's Shortage," it argued that all things considered, history may decide that Germany's fatal shortage was neither in flour nor raw materials but in humor: "The Allies could never escape the feeling that, in addition to being terrible, Germany was also rather ridiculous." A discerning Englishman once observed that "even in her invasion of little Belgium, the spectacle she presented of a huge, whip-cracking bully striding into a room and stumbling over a doormat had in it a disastrous element of the comic." And as to the Kaiser: "Wilhelm, in any country with a sense of humor, would never have been able to play his role out to its ghastly conclusion. He would have been laughed off the stage in the prologue." The Germans could not appreciate—being laughless themselves—the British, "who could catch the Kaiser's sneer and make a fond and jubilant war cry out of 'The Old Contempt-ibles.' " And the French, "whose gayety had misled the Germans into thinking them negligible and frivolous, proved to be quite a serious people on the hills before Verdun." The American doughboy seemed to regard himself fully equipped "so long as he could go into battle armed with a toothbrush and a grin; and it is probably true that his army laughed more per kilometer than any other army in the field." Indeed, the Germans must have often wondered at the fact "that the Yank was the most baffling and most deadly of all offensive weapons—the soldier who fights with a smile" (10 January 1919).

But with Germany defeated, *The Stars and Stripes* had to answer the doubters already asking questions as to what had been accomplished and why America had been involved at all; wasn't the war, in truth, fought in vain? Decidedly not, was the usual retort. "America's chief reason for going to war—also France's chief reason and England's—[was] self-defense," one response began. "It was to avoid capture and enslavement by Germania on a tout. It was the same purpose which animates every posse of citizens who are out to catch a maniacal burglar." That aim was attained: "The burglar-nation is in the lockup." If the posse, before it broke up, was able to "adjust the affairs of the neighborhood so as to discourage future burglarious enterprises," so much the better. But the Allies did not fight the war in vain. "It was Germany who did that" (2 May 1919).[9]

Nevertheless, *The Stars and Stripes* could recognize good in the Germans, at least in some of them, and often differentiated between individual Germans and their leaders. Accordingly, it reprinted a letter that a German soldier, Hans Pern, had written to Mrs. Gertrude Bostrom of Santa Cruz, California: "I will communicate briefly the sad news that your son, Walter, fell in battle on the 2nd of October, 1918. I myself gave him assistance, but he fell asleep in my arms and was buried by German comrades in Wenn Wade, near the village of Tonel, Northern France." He hoped that Mrs. Bostrom would answer his letter, "even if it is not until after the war." This would, he continued, "give me sincere pleasure." He concluded: "With heartfelt sympathy for your fallen son, [I am] enclosing two letters and a photograph he left." To the editor this was a significant gesture, indicating that "every once in a while something happens which, to the great annoyance of statisticians and propagandists, reminds us all that the late war was a mighty clash of peoples which, unfortunately, involved human beings" (28 March 1919).

In fact, there was the problem of the "good Germans" and the "bad French" with which the paper had to cope late in its career. There surfaced considerable evidence within the AEF of a great deal of anti-French sentiment, which was a cause of considerable worry at Chaumont. This was especially strong among the men of the Third Army, the American force occupying the American zone in the Rhineland after the Armistice, headquartered at Coblenz. Troops there seemed inclined—and many in France found this attitude incredible—to see the Germans in a more positive light than they saw the French. Alexander Woollcott, of the paper's staff, who functioned for a time in Coblenz as its resident correspondent, reported to Watson that this "mild but genuine animosity toward the French," was related to the feeling of increasing amity felt toward the Rhinelanders. These feelings were present among both the officers and men, though they derived from different sources. As to the officers, they were extremely exasperated because the French had blatantly pushed into the American bridgehead, and there evinced a disposition "to take the curtain calls with us, [and] from the French decision to indulge in the sort of triumphant display in Coblenz which the Americans had, from policy or instinct, sedulously avoided." *The Stars and Stripes*, in fact, had reported that "nothing could have been much more striking than the contrast between the French and American methods of entering Coblence [*sic*]. The Americans sort of dropped in in their casual manner [on 8 December 1918], which so grievously disappoints those who crave a grand entry." The Americans had merely "trundled in on a slow-poke German train, dropped out at the railroad station, marched to the nearest barracks and went to sleep." But when the French came, they came by river boats at high noon, with "the kind of music that sets the blood a-dancing, the drums thumping an accompaniment to the horns, while the cymbals crashed and the shrill whine of the Arabian reed-pipe sounded clear from shore to shore." In these circumstances it was perhaps disconcerting to the French that, before the American commander, Gen. Joseph Dickman, could meet them, they "were met (accidently) by a detachment of sixteen American soldiers ambling along the quay." The paper hoped that the

French never learned that this was no official deputation, but was rather, "the local AWOLs out for an airing under guard" (27 December 1918).

The troops, on the other hand, Woollcott continued, harbored a much deeper feeling, "and one likely to infect more people." Beginning in June, and reaching its height in September, he observed, "the troops in the combat units developed the habit of expressing a growing dislike for the French. This dislike can be traced, of course, to the natural friction between alien peoples. It was heightened by the forlorn and dirty parts of France the American fighter has been obliged to see and smell, by the uncooperative spirit of many French soldiers as manifested in the amenities of the highway, by the indifferent quality of the dulled and weary French troops with whom, for military reasons, the vigorous young American divisions were for the most part, associated and by the disposition of many French shopkeepers, like many American shopkeepers, to mulct the doughboy." Ironically, the Rhineland shopkeeper is prevented, whatever his inclination, by the American military authorities from "jockeying prices to the disadvantage of the soldiers." Hence he comes off much better in the comparison.

Woollcott also remarked upon the fact that the sense of friendliness between the American troops and the Rhinelanders was "something quite separate from the policy of our staff and could not be greatly altered by any change in that policy." Indeed, it did not derive to any great extent "from the shrewdly agreeable manner of the Rhinelander—to his natural effort to please." It arose, rather, "from a kinship in the little customs that make up existence, a kinship which extends all the way from architecture to apple-pies. The dress of the people, the cleanliness and width of the streets, the arrangement of the shop-windows, the very bathtubs and water closets along the Rhine call out to the homesick Yankee: 'We are of one blood, ye and I.' " In short, "the American soldier is at ease in Germany because it is a country contemporary with his own, that is, a country which, by expanding during the same half century that saw America's expansion, is similarly adorned and equipped." When Christmas rolled around, as *The Stars and Stripes* recorded, the Yanks in Germany were even more poignantly reminded of the similarities, observing "the rows upon rows of Christmas trees for sale in the public squares. Their high fir points, where one might easily conjure up the topmost, wobbly candle—Mother would be in such panic for fear it would set the tree afire—these points it was that pierced the Yankee to the heart" (27 December 1918).

Contrastingly, "the American ill at ease in France is just a case of crabbed age and youth," Woollcott observed. America and France were, to be sure, "kin in thought." But Germans and Americans were "kin in customs." He elaborated: "It may be kinship in thought which links two peoples when the Atlantic separates them. [But] it is kinship in custom which avoids friction when those peoples are, through war or immigration, pitched into the same territory. France, then, would, even if matters were to become far worse than they are, reestablish, in time, her greater claim on our national affections and her true place in our national perspective. But, unless a pretty active and able propaganda is set at work, a large number of Americans in Europe will go home loudly and perversely expressing their preference for the Germans." Woollcott, for his part, hoped fervently that the Army of Occupation would "go home to leaven the lump of hate for Germany. I should be sorry to have any American take home an irrational dislike for France. A good many Americans are sure to take home at least a deep irritation against the French and a quite undeserved irritation. Millions of letters home must reflect it now." Woollcott had some suggestions. He felt that, in the first place, Paris and Chaumont should realize "how Murman-like is the remote isolation of the Third American Army." He instanced that "we at Coblenz caught only the faintest echoes of the stupendous welcome accorded to America in the person of the President," when he arrived in Europe for peace talks. Furthermore, "the divisions on the Rhine are scarcely touched by the currents of opinion and emotion which flow in France. Much moody and misguided thinking in those divisions would be avoided if, by strenuous effort, they were flooded with enough fresh newspapers to go round." The circulation of *The Stars and Stripes*, then, must there immediately receive "a great impetus from Paris."[10]

Watson saw the problem plainly; an emergency of some magnitude existed. Germans must not be permitted to displace Frenchmen in America's affections, if it could be avoided. Accordingly, he proposed to greatly increase the circulation of *The Stars and Stripes* in Germany. Furthermore, he would "publish an occasional reminder what the gentle German people did to Belgium [*sic*] women, children and priests in 1914." He would also highlight the losses incurred by the French during four and one-half years of war. His remedies were accepted at G.H.Q., Capt. Donald L. Stone, the assistant chief of G-2-D, feeling that his reminders would "be admirable if not over-done," and was confident that Watson could be trusted "not to be too obvious about it."[11]

Subsequently, Watson followed up on his proposals. To assist him in the greater circulation of the paper in Germany, he received additional trucks and other help. As to his subtle propaganda, a clever representative article appeared in the 7 Feburary 1919 issue:

When Bismarck enunciated the principle that the best place to have a war was in somebody else's territory he said a sage and far-sighted mouthful. And Germany sagely and far-sightedly did her best to follow that principle from 1914 to 1918, with the result that only her fringes have been touched—amid the smoking ruins of her neighbors, her own hearth, for all its sorrows, is clean-swept and unmolested. The Chemin des Dames is gutted and black with the ugly aftermath of war; the Rheinstrasse is as neat as ever.

In Coblenz you will walk along a clean street (that was never splattered by a Bertha's iron scales) into a neat café (that never shook from a Gotha's bomb) and drink a tall one from a brewery which has been assaulted by nothing worse than a war tax. It is good. It is comfortable. It is clean.

With its roofs and walls intact, why shouldn't it be?

The course of the Franco-American alliance, then, was not altogether a smooth one. Though there is no doubt but that the French and their land would never be forgotten by those Americans who served there in the greatest adventure of their lives, other peoples excited their respect and admiration. When these included the late foes, the Germans, to an extent regarded as excessive, *The Stars and Stripes* was mobilized to counter it, hoping to inculcate, as it so often did, the correct attitude within its charges—the men of the AEF.

8

Sports and Entertainment

What care we for "Y" hut dances?
    There's a thrilling in the glen.
What care we how muddy France is?
    Blithesome April's here again.

April days of springtime glory
    Sending out to youth the call,
April—leading summer's story
    With a glove, a bat and ball.

                    (4 April 1919)

Shades of Spaulding, Walter Camp,
    And others who our sports enhance;
Who would have thought two years ago
    That we'd have pigskin days in France!

But when the fighting doughboy came
    He brought his shifts and forward pass,
And he can drop-kick just the same
    As when he played on Yankee grass.

                    (14 March 1919)

Wherever the American soldier goes, he seemingly must have his sports and entertainment, and in order to help maintain morale, his commanders are usually willing to abet him, even in times of fiercest battle. Indeed, "one of the wonders of the world war is the way the Americans have carried their sports to the battle fields of France and Belgium," the column, "Passing The Buck," by "Franc Terror," once began. No question about it, it amounted to a veritable "sports invasion," and Yankee athletic activity was soon quite apparent. Indeed, to one observer, American sports even seemed to be catching on in England, which had "taken quite a liking to our basketball game and in some places baseball is making a feeble fight to gain a foothold in the land of cricket and tea" (11 April 1919). The future would reveal that such appearances were deceptive, but for the moment Americans deluded themselves that their presence was not only a major factor on the battlefield but elsewhere "the American way" held sway. To be sure, there were exceptions as to the extent that American sports were catching on:

You're Not a Fan, Pierrette

I'll take you to the Follies, dear,
  If there you think you'd like to go;
I'll buy you *beaucoup* wine and beer
  Down at the gay Casino show;
In short, I'll do whatever task
  Your little heart desires to name,
Save one: You must not ever ask
  To see another baseball game.

. . . .

When you and I were watching while
  The Doughboys battled the Marines.
Did classy hitting make you smile?
  Did you rejoice in home run scenes?
Ah, no; When Meyer slammed the pill—
  They couldn't find it for a week—
You turned to me and said, "Oh, Bill,
  I zink hees uniform ees *chique*."

. . . .

Sgt. Stuart Carroll
(8 March 1918)

The Stars and Stripes accepted the fact that any American newspaper worth its salt must have a respectable sports page printing the latest sports news. Therefore, from the beginning, sports reports were included in the cables reaching the paper from New York. The first sports editor was B. F. Steinel, lately a Red Cross ambulance driver, who had had twenty years' experience as sporting editor on *The Milwaukee Evening Wisconsin, The Sentinel, The Journal, The Free Press, The Daily News,* and *The Chicago Inter-Ocean* (22 February 1918).

Nevertheless, much of the sporting news was generated by men of the AEF, and it seemed only natural that baseball should be played within the sound and range of the guns at the front (29 March 1918). It was also immediately recognized that the American experience in sports could help the soldier to relate to the war experiences that were soon to be encountered. Such sports as field, track and baseball had already helped prepare the men for the approaching ordeals at the front. The Iron Duke had once recalled that the battle of Waterloo was won on the playing fields of Eton. "Similarly it may be said in time that the battle of _____was won upon the diamonds and cinder tracks of America." The reasons were obvious: "Baseball [for instance] makes for self-reliance, for quick thinking and quick and sound judgements. It develops speed, endurance, strength of arms and backs and legs—in short, all the physical attributes of the really effective soldier." Therefore, it would be well for all soldiers to be toughened and refreshed by "that best of recreation and exercise," sports. By the same token, "it will be very bad for the Boche to face an army of baseball-trained, grenade and bomb-tossers; and, in playing with the Boche, spiking, too, is perfectly within the rules!" (8 March 1918).

The point was made by a poet in his "World's Series Opened—Batter Up!":

> He's tossed the horsehide far away to plug the hand
>   grenade;
> What matter if on muddy grounds this game of war
>   is played?
> He'll last through extra innings and he'll hit as well
>   as pitch;
> His smoking Texas Leaguers'll make the Fritzies seek
>   the ditch!
>
> . . . .

Anon.
(22 February 1918)

Truly, the war was *the* world series:

Uncle Sammy in the Box

> Oh, just watch me when it's Springtime
>   and the sunshines on the bleachers,
> When the Big Game starts, my laddie,
>   On the di'mond Over Here—
> See the grin of joyous rapture sneaking
>   o'er my classic features
> As I'm thinking how Our Boys will
>   win the bacon and the beer.
> Tho' the Gothas play a savage game
>   and lately they've been winning
> From some pitchers not in training
>   and who couldn't stand the knocks,

> You will hear 'em shouting "Kamerad"
> about the second inning
> When Uncle Sammy dances to the box.

....

The pitcher would send "the old horsehide" over the plate "To greet the chinless Kronprinz / who misses it a mile," and the "Hun Bench-warmers" would wonder, "Vot der hell is dot he's serving?", and "He can give them any brand of ball / and any place they want 'em / Around their neck one minute and / the next around their socks." It would certainly be something, "When Uncle Sammy dances to the box" (15 February 1918).

An editorial, entitled "The Real Thrill," attempted further to help those apprehensive men anticipating the uncertainties of combat to dispel their fears: "For most of us the thrills of soldiering have thus far been little ones. We had our first pleasant shiver the day we took the oath of allegiance. Then came the memorable morning when we first donned uniform, the first time we paraded down the avenue in ranks with colors flying at the head of the column and the band a-blare, and the first time we set foot on foreign shores with the A.E.F." However, "the thrill that comes but once in a lifetime" would be the first sight of the front. Yet, "the actual entrance to the trenches is, oddly enough, not nearly as inspiring as that first glimpse from afar. Away off you see the guns flashing. The whole sky is vibrant. The weird light of the star shells stirs the imagination. You have a sensation much like that just before you go into a football game—the same nervous tension, the same doubts about whether you will be able to hold your bit of the line." Just as in a sporting event, one would soon have so many other things to think about "that you forget your uneasiness. After all, these trenches are just like the ones back home in the training camp." The only real difference "is that the Boches are shooting at you." Thus, "the game is on! All you have to do now is to watch your opponent and keep your ears open for the quarterback's signals. Remember how it used to be in football games?—Once you mixed into a scrimmage and got roughed up a bit your dander was up and all stage fright was forgotten. And so it is in this game of war" (8 March 1918). The "game of war" accordingly should hold no terrors for the average American soldier already trained in sports. That familiar experience of the playing field was a framework for war experiences—the parameters were set, terror circumscribed; fear and uncertainty, and even the horrors of conflict, were thus rendered familiar if not innocuous.

Given this state of affairs, it is not surprising that certain attitudes would surface towards sports heroes who confined their sports, as in the past, to the diamonds, cinder tracks, and rings at home when the sports arenas that now mattered were in Europe. An editorial, "Heroes in Wartime," in the 15 March 1918 issue, explained that *The Stars and Stripes* had, "as a matter of news," printed in full the account of the Frank Moran–Fred Fulton boxing bout held in

New Orleans on 26 February. It was, in fact, given "all of the prominence as a sporting event that it deserved." However, the editor hastened to add, "let no one suppose that we have the slightest disposition to make heroes of this pair. To our notion the proper belt for a fighting man to wear in war time is of regulation canvas web or fair leather—not green silk. We may be doing somebody an injustice (and if we are we will make due apologies for it), but to the best of our knowledge neither Fred Fulton nor Frank Moran has yet seen fit to hold up his right hand and swear to defend the United States against its enemies." The editorial noted that "an athlete with the extraordinary reach of a Fulton should be a mighty handy man with a bayonet." And, "a husky fellow with four years' service in the United States Marine Corps [the reference was to Frank Moran] . . . should win more enthusiastic plaudits from the A.E.F. if we could behold him in his old 'sea-goin' blues' or a suit of forest green." It simply would not do that a boxer would plead that service in the army would separate him from his family and a fat income." Indeed, "thousands of other Americans in France and in the training camps back home are making such sacrifices and making them cheerfully." Thus, "a trained athlete, particularly one who has had the opportunity to lay away a tidy fortune at fighting, owes it to his country to do something in return." Therefore, "as we see it, . . . Fulton and Moran are anything but heroes" (15 March 1918).

This was the opening salvo of what became a full-scale barrage against athletic "slackers." The next to feel the paper's wrath were not only Fulton again, but also another boxer of note: "The managers of Mr. J. Willard and Mr. F. Fulton, our most celebrated pacifists—pardon us, the typewriter slipped, of course we meant pugilists—say that their respective champs were never in better physical condition. . . . So, having that worry off their minds, we can expect to see Jess and Fred with the A.E.F. 'most any day now" (10 May 1918).[1]

When casualties in the AEF began to mount, as more and more units were committed to combat, the editorials became more strident. One, entitled "Sport For Who's [sic] Sake?", observed that "we can only shout 'Bravo' in a faint and unconvincing voice when we learn that Ty Cobb is quoted as saying that he will enlist in the service at the close of the present season." And, "we are moved to blush when Eddie Ainsmith [catcher for the Washington "Americans"], called in the draft, appeals to the Secretary of War." His plea, and other developments and incidents, generated a great debate in the United States, as well as in the AEF, as to whether or not baseball should be considered an "essential industry" in wartime. The editors of the paper put their views strongly, asserting that "unless the whole petty, unpatriotic squabble stops," the paper might "mysteriously lose its sporting page" (26 July 1918).

Events rapidly came to a head. The Secretary of War soon ruled that baseball was a nonessential occupation, an event which "caught the magnates without umbrellas, though weather prognostications had been decidedly bad for a long while." It was in fact Ainsmith's appeal that had "precipitated the deluge," leading Baker to state that ballplayers are men of unusual physical ability, dexterity and alertness, "just the type needed to help in the game of war at home and abroad." Furthermore, "the people at home could very well do without a recreation that depended for its existence upon a class or type badly needed for the greater game of winning the war." The watchword, "Work or fight," did not mean getting two-base hits or catching fly balls between the hours of four and six. It was obvious that the Secretary of War saw only one Big League and that was in France (26 July 1918).

The Stars and Stripes heartily cheered Baker's decision, announcing that the sporting page of the 26 July 1918 issue would be the last to appear until an Allied victory was secured. To be sure, the paper understood the value of sports in developing the physical stamina and morale of the Army, recognizing that "it was sport that first taught our men to play the game, to play it out, to play it hard," it was also sport "that brought out the value of team play, of long, hard training and the knack of thinking quickly at a vital point of the contest." Certainly, sports among the troops must go on, then, "for that is part of the job." Furthermore, "sport among the youngsters back home must go on—for that, too, is part of the training job." But now, with the AEF rapidly growing in size, it would be impossible to report all of the news of its sports events, and those left out would remember the offense. As to developments at home, *The Stars and Stripes* was printed for the soldiers of the AEF, and "not to help perpetuate the renown of able-bodied stars, who, with their unusual physical attributes elected only to hear a 'Business as Usual' slogan above their country's call for help in the greatest war she has ever known." The only Big Leauge the paper henceforth recognized was in France. There was no space left "for the Cobbs, the Ruths, the Johnsons, the Willards and the Fultons in the ease and safety of home when the Ryans, the Smiths, the Larsens, the Bernsteins and others were charging machine guns and plugging along through shrapnel or grinding out 12-hour details 200 miles in the rear." Back home, "the sight of a high fly drifting into the late sun may still have its thrills for a few." But in France the all-absorbing factors were of a different kind, and "the glorified, the commercialized, the spectatorial sport of the past has been burnt out by gunfire. The sole slogan left is 'Beat Germany.' Anything that pertains to that slogan counts. The rest doesn't. And that is why this is the last sporting page *The Stars and Stripes* will print until an Allied victory brings peace" (26 July 1918).[2]

The new mood was highlighted in a poem, "The Old Game And The New":

> This game is not the game they knew
>   Before they faced the guns;
> The game that called for tackle drives,
>   Or cracking in the runs;
> The game they played on friendly sod
>   Beneath a friendly sky,
> To poke a double down the line,
>   Or snag the winging fly.
>
> . . . .

A new game? Yes, but still a game
    For those who had the heart
To crack a line or spill an end
    Along the sportive mart;
And so the slogan, born of old,
    Shall be their final aim—
"Come on, and show me something, kid;
Heads up—and play the game!"

                                                            Anon.
                                        (9 August 1918)

However, if the sports page was now absent, the sports idiom was not thereby laid aside, and furthermore, there were sports heroes, such as the baseball star, Hank Gowdy, worthy of discussion. The former catcher, engaged in action at the front lines, was finding that the Germans were "noisier and meaner than [the] old time pitchers." But nothing daunted, he seemed to be meeting the tests well; indeed he appeared as the very epitome of the best of American youth and its sports mystique, as he came, "swinging down the road just back of the lines with the same old grin." He had been under fire, and hard at it for some time, but even war had been unable to transform "Lank Hank Gowdy from the old Lank Hank of baseball days." "This game over here is all right," Hank was made to say, "But for a steady job all the rest of my life, I guess I'll take baseball. We are going to see this one through to a finish till the winning run goes over in the ninth, but after that I don't mind admitting I'll be ready to change the gas mask for the catcher's mask and take my chance against Walter Johnson's fast one rather than one of the fast ones from Fritz." Hank had some observations on the Germans, turning in a scouting report: "At that, Fritz hasn't got much more speed than Walter has and no better control. But he's noisier and meaner, and I guess we'll have to drive him from the box, or help in doing it. Fritz won't follow rules and he wants to do his own umpiring, but we've been landing on him lately and he's about given up hope for any lucky seventh. He had a rally going, but he couldn't keep it up." As to the hero, he "looks just as he did in the old days. His uniform isn't the same color or shape and neither is the mask he wears, but the change hasn't affected that world-embracing grin nor the cheery call along the road" (23 August 1918).[3]

This "approved athlete" was frequently compared with those who persisted in their unpatriotic stance and activities, and readers were not allowed to forget the likes of Jack Dempsey, Frank Fulton and Jess Willard. Willard, for instance, was castigated for "sulking in his tent until a bigger purse is offered"; he was compared with a young soldier named Scotty, aged sixteen, "lying dead across his beloved 'sho-sho' [Chauchat—a French light machine gun with which some Americans were equipped] with a bullet through his brain, and out beyond him 30 German dead who had fallen before his fire." One reads, the paper continued, that thousands acclaimed Dempsey's victory over Fred Fulton; but "there were no thousands to acclaim Scotty's fall, for his place was out in a French forest, where thousands around him were too busy fighting themselves to speak through any voice save the rifles'' (9 August 1918). Indeed, ''Those boxers or fighters back home who have failed to enter the service are going to have a hard time carrying the old trade mark forward when the war is over. Explaining that you were a 'fighter' when you never had on khaki will call for one of the most agile brains of the decade'' (23 August 1918).

The paper's crusade against the sports slackers suffered a setback, however, when Secretary Baker, no doubt under considerable pressure, consented to allow professional athletes to take up war work at home rather than enter the fighting forces. Many of the men in France, feeling betrayed, did not see how that could be fair. Contemptuously referring to these men as ''shipyard patriots,'' one bitter editorial observed that ''shipyard work is a great institution at all times. So is baseball—in the Army. But when hundreds of husky, alert, able-bodied professional ball players begin to scuttle from the diamond into shipyard work to escape the draft, the time is ripe for a lusty roar.'' When thousands of their countrymen were engaged in mortal combat, ''it seems beyond belief that any well trained athlete . . . should be guilty of such yellow-hearted cowardice, traitors to their country's good, and worse than traitors to their own souls.'' Furthermore, Ty Cobb's ''thinking of enlisting later on,'' was not acceptable. ''Suppose every American had decided to make it 'later on?' '' (2 August 1918).

Neither were these critics mollified when the Big League owners proposed sending professional teams to Europe to play exhibition games for the men in uniform. There was no need for them, as ''the A.E.F. has . . . perfectly good talent within its own ranks. There is, for example, a tolerably fair battery in Hank Gowdy and Grover Cleveland Alexander, both in France—and both in khaki'' (30 August 1918).

The paper found allies who supported its position and applauded its decision to suspend the sports page for the duration, though there was ridicule and opposition as well. E.W. Dickerson, president of the Western Baseball League, of the minors, in a letter to the paper, demanded a thorough overhauling of both the National and American Leagues, insisting that one of the most glaring ''sins of baseball'' had occurred when Ben Johnson, president of the American League, had formally requested of the government that baseball players be exempted from the draft. Dickerson professed outrage, asserting that it was just as reasonable for the billiard hall owners or the National Tennis Association to ask for the exemption of all those who played pool or tennis. He hoped that the boys in service would recognize the difference between the majors and minors in the matter of patriotism, pointing out that the minors had voluntarily suspended play ''so that not one man might be kept out of the service who might be helping to win the war.'' Warmly praising the paper's stand regarding baseball, he proposed a boycott of all players who quit the game to go into some other occupation—such as shipbuilding—to escape military service (11 October 1918).

There were other sports reformers in the United States, among them John D. Rockefeller, Jr. Speaking for the committee heading a campaign in November 1918 on behalf jointly of the YMCA, the Knights of Columbus, the Salvation Army, the YWCA, and the Jewish Welfare Board, he refused to permit a planned national boxing carnival designed to raise funds. This was in response to a great concern that had surfaced in the United States against boxing, "on account of its brutality." Rockefeller's committee also adopted resolutions stating that money derived from social games, golf tournaments and the like, held on Sunday, would not be accepted even for such worthy causes. This Puritanism hardly met with a favorable response among the doughboys in France, who could only swear in response to these inexplicable actions of "well-meaning but misguided fellow citizens" (8 November 1918).

Subsequently, some weeks after the Armistice, the paper's editors felt that the time had arrived to reestablish the sports page. Though no definitive peace had been signed, this was regarded as a technicality, since "the fighting is over—the greatest world series in history is finished and the Allies have got the pennant—and in these days of occupying Germany and marking time the great value and necessity of healthy exercise and recreation is fully realized" (20 December 1918).

The new page would emphasize sports in the AEF since, hopefully, "the average American soldier has lost his interest, for the time being at least, in professional and other sports at home, for the top notchers of the sporting world are in Europe wearing khaki and for the past year or more the sport of soldiering has been enough to keep the doughboy's mind and body fully occupied." Also, now that peace had arrived, Uncle Sam was determined to introduce a broad athletic program in the Army, and it would only be a matter of days before afternoons of many days, if not every one, would be devoted to some line of sport, the paper promised the men (27 December 1918).[4]

Baseball would once more appear when spring rolled around. But boxing had received great impetus during the war since it had been strongly encouraged by Army and Navy officers as a helpful means of developing young manhood. This sanction had done much to lift the odium which surrounded it previously, despite the number of slackers associated with it (27 December 1918). However, Chaumont did balk at one boxing scheme planned. For a brief moment *The Stars and Stripes* smelled a sensation which it eagerly took up: two chaplains were pitted against each other in the boxing ring, or rather a match was planned and scheduled. The combatants were Earl A. Blackman, the "fighting parson" of the 130th Field Artillery, of the 35th Division, and the Rev. Charles Reprode, chaplain of the 316th MPs of the 91st Division. It had been planned by Jimmy Bronson, of the YMCA's "pugilistic emporium" in Paris, the Palais de Glace, scheduled to come off on 11 February 1919. The paper waxed ecstatic: "The scrap will mark an epoch in the boxing game. If not the first battle of its kind, it will be at least one of the very few of its kind ever held anywhere. Nothing could be more of a boost for the game, nothing could prove a better testimonial to the cleanliness of the sport when properly conducted, than this contest between two Army chaplains'' (7 February 1919).

A poet was also impressed:

....

Preachers scrapping! What a lark
   To greet on balmy Sunday morn
A shepherd preaching to his flock
   With two black eyes and ears all torn!

Anon.
(7 February 1919)

But such was not to be. Though both men had considerable ring experience and were of similar age and weight, and thus it was no mismatch, army officials felt that it was "unseemly" and it was accordingly cancelled. Apparently the statement, "turn the other cheek," was still the norm for parsons; smiting each other "hip and thigh," was meant for others. Chaplains with "pugilistic zeal" were apparently not desirable in the AEF (7 and 14 February 1919).[5]

The paper continued to follow closely the career of Hank Gowdy, "the first major league baseball player to enlist in the U.S. Army," and rejoiced with him when he sailed for home on the *Leviathan*, revealing that he had signed a new contract with the Braves baseball club (2 May 1919). In other respects, the running fight that the paper had indulged in with professional baseball continued almost to the end of its career. It was pleased to learn that an "outlaw" baseball circuit was planned in the United States, called the Allied League, which would hopefully supplant the established major leagues. Counterattacking, hoping to attract the disaffected doughboys back to the fold, the president of the Chicago White Sox, Charles A. Comiskey, announced that any soldier with a wound stripe could enter major league games in Chicago free of charge for the 1919 season. This was singularly amusing to "Franc Terror," who observed that "we can almost see major league magnates with ears to the ground and eyes strained across the Atlantic to learn what the attitude of the A.E.F. will be this year toward baseball players who ducked their duty to their country and rushed for shipyard jobs" (16 May 1919).

Naturally, the men of the AEF obtained, in due course, opportunities to go on leave, or "*permission*," as the French called it.[6] *The Stars and Stripes* was the logical bulletin board, publishing a great deal of information on regulations as to leaves, identified and described various designated leave areas, and on occasion lectured the *permissionnaire* on his conduct while on leave. For instance, the "Oo-la-la! This is France!" attitude should be shunned. The times were too serious and "undue hilarity, undue familiarity, undue roisterousness, wearies the soul of France," that has so many months been "fed on tragedy."

The men must therefore not expect too much of the French, nor were they to consider France frivolously, as "her enemies would have us think of her . . . as a 'daughter of joy.' " Certainly, "nobody . . . expects the American soldier on leave to go about with a prayer-book neatly folded between his hands and a millstone hung about his neck." Rather, "far from it. He will be a better fighting man after his leave if he gives his body and mind a holiday and seeks the things such as outdoor exercise, reading and sightseeing that interest him without impairing his efficiency." For those perhaps not inclined to those pursuits, or those too dense to get the point, a firmer exhortation was made: "The things that are expected of the A.E.F. man on leave are: That he conduct himself as a gentleman. That, like the knights of King Arthur's Round Table—whose spiritual successor, from the nature of his task, he most certainly is—he consider himself bound 'to hold all women as sacred.' That he allow himself to indulge in no excesses that will impair his efficiency as a member of one of Uncle Sam's combative units. One can have a bully good time in France—or anywhere else, for that matter— and still live up to those three cardinal principles." Certainly, the man who let his vacation time go by without visiting some of the famous spots in France where world history had been made was missing "one of the most splendid opportunities of his life." In fact, "from now on forever, the man who does not know France, 'the best beloved of nations,' is sure to be set down as a 'lowbrow' indeed!" (22 February 1918).

It would not be until after hostilities were over that many men would get the opportunity to see Paris, the great lodestone drawing all to her. The official leave areas were located, for the most part, far from the magic capital. One of the reasons was that Paris in wartime simply could not absorb a great crowd of sightseers; France was in the midst of a major war and her capital was hard pressed in many ways. Still, Paris remained the goal of almost every man seeking a leave or a pass. An anonymous poet captured something of the spirit of the thing:

Make Mine Pink

> They may bull about their leaves to Aix–
> les-Bains,
> They may flash their nice white tickets
> for Savoy,
> They may work the song and dance about
> other parts of France,
> But they rouse in me no feeling kin
> to joy,
> They may prate of climbing mountains
> for a change,
> They may hint of dulcet bathing in the
> sea;

But the only thing I crave for, in the
                line of leave-time favor,
        Is the little old pink ticket to Par-ee!
                                                        Oh, Gee!
That little old pink ticket to Par-ee!
. . . .

After wallowing in sloughs of endless
                mud,
        After hiking with a pack upon my
                spine,
All the privilege I ask is in Paris sun to
                bask,
        And, perhaps, to take a little sip of
                wine!
After walking post from midnight unto
                dawn,
        After being wet and hungry as can be,
After standing sergeants' houndings I
                want civilized surroundings,
        And that little old pink ticket to
                Par-ee!
                                                        Ba-BEE!
That little old pink ticket to Par-ee!
. . . .

                                (8 March 1918)

    The first leave area officially designated was in Savoy around Aix-les-Bains, including the *arrondissement* of Chambéry (8 March 1918). This was followed shortly by the designation of the second on the northern coast of Brittany, centering on the towns of St. Malo, Dinard and Paramé, and consisting of about forty square miles of territory. By October, the area was able to accommodate 2,600 men per week, while Savoy was entertaining about 4,500. In Brittany, the YMCA had leased the High Life Casino at Dinard. This possessed a 700-seat theater, a cafe, concert hall and library. Vaudeville was one of the theater's main features, with the promise that it would continue "as long as jazz-loving Yanks visit the region." Excursions along the Côte d'Emeraude were featured, culminating in a visit to the famed Mont-St. Michel. The government picked up the tab for food and lodging for the men on leave (23 August 1918; 13 September 1918).
    A third leave area was soon established in the province of Auvergne at La Bourboule and Mont Dore, just south of Clermont-Ferrand. It would accommodate 5,000 men at a time and featured winter sports (6 September 1918).
    After the Armistice, leaves were encouraged even more, partly to ease the

restlessness among the troops desiring to return home. As many of these as possible were given a chance to see Paris on short three-day passes, or for extended leaves (29 November 1918). Eventually it was possible for Paris to entertain some 12,000 men with the Y and the Red Cross making many of the arrangements. The cost for the men was minimal, the average expenditure for a night's stay being three francs, with breakfast and lunch costing fifty centimes and an outlay of seventy-five centimes purchasing an adequate dinner. One of the hotels taken over was the Grand Hôtel de Louvre, which was managed by L. M. Boomer, manager of the Waldorf-Astoria and the McAlpin hotels in New York City. Mary Elizabeth Evans, the famous New York candy maker, was placed in charge of making cakes and pastries at the hotel (31 January 1919).

Other new leave areas were established in the Pyrenees, which could take in 8,000 men. These included Luchon, only six kilometers from the Spanish border; Cauterets; Eaux-Bonnes; and Bagnères-de-Bigorre. These were fashionable watering places which the doughboys could enjoy. The men were reminded that both Foch and Joffre were born in this region and that Lourdes would be a highlight of the visits to this area. Escorted group tours into Spain were also available (13 December 1918). In the Department of Haute-Savoie other centers opened up were Chamonix, Annecy, and St. Gervais where skiing on the slopes of Mont Blanc and other winter sports were features (20 December 1918).

Meanwhile, troops of the Third Army in Germany were soon taking free sightseeing trips on the Rhine, on such excursion boats as the *Frauenlob, Borussia, Goethe*, and the *Hindenburg* among others, the boats retaining their German names after the war. The craft were commanded by U.S. Marine officers with German crews, all under the control of the Army Transportation Service. The boats possessed guides, bands and eating facilities, and undertook day-long cruises to many of the Rhine's storied sites. They were stationed at Coblenz, Remagen, Andernach and Neuwied (24 January 1919).

By late January 1919, leave policies were modified so as to accommodate even more officers and men. Prior arrangements provided for seven days' leave every four months, with twenty-four-hour passes being given at the discretion of commanding officers. General Order 14, G.H.Q., AEF, of 18 January 1919, established five classes of leave. Class A passes provided for seven days' leave, travel time not included, to the specified leave areas described earlier. These were for enlisted men only. The Class B was for either officers or men, providing for leaves not to exceed fourteen days in Great Britain, Italy, Belgium or France (excluding Paris), travel time included. This leave also granted an allowance of sixty cents per day for rations. A Class C pass, for officers and men, was for three days in Paris, travel time excluded. The Class D *permission* met the needs of casual officers and men, giving them a ten-day pass. Class E passes were for three days, for officers and men, to be taken in France but excluded Paris. One of the purposes for the extended privileges was to enable American troops to visit relatives in various countries. There were restrictions, however: no leaves could be taken in Alsace or Lorraine without French permission. It was further stipulated that no more than 20 percent of troop strength of any unit could be gone at any given time, nor could any organization be crippled by the absence of too many officers. Also only Class E leaves would be granted to men with less than four months in Europe (24 January 1919).

One of the most popular leave centers later established was on the Riviera, at Cannes, Nice, Monaco, and Menton. In order to transport the Yanks to those fabled areas, special leave trains were operated by the Leave Train Bureau, AEF. "The American Express" left Paris daily from the Gare de Lyon with 240 third-class and 300-first-class seats. No other passenger trains were to be used by American personnel unless the leave train was filled. Another train ran from Dijon to the Riviera; one ran between Bordeaux and Cauterets in the Department of Hautes Pyrénées; yet others went to Bordeaux and Biarritz from Paris, famed Biarritz having been opened on 1 March 1919 (14 February 1919). In the Army of Occupation area of Germany, leaves were normally taken at Coblenz, Andernach, Neuwied, and Neuenahr on the River Ahr, the location of famous sulphur baths (14 February 1919).

Of the more than 2,000,000 men shipped to Europe during the course of the Great War, figures maintained by the YMCA's Soldiers Leave Department revealed that by April of 1919, over 400,000 soldiers had taken advantage of the leave facilities (2 May 1919). During the first year of leave operations, some 75,000 troops went to the Savoy area. The Riviera had entertained 30,000; the Auvergne area had seen 25,000; the Brittany coast, 40,000; the Dauphiné-Grenoble area, 20,000; and the Pyrenees, 10,000 (7 March 1919).

Franklin S. Edmonds, head of the YMCA's Soldiers Leave Department, felt that the effects of the leaves were significant and positive, not only regarding the men themselves, but for international goodwill. He predicted "that the demonstrated example of organized, wholesale recreation furnished by the Army in France may lead big industrial concerns in the United States to establish similar vacational systems," for employees (7 March 1919). Such was not to be in the United States, but the German government later introduced such a system in its "Strength Through Joy" program under Hitler, as did Italy under Mussolini.

As the men began to return home, many of the centers were closed as rapidly as they had been opened, and by the end of April 1919, the major ones left open included Aix-les-Bains, Chambéry, Nice, Annecy, St. Malo, Cauterets, and Biarritz. These could still accommodate 17,000 *permissionnaires* at any given time (25 April 1919).

Regarding entertainment, music was popular in the AEF, and bands were numerous. Initially, bandsmen performed as stretcher bearers as frequently as on their instruments, though G.H.Q. soon ordered that they were not to be used in this capacity except in extreme emergencies. This was the case since bandsmen were not a mere adjunct to other branches of service, and in fact had the primary duty of making music, which "has a definite military value, . . . is an essential part of the Army's spiritual equipment, and is so recognized by those whose business it is to build up a fighting force to the maximum of effectiveness'' (13 September 1918).

The era of World War I corresponded with the coming of the jazz age as well, and this musical form was quite popular among the doughboys. One anonymous poet well understood its appeal:

Jazz in Barracks

I can stand their hiking and their firing
    on the range,
I can walk a lonesome post or do K.P.:
Nothing in this army life to me is new
    or strange,—
I'm as seasoned and as hardened as can
    be.
Yet, with all my boasted toughness there
    is one thing I can't stand,
Though over all of Europe I may roam;
When a ham piano-artist bangs the box
    to beat the band,
Playing jazz—oh, gee! It's then I long
    for home!

. . . .

(29 March 1918)[7]

Another musical development was deplored, however. The Y issued a book, *Popular Songs of the A.E.F.*, with the songs sanitized and rendered ''stingless.'' The men were not accustomed to singing the words of certain songs as the book presented them:

Hail! Hail! the gang's all here,
What the deuce do we care, what the deuce do
    we care,
Hail! Hail! we're full of cheer,
What the deuce do we care, Bill!

''Next thing somebody will suggest that there might be room for reformation even in 'Home, Boys, Home,' or 'You're in the Army Now,' and more idols will be shattered. But what the deuce do we care?'' sarcastically retorted one writer (28 March 1919).

Movies were perhaps the most popular form of entertainment, the doughboys having become accustomed to seeing films before they entered the army. Indicative of their popularity was that after the Armistice, the First Army transformed sixty ambulances into mobile projection booths which carried their own portable screens or were simply backed up to a hangar or a wall and proceeded with the show (14 February 1919).

To cope with the great demand for films, the Y maintained the Community Motion Picture Bureau in Paris, which also involved the Salvation Army, the Knights of Columbus, and the Jewish Welfare Board. The bureau's 1,596 personnel were engaged in distributing films throughout France, into the occupied zone of Germany, likewise supplying films to the troops of Great Britain, New Zealand, Australia, Canada, Italy, France, Russia and some Balkan areas, as well as American personnel on over one thousand ships. Up to the spring of 1919, some 90,000 showings in France and 4,000 in Germany were screened weekly (9 May 1919).

Some of the films then popular included Douglas Fairbanks in "Habit of Happiness," and "Reggie Mixes In"; Norma Talmadge in "De Luxe Annie"; Constance Talmadge in "Up The Road With Sally"; and the production "My Own United States," based on Edward Everett Hale's *The Man Without A Country*. D. W. Griffith made available to the AEF three of his most famous films, "The Birth of a Nation," "Intolerance," and "Hearts of the World." These premiered at the soldier theater in Paris, the Albert Premier, in the Rue de Rocher (31 January 1919). Other popular films starred W. S. Hart and the most delightful of all, Charlie Chaplin. The best-liked of the latter's films was undoubtedly his "scream," "Shoulder Arms" (9 May 1919).

The AEF was a reading army as well, and the American Library Association (ALA) undertook to supply the almost unlimited appetite for books. After the Armistice, it became possible for any soldier, wherever based in Europe, to obtain any two books at a time by mail simply by writing a letter or postcard to the association's headquarters at 10 Rue de l'Elysée in Paris. By March 1919, there were also about one thousand branch libraries in France with others in Germany and elsewhere (28 February 1919).

As to what the boys were reading, the ALA claimed that those in Europe were reading heavier stuff than their contemporaries in the United States, checking out books on business and agricultural subjects, as well as reading much history and poetry. In fiction, love stories and westerns headed the list; war stories, however, were in low demand. The Yank reader, much to his surprise, was in fact dubbed a "highbrow" by the association (6 June 1919). A poem, "Old Kip," appearing in the 21 June 1918 issue, took exception to that description, however:

> Oh, they ain't long on the highbrow in this Yankee gang
> of ours,
> And they don't read Walter Pater in their precious
> leisure hours,

But they do like simple soldier-songs, a-full of pep and
zip—
And the guy what's wrote the best of 'em is Mister
Rudyard Kip!

So, it's good old cheery Kip—(you will pardon us our lip,
But we like your stuff so mighty well formality we'll
skip)—
You have lightened many a load with your poems of camp
and road,
And you've kept us grinnin' cheery 'neath the Top's
or Skipper's goad!

We get thrilled on "Danny Deever," and, before we hit
the hay,
There's a chorus round the fire singing "Road to
Mandalay";
When we're feeling sentimental, there's that "Mother" thing
o' yours.
That just lifts us out o' France back to our own Atlantic
shores!

We have felt like little Mowgli—oh, a lot o' times this
year!—
All so helpless in the jungle, but your song has brought
us cheer;
For when shells is bustin' round us, and it's mighty hard
to grin,
We can gather heart and courage from the tale o' Gunga
Dhin![8]

. . . .

One of the gratifying things about the entertainment world was the willingness
of established actors in the United States to follow the men to France and to
perform on the make-shift stages, often near the front lines. Initially, some 9,600
vaudeville players volunteered to go to France, including such established stars
as Maude Adams, George C. Cohan, Jimmy Powers, Marguerite Clark, Joe
Weber, Lew Fields, Elsie Ferguson, Otis Skinner, Lillian Russell, and Billie
Burke, among others. As a consequence, the Yanks resting up between stints
in the trenches could look upon the loveliness of Elsie Ferguson, listen to the
writer of "Over There" sing "his own ditty through his own nose," and watch
Lew Fields at his ancient task of choking Joe Weber to death (17 May 1918).
However, as *The Stars and Stripes* rather sarcastically reported later, not all
of the volunteers followed through on their hasty volunteering, often done in
the midst of the enthusiasm for the war following America's entry therein.

Though eventually about 700 actors and actresses appeared in Europe, some at great personal sacrifice, many of the great names of the American theater and vaudeville circuits were missing. In short, "the luxury-loving, overpaid, over-praised crowd, the spoiled children of America—they are strangers to the A.E.F." In the future, it was to be hoped, therefore, that the greatest applause in some all-star performance that "will fairly stop the show," would be accorded, not to the most celebrated of the stars, "but to some little *soubrette*," recognized by the soldiers in the audience as one who once upon a time had been "one of them in France" (28 Feburary 1919).

Such attacks were not altogether fair, however. Some of the stars were absent because they were not invited or their specific performance could not be accom-modated. As soon as it was clear that theater acts were desired in France, Winthrop Ames, the director of the Little Theater in New York City, and E. H. Sothern, the well-known Shakespearean actor, visited the AEF and "decided that only the fly-by-night entertainers who could chase the troops all over the map of Europe would stand a chance. Therefore, the unfortunate impression was created that the A.E.F. could use only light, extremely mobile artillery in show business." This was perhaps a mistake. If other arrangements had been made, certainly at the more or less permanent base camps, such performers as Maude Adams could have appeared as "Peter Pan" for six months at a time, or Laurette Taylor could have played in "Peg o' My Heart" every night, perhaps at St. Nazaire, and Fred Stone might have put on "Chin-Chin," at St. Aignan, "which would have improved St. Aignan quite a bit" (28 Feburary 1919).

As it was, the AEF looked with pride and admiration on the vaudeville people, "the good old two-a-day [performers], at which the high brow scoff, which [gave] the A.E.F. the great majority of its entertainers." Some 200 of these were brought to Europe under the auspices of the Over-There Theater League under the direction of the American playwright, James Forbes. Many of the others performed on the YMCA's theater circuit, dressed in the Y's distinctive uniform (17 May 1918).[9]

One famous star did arrive in France: Elsie Janis, "The Sweetheart of the A.E.F." The first American musical comedy star to come to France to entertain the troops, she became World War I's version of Betty Grable, Bob Hope, and any number of other stars of the World War II era, rolled up into one bouncy bundle of female charm.

In her memoirs, Elsie noted that she sailed for Europe early in February 1918, "to make my debut in the only really vital 'part' I have ever played in life!" She refused to wear a Y uniform but was sponsored by that organization. She was soon doing from two to seven shows a day and every so often would return to Paris where she kept an apartment at the Hotel Crillon, taking advantage of the time of *repos* to have hot baths, and kept open house, "buying cocktails for every lad in khaki who happened to drop in at the Crillon feeling a bit 'fed up' with war, light wines and beers!" However, Paris at the time was frequently being shelled by "Big Bertha," and experiencing air raids, which made her short respites less than restful at times.[10]

Her performances featured dances, songs, rope throwing acts, and impersonations, among other vaudeville routines. Her *spécialité de la maison* was turning cartwheels on the tailgate of army trucks. Many of her songs were quite popular. She had changed "Over There" to "Over Here," and her favorite, sung at every performance, was "All We Do Is Sign The Payroll, And We Never Get A God Damned Cent." Her opening yell was invariably, "Are we downhearted?", which always evoked the expected response, a resounding "No!"

One of the reasons for her being frequently written up in *The Stars and Stripes* as she was, was the close attention bestowed upon her by Alexander Woollcott. She had known him earlier, observing that his criticisms of her plays at home, "I had always valued and feared." But there was nothing to fear from him in France, as she herself admitted: "Alec was most enthusiastic about what I was doing and later when he became [an] editor of *The Stars and Stripes*, the betting among the fellows was that if my name didn't appear somewhere in the paper, Woollcott was 'on leave.' " But to Viskniskki, there could be too much of a good thing, even Elsie, and he once felt compelled to write to a Y secretary that "you are advised that we have written Elsie up to beat the band, and inasmuch as our space is limited, we cannot give her a write up every time she performs."[11]

She also attracted the attention of the highest brass, Pershing once saying to her, "Elsie, when you first came to France someone said you were more valuable than an entire regiment, then someone raised it to a division, but I want to tell you that if you can give our men this sort of happiness, you are worth an Army Corps."[12] Indeed, he saw to it that she had an army Cadillac limousine, chauffeured by a soldier, and armed her with an unlimited pass.

One of the paper's editors was equally enthusiastic, observing that instead of lecturers on such topics as "Why We Are At War," "The Mining of Carroway Seeds in Argentina," "The Fiscal System Under the Emperor Justinian," or "Fascinating Facts About The Income Tax," there was now Elsie Janis. Thus, "to an Army that has been persistently told that it can't be happy and be good at the same time; to an Army that has been overwhelmingly 'informed' and otherwise edified, Elsie Janis comes as a distinct relief. She is an oasis of color and vivacity in the midst of a dreary desert of frock-coated and white-tied legislators and lecturers who have been visited upon us for our sins and the sins of our fathers." It was obvious that "more entertainment by her and 'the likes of her' and less instruction by people who take themselves seriously—[was] one formula for winning the war!" (15 March 1918).

Somewhat later, in an open letter to her boys, published in the paper, Elsie confided that since she had not been gainfully employed for the several months that she had spent in their midst, she had to make her way to London to replenish her bank account. She was soon employed by the Palace Theater, but promised that she would still "be thinking about you and pulling for you." To those she had met she hoped that they would "keep the pep that you had when I saw you," and to those she had not met, she hoped to return to France sometime in the future. The letter included "Love from Mother," a reference to her constant companion, her mother, the closeness of the two being frequently remarked upon (13 September 1918). When the AEF began to push forward in early September of 1918, Elsie wired her beloved troops: "Congratulations on your big show. Sorry not to be in the cast. Hope to join the company in Berlin. Our regards" (20 September 1918).

In December, she wrote again, wishing all a Merry Christmas, and observing that her new show, "Hullo! America!", was being well received. She would like to change its name to "Bravo! America!", so proud was she of her country, now victorious over the Central Powers. The London audiences were enthusiastic, but "no audience can ever take the place in my heart of the A.E.F.— no bull!", she concluded, enclosing "more love from mother," and hoping to see one and all when "we all get home" (20 December 1918).

But perhaps as important as any professional entertainment in the maintenance of morale were the shows that the doughboys put on themselves. With the assistance of the Y and other welfare organizations, their appearance dated from early in the career of the AEF. Shortly after the Armistice, Chaumont issued a general order providing for more general support of the "Olive Drab" shows, based on the premise that not even Elsie Janis could compete with them, nor could professionals "hand an outfit as many laughs as its own privates in petticoats, [or] its own sergeants in skirts," this being the type of performance most commonly put on (24 January 1919). These shows were well publicized by *The Stars and Stripes*, and when they burgeoned after the Armistice, Alexander Woollcott took over the tasks of reviewing them in a regular column called "A.E.F. Amusements." He was well fitted for the job, having been a drama critic earlier in his career.

At many of the larger bases, especially those in the S.O.S. which were more or less permanent, the slogan became a "show a night," with the amateur performances being staged in hangars, barracks and even barns converted to theaters. Many of the productions soon took on a professional air and toured widely. Indeed, the ultimate goal of many of the groups was the Albert Premier Theater in Paris, and the headquarters of the S.O.S. was obliged to instruct all performers that their troupes must play their own areas before embarking upon larger stages. It was decided also to limit the groups to about twenty men who were to be largely self-sufficient. This was necessary because gigantic productions were planned by some outfits which threatened to eclipse their regular activities (7 February 1919).

Some of the troupes became widely known for all that. One which first appeared at Bordeaux's Franklin Theater was the "Mess Line Breakers," a group featuring close harmony, soft-shoe dancing and "hokum" performed by nine blacks from a nearby labor battalion. The star of the group was a pianist, "who unloads freight cars by day and ragtime by night." It was said that his height was exactly four feet and his name, "his real name," was Booze (31 January 1919).

Another group which gained some fame, since it was seen by President Wilson and numerous dignitaries attending the peace talks, was "The Argonne Players," who ridiculed those at home attempting to write about the war. They featured material which truly represented the conflict for what it was (31 January 1919). Equally famous was "The Rainbow Revue," of the 42nd "Rainbow" Division. It featured a real Salome dance, the "naughty lady" being impersonated by William A. Dole of Kansas City, then of the 117th Signal Corps. As Woollcott observed, since the rainbow was supposed to have all colors, there was "no reason why it should not have a dash of lavender" (7 February 1919). The 82nd Division's show, "Toot Sweet," featured a song hit entitled, "Duck for the Dugout, Douglas" (7 February 1919).

Another celebrated group, producing a musical extravaganza, "Let's Go!", was recruited from the U.S. Army Ambulance Service. One of its song numbers, "Bring Me a Blonde," featured costumes costing 30,000 francs, which were contributed gratis by the *modistes* of the Rue de la Paix in Paris. Another elaborate number in the show was "When Mlle. Eiffel Tower Chats With Miss Liberty," in which, Woollcott observed, "six ambulance drivers, dressed like the Eiffel Tower, stand in a row and warble in the general direction of six other drivers, all trying to look as much like New York Bay as possible" (14 February 1919).

A rather more violent musical production staged in Luxembourg was "Gazook's Charge" which included all the noise of a battle (21 February 1919). The musical, "Die Wacht am Rhein," produced by the 1st Engineers, may have transcended that however, featuring a large mechanical cootie "with three service stripes," calculated to make the entire audience itch at the mere sight of it (14 March 1919).

Some idea as to the extent of the O.D. theatricals can be gained by noting that in the Third Army alone in Germany there were, in March of 1919, some 134 soldier troupes active, consisting of a total of 3,618 players. In February, the companies gave 2,626 performances (28 March 1919).[13]

In addition to doughboy troupes and professional groups from America which toured through the AEF, German opera companies were booked. One, the Niemeyer Opera Company, was nonplussed to encounter at first hand the enthusiasm of a doughboy audience. The overture was once received with tremendous approval by the men, "who stamped and whistled with flattering violence." But, as *The Stars and Stripes* reported it, "as these queer foreigners persist in regarding whistling as a sign of disapproval, the orchestra leader almost wept." " 'My God,' he said, 'if they think the overture is as bad as that, what will they think of the rest of the music?' " It took the authorities some time to convince the performers that they were in fact being warmly applauded (7 February 1919).

9

Education

"Private Perkins, take the floor;
Scan this philosophic law,
Who was Kant and who was Locke?
Why did Hick'ry Dick'ry Dock
Run about and play when he
Might have read philosophy
And learned to talk in high-brow strain?
I dare you, sir, to make it plain."

Now ain't that a scrumptious way
For a hulkin' man to play?
Next they'll teach us how to dress.
HELL! YES!—HELL! YES!

Cpl. T. G. Brown
(14 March 1919)

For a considerable time, the emphasis on education in the AEF naturally was on military subjects such as, for example, the five-weeks' intensive advanced training course given to the men arriving in France before they were sent up to the lines. This instruction gave troops their "Bachelor of Arts of Fighting," i.e., their "BAF" degree (15 February 1918). But in time, Army officials and the Army Educational Commission of the Y proposed that when conditions permitted, greater educational opportunities of a more traditional nature should be provided (27 September 1918).

After 11 November, the Army established some order in military instruction as an aid in maintaining discipline and to keep the forces combat ready, the Armistice being only a cease-fire, not a peace treaty. General Order 207, G.H.Q., AEF, 1918, specified that military drill was to be instituted five days per week for at least five hours per day. Each drill day would see from fifteen minutes to one hour's close order drill; daily practice with weapons firing live ammunition; and tactical exercises were to be undertaken. Artillery units were to fire the "75" light artillery piece daily. A standard instruction and drill program was set up requiring four weeks to complete, at which time it was to be repeated. Saturday mornings were given over to "spit and polish" inspections (6 December 1918). However, the afternoons could be used for other activities such as sports or educational pursuits. Furthermore, opportunities arose for detached service for attending courses at schools, colleges, or universities. At these, military drill was kept at a minimum. It was no doubt to avoid such that many men availed themselves of the schooling opportunities which they were soon to be provided. Even textbook drill seemed preferable to "squads east and west." *The Stars and Stripes* took close interest in educational matters, urging the men to improve themselves, enabling the Army to send home "men with definite purposes, rather than an Army whose collective mind has decided 'to loaf four or five months and see what turns up.' " In short, it must not be said of any doughboy that "he checked his brains at Hoboken on the way over" (7 March 1919).

In order to give the men these opportunities, a systematic program was needed. This was developed collectively by the Army Educational Commission of the Y and the Army itself, with the former taking the lead. Soon after the Armistice, several prominent American educators came to France to assist in establishing the program. Among those involved were Professors John Erskine of Columbia; P. A. Appelbloom of Kansas State; Everett Green of the University of Illinois; President Kenyon L. Butterfield of the Massachusetts Agricultural College; and Dean Louis E. Reber of the University of Wisconsin. The planning was rapidly accomplished, and in January, General Order No. 9, G.H.Q., AEF, 1919, set forth the general program. Post schools were to be established at all bases where 500 men or more were stationed. Courses at various levels were provided, taught, for the most part, by schoolmasters then in the Army. Books and instructional materials were provided in part by textbook publishers making special rates on their publications. The ALA was also of great assistance in collecting books.[1] Enrollments were voluntary except for non-English-speaking men and illiterates; these were ordered into basic English and composition courses. However, men enrolling in classes were required to complete those undertaken. If duty assignments or transfers interrupted a course, progress reports were attached to the soldier's service record and he could resume his study at his new duty station. The subjects taught at the post schools ranged from elementary subjects to modern languages, U.S. history, history of modern nations, civics and citizenship. These schools were under the supervision of the training section of the General Staff, i.e., G-5 (24 January 1919).

For posts with less than 500 men, correspondence courses were available. In general charge was J. Foster Hill, who for many years had been with the International Correspondence Schools. These courses were administered by the Army Educational Commission of the Y. Initially, courses were available in business, commercial, engineering and industrial subjects, though they were greatly expanded.[2]

General Order No. 9 also made it possible for officers and men who spoke French and were otherwise well-qualified, to attend the Sorbonne and other French universities. Others in restricted numbers could pursue studies at Oxford, Cambridge and other selected colleges and universities in the British Isles. Those selected were placed on detached service, drawing their usual pay, and paid commutation of quarters at the rate of one dollar per day, and rations at the rate of two dollars per day, but they had to pay their own tuition. When their units departed for home, they were given the option of completing their studies or returning to America (14 February 1919). For many men, this was a golden opportunity and soon O.D. was seen in unfamiliar surroundings. One of the first of the French universities to see Americans in some numbers was the University of Bordeaux, and by early February 1919, some 500 Yanks were enrolled in the law school, with 200 in the medical school and 200 each in the scientific and liberal arts programs (7 February 1919).[3]

Meanwhile, the post schools began to attract large numbers of students. By early February, almost 50,000 men were enrolled, of which about 20,000 were in the Third Army in Germany; 19,000 in the S.O.S. area around Bordeaux; and 11,000 in the St. Mihiel area (7 February 1919).

As time elapsed, additional opportunities were added. General Order No. 28, G.H.Q., AEF, 1919, stipulated that in each army, corps and division, and in each S.O.S. section, educational centers were to be established specifically to teach vocational courses. These were to include carpentry, telegraphy, road construction, horseshoeing, auto repair, cobbling, barbering, and cooking and baking. Special provisions were also made for the teaching of agriculture, as well as advanced courses beyond the post schools' offerings, focusing on such courses as algebra, trigonometry, mechanical drawing, salesmanship, economics, languages and advanced history. This order also provided that up to fifteen percent of any command could go to school at any given time, and if they were in class attendance for five hours of instruction for five days per week and signed up for at least a three-month course, they would be excused from other military duties.

Yet additional refinements were provided for in Bulletin No. 9, G.H.Q., AEF, 1919. This outlined the establishment of farmers' clubs, institutes and short courses on agricultural topics. The clubs were to consist of ten or more men and would hold regular meetings and conduct discussions, debates and attend lectures on such topics as marketing, rural credit, farm community life and the place of the farmer in national and world affairs. The short courses would feature lectures based on the chautauqua idea, drawing from men knowledgeable on agricultural subjects. These experts were also to be sent into the areas where post schools were not available. Many films and educational lantern slide programs were to be developed as well. The farmers' institutes would consist of concentrated three-day sessions (28 February 1919).

The Army Educational Commission of the Y matured along with the burgeoning school system. It soon consisted of around 300 people, about half of whom were attached to various post schools supervising and evaluating their work. Many of these were school superintendents or teachers in America. They were brought to Europe at the YMCA's expense, and the same agency provided for their maintenance, housing and supplies. The Commission was also charged with mapping out programs, outlining courses, selecting texts, and preparing syllabi. The actual organization, staffing and operation of the schools was the Army's responsibility, under the command of Brig. Gen. Robert L. Rees. Somewhat later, in the spring of 1919, the YMCA's educational tasks ended when the Army took over all such operations. This was effected by General Order No. 63, G.H.Q., AEF, 1919 (25 April 1919). The former Y educational personnel became in the process "militarized civilians," with a distinctive arm insignia (28 March 1919).

In the meantime, another dimension of the Army's educational system appeared: the Technical Trade Centers which were opened at several bases and camps. This scheme was to enable trainees to take advantage of the skilled personnel and often elaborate equipment and installations at various places. For example, at the great railroad shops at Nevers large numbers of men in classes of up to 500 were taught various metal trades. At the Motor Reconstruction Park at Verneuil, some 1,700 students could be accommodated at a time, being taught auto, truck and motorcycle repair and rebuilding. A similar park at Romorantin could handle 1,500 students. At Gièvres, telephone and electric repair was taught to classes of 250. At Mehun, 600 men could be enrolled in courses teaching carpentry, woodworking, printing, optical instrument repair and laundrying at the great ordnance shops located there. At Decize, another 600 men were taught motor operation and auto repair. At Sougy, the large AEF remount station, 300 soldiers at a time could be taught blacksmithing, horseshoeing and related trades (28 March 1919). While the Army stood to gain by this instruction, much of it was undertaken with an eye to making the men employable in civilian life following their discharges.

But the most ambitious educational scheme that the Army undertook was the establishment of the AEF University at Beaune, located southwest of Dijon in Burgundy, eastern France, which would sometimes be called the University of Beaune. It took over buildings that had belonged to a large hospital center, planning to enroll a student body of between 10,000 and 15,000, making it thereby the largest university in the world. Three regiments of stevedores and an engineer batallion were detailed to renovate the structures and modify them for classroom use.[4] The labor force soon had things in order, and classes began on 10 March, with the elaborate formal opening ceremonies coming five days later (7 March 1919).

The university was commanded by Col. Ira L. Reeves, a former professor of military science at Purdue University, and later president of the faculty of Norwich University. Professor John Erskine, professor of English at Columbia, was the new institution's president. The university consisted of fourteen separate colleges in addition to a special prep college for some 300 men who had been appointed to West Point. Among the colleges were those of music, education, business, journalism, engineering, law, art, premed and dental, agriculture and the correspondence school, identified as a separate college. The faculty consisted initially of 500 instructors drawn from the 50,000 or so in the AEF who had been found qualified by G-5 to teach at the university level.

The students, with their distinctive insignia, were organized into regiments for administrative purposes and each 100 students had a tactical officer assigned to them. While in class no distinctions in rank were made; outside of the class-room, military courtesy and discipline prevailed. Reveille was not forgotten, being at 7:00, and at 8:00 military drill commenced for an hour prior to dismissal for classes, and the remainder of the day was devoted to study.

One of the pressing needs was for textbooks and an adequate library. Regarding the former, the War Department asked the War Industries Board to lift bans on the manufacture of pulp and paper for textbooks. This was speedily done, and soon texts were being rushed to France (21 February 1919). The ALA, the Y and the Army combined their efforts to fill the planned 500,000-volume library, but in the institution's short life only about 26,000 were actually obtained (16 May 1919).

Among the university's more interesting schools was that of the Beaux Arts. This was located at the famous Pavilion de Bellevue, near Sèvres, in the environs of Paris, "where earlier maidens in diaphanous gowns danced underfoot under the direction of Isadora Duncan." The first class of advanced students numbered 230 men pursuing the study of architecture, art and sculpture, as well as landscape design, interior decorating, industrial and commercial art, ornamental modeling and city planning (7 March 1919). Instructors were noted artists and architects from the United States and France. The contingent was commanded by Maj. G. H. Gray, with a staff and service company. "But," one account noted, "military discipline . . . does not interfere with artistic atmosphere." In fact, a student council takes care of many of the problems. There was one hour's physical and military drill each morning, but "artists are artists, be they temporarily in the uniform of the fighting man or not, and Major Gray is enough of an artist himself to appreciate that."

Lloyd Warren, a noted New York architect, was dean of the school. He was assisted in his professional instruction by Archibald Brown and John Galen Howard of San Francisco. Leslie Cauldwell was the instructor in interior dec-orating. Sculpture and painting classes were conducted by Capt. Ernest Peixotto of San Francisco, one of the AEF's official artists, assisted by Solon Borglum and Laredo Taft, both well-known artists as well. French classes were also held at the Pavilion, which all students had to attend. Afternoons were devoted to studio work, and field trips into Paris by various groups was a daily occurrence. The students were enrolled in a three-month course of intensive study. Of these, about two-thirds were enrolled in the architecture classes, with about 30 per-cent studying painting and the remainder in sculpture classes. Certain it was, however, that there were "no garrets for [the] soldier students of arts in Paris" (2 May 1919).

The correspondence college rapidly expanded its holdings as soon as it was attached to the University of Beaune. In addition to mathematics and business courses, students could choose such offerings as British geography, economics and modern European history. Some 300 to 400 applications rolled in per day, the most popular courses being salesmanship, auto repair and farm management. So popular did the correspondence courses become that each student was limited to one course at a time (21 March 1919).[5]

The agricultural college at Beaune was under the directorship of Professor Kenyon L. Butterfield of the Massachusetts Agricultural College. In addition to this college, the Army also created the Army Farm School at Allerey, France, opening its doors on 1 April 1919. Though it cooperated with Beaune, it emphasized the practical aspects of farming on the 350 acres of land at its disposal. Other U.S. students were also studying agriculture at French agricultural colleges at an advanced undergraduate or graduate level, though they had to understand French, since lectures were only given in that language (21 March 1919).

The University of Beaune also boasted its large mechanical and electrical engineering laboratories. It also obtained three locomotives and five aircraft, together with a large collection of motors, gas engines, boilers, and road-making and repairing equipment for instructional use (28 March 1919).

The business college had several clubs as a jewelry club, drug club and a men's clothing club. These took field trips, visiting establishments of interest, such as the watch factories in Besançon, and in Lyon (16 May 1919).

The university's department of French boasted a twenty-five-man, all-soldier detachment, the *Mission Militaire Française*. All of its members had won the *Croix de Guerre* and some had in addition acquired the *Médaille Militaire* or the *Légion d'Honneur* (16 May 1919).

The journalism school had planned to establish its own newspaper, *The A.E.F. News*, but failed to get it launched. It did make a collection of all the AEF newspapers that it could locate, asking to be placed on their mailing lists. In addition, the school took advantage of the fact that a large number of the world's prominent journalists were covering the Paris Peace Conference to invite a number of them down to lecture to the students. The first to arrive was William Allen White of Kansas fame, who lectured on "Reporting the Peace Conference." He was followed by Patrick Gallagher of *The New York Herald*, an expert on the Far East; Reginald Wright Kaufman of *The New York Tribune*, who lectured on "The Newspaper and the Novel"; and Herbert Bayard Swope, city editor of *The New York World*. The journalism school had 517 students registered in the seven courses offered (16 May 1919).[6]

The University of Beaune, despite its elaborate setup, closed its doors on 7 June. Colonel Reeves explained that the reason for the precipitous closing was that the student body was rapidly thinning out as the homeward flight accelerated. The S.O.S. was breaking up as well and he concluded that the university had met its primary aim of giving "to the soldier the greatest possible benefits to be derived in utilizing his time while waiting for transportation home." In fact, he added, the institution was never intended "to delay for one moment the return of any soldiers to the United States." The venture had been an interesting one and had no doubt benefitted many men. Of the students remaining, he concluded, they were to be organized into a special university regiment for shipment home (9 May 1919).

The final figures revealed that 9,319 men attended classes at the university, with the business college well in the lead with the total of 1,973 students. The engineering college was second with 931; letters had enrolled 843; the agricultural college had 717 students. The college of education was the least popular with only eighty-two students. In the university's short life, a total of 303 courses had been offered in 538 classes in the forty-one departments of the institution's colleges.

In addition to the men of the AEF enrolled at Beaune, almost 2,000 attended various classes at the Sorbonne. There, they had two sorts of courses available: the public lectures, which charged no fees and with no regular attendance required, and the closed courses which required matriculation (7 March 1919). Of particular interest to many of the men was a special series of lectures presented in the Grand Amphitheater at the Sorbonne, especially for their benefit, by both American and French lecturers. Among the subjects dealt with were: "French Public Opinion"; "The Cathedral at Reims"; "The Battle of Verdun"; and "The Modern Theater" (25 April 1919). Most of the students attending the Sorbonne lived in the Latin Quarter, around the Boulevards of St. Germain and St. Michel. Some lived with French families; others were in hotels or flats. Many were taking French lessons taught by the Alliance Française. So pleased were they with the opportunities for improving their education, that only a relatively few of these sailed for home, many planning to continue in Paris. Some of these doubtless helped to swell the large American expatriate colony in Paris (2 May 1919).

A large number of Americans also attended the French universities at Bordeaux, Dijon, Toulouse and Grenoble (14 March 1919). In addition, 2,000 more were enrolled in British universities.

In any event, the Army had certainly exerted a great deal of effort in its educational program. *The Stars and Stripes* was a warm supporter and careful recorder of this venture, well pleased that the enforced stay in Europe had been rendered both pleasant and profitable for so many doughboys.

10

Dénouement

It is the snappiest and most vigorous paper I have seen,
and reflects the spirit of the A.E.F. at the front, in training,
and *en route.*

Pvt. Meyer Agen
(5 April 1918)

In his final report to the War Department, General Pershing praised *The Stars and Stripes* for "providing a common means of voicing the thought of the entire American Expeditionary Forces." He commended the enlisted men of the staff, most of whom desired to remain in the ranks, "in order better to interpret the spirit of the Army." The paper, he was pleased to acknowledge, "was a great unifying force and materially aided in the development of an espirit de corps." Furthermore, it had lent "loyal and enthusiastic" support to Army athletics and the educational program. But perhaps its most significant contribution was that "in leading the men of our Army to laugh at their hardships, it was a distinct force for good and helped to create a healthy viewpoint."[1]

An unnamed high official in the War Department went even further, avowing that the paper was one of the three outstanding contributions of America to the art of war. What the other two were was, unfortunately, not recorded.[2]

British Prime Minister David Lloyd George, who had been sent copies of the paper, was of the opinion that it was "an excellent thought to meet the needs of the troops in this way."[3] And the publication of the anniversary issue of the paper on 7 February 1919, gave ample opportunity for well-wishers to commend the paper. President Wilson wired his congratulations, and the Secretary of War, Newton D. Baker, informed Pershing of his satisfaction with the paper, observing that "it has been not only a medium of communication, but a strong force in making for our Army abroad a united spirit, and the copies which have reached America have been the best evidence our home people have had of the spirit of the Army.''[4] Gen. J. G. Harbord, the commanding officer of the Services of Supply, remarking on this ''undertaking unique in the history of journalism and warfare,'' stated that it had at once ''instructed, inspired and amused.'' In short, *The Stars and Stripes* ''has played an important part in the highly organized business we have carried on to defeat Germany'' (7 February 1919).

However, most interestingly—and rather strangely—*The Stars and Stripes* requested that General Pershing congratulate it on its anniversary. Captain Early, who initiated the matter, felt that ''the result will more than repay us for any embarrassment felt in submitting the request. Certainly it proves that we are not at all modest.'' This rather pushy procedure succeeded; Pershing complied, perhaps more or less gladly, emphasizing that the paper was fulfilling its intended function, and in the process, was maintaining ''all the best traditions of journalism.''[5]

On the occasion of its anniversary, a dinner for 220 persons was held, paid for by the paper at the cost of fifteen francs each. The outlay was justified as a ''benefit to morale.''[6] Nolan, whose duties prevented his attending, nevertheless took the occasion to congratulate a ''newspaper stalwart of international repute, the Infant Phenomenon of the journalistic world.''[7]

But the paper was not meant to impress officialdom.[8] It was intended primarily for the AEF of all ranks and stations. That it attained its goal in a praiseworthy fashion is abundantly clear. The letters column frequently included missives of praise for the paper's accomplishments. Just prior to his leaving France, a ''2nd Loot'' warmly thanked the paper, recognizing it as ''something human; something one can shake hands with, slap on the back, borrow five francs from and offer to buy the drinks for,'' a tried and true bosom buddy and close companion (28 March 1919).

Another enthusiastic reader, David R. Erwin, exclaimed that the paper was ''one good, snappy, readable sheet with punch and pep, the *sine qua non* of modern journalism, scintillating in every column.'' He confessed his apprehension when he first heard that a newspaper was to be published for the troops, fearing that it ''would be one of those typical 'army' publications with heavy wit sandwiched in between dreary selections from the [regulations] and incomprehensibly technical dissertations on the avoidance of venereal diseases.'' He himself was a former newspaperman and ''so possibly appreciate a sheet like yours a little more than the man who hasn't learned to love the smell of printer's ink and the rattle and clatter of typewriters and linotype machines.'' The many warm comments that he had heard indicated that ''*The Stars and Stripes* is going to go good, and mighty good, with the A.E.F.'' He urged the paper to ''keep up the good work, make *The Stars and Stripes* a bright, breezy sheet, kid us along a little, don't let the publications get too serious, for most everyone over here in uniform has enough of the serious and needs more of the frivolous; and, for the love of Mike, don't let anything happen to that artist [Wally], for we need his stuff'' (12 April 1918).

His sentiments were echoed by Capt. Will K. Chase, an infantry officer, also a former newspaperman, who was likewise duly impressed with the paper: "The last thought that ever entered my head was that I would have to come all the way over to France to find a sure-enough, honest-to-goodness editorial page." He predicted a bright future for the sheet, "unless this is just a flash in the pan," because in his experience, he concluded, "a successful editorial page means a successful paper" (19 April 1918).

Civilian readers in Europe and America similarly recognized the merits of the paper. An American woman living in Paris with her French husband was enthralled by it: "I read every word in every story because the voice of *The Stars and Stripes* has the Yankee twang and it does me good to hear it." She explained that "once in a while a phrase or a word, which you use unconsciously, but which I have not heard these many years, conjures up a picture of the places I used to know and I read on with a mist in my eyes." To her, then, the Atlantic was "not quite so wide since you started to publish" (17 May 1918). A woman in Los Angeles observed that the paper was the only one able to convey successfully to the civilians the real atmosphere of the war zone (18 October 1918).[9]

At least one subscriber in the United States posted the paper in a local drugstore window where a crowd could be seen gathered around to read it (24 May 1918). In another instance, sixteen copies of *The Stars and Stripes*, autographed by the staff, were auctioned off in New York City on behalf of the Red Cross during a fund drive. The copies realized a total of $13,000, or about $812.50 per copy (31 May 1918).

The staff of the paper was especially gratified by the many indications in the American press at home that their paper was acclaimed a success. To be recognized and praised by one's peers is more than acceptable. To *The Editor and Publisher,* the foremost "newspaperman's paper," "*The Stars and Stripes* is more American in tone and style than many of our home newspapers, and it mirrors the spirit of the American Army" (10 May 1918). And almost immediately after the paper was launched *The Kansas City Journal*, having received a copy of the first issue, liked what it saw, and in its 10 March 1918 issue stated: "There is little if anything of glorification of American patriotism [in the paper], for the publishers of that paper are too heroic to be boastful and too good to be self-righteous. There is a significant abundance of 'funny stuff,' little jests and jingles, jokes and quips, which might not 'sell' to the American 'funny' magazines, but which testify eloquently to the American soldier's light-heartedness, as well as to the necessity of laughing at a time when tears would be more natural." In truth, "to laugh as one stands on the brink of hell and gazes down into the pit of torture and suffering does not betoken indifference, but quite the reverse. The preservation of reason and sublime purpose which animates the men in khaki demand these laughs which mask the righteous curses that are directed toward the barbarous enemy." The writer felt that the paper should be read by all Americans who would feel a new measure of pride in the men "who are so worthily representing the greatest democracy in the world in this gigantic war against the greatest autocracy in the world. Nor could he read it without feeling a new consecration to the task of doing over here everything that is necessary to bring victory to the boys 'over there' '' (12 April 1918).

The New York Globe, on 2 July 1918, applauded the paper's "inestimable value" in portraying the American Army overseas. The paper also breathed "freshness, virility, [and] wholesomeness.'' The men at the front were depicted as "young men buckling earnestly to the job in hand as ambitious young men in peace-time business would do, seeing their aim clearly and not letting themselves be diverted. They are shown to us as intensely wholesome and almighty human. Even the wounded hop along gaily on the crutch of unfailing humor'' (27 September 1918). Indeed, the *Globe* insisted on another occasion, that the most American of newspapers was not in fact being published in the United States. That worthy was *The Stars and Stripes*, which "reeks of Americanism,'' and the advice the *Globe* gave to any American plagued with "a touch of liver,'' or who felt gloomy, or "despairing as to the outcome or the worthwhileness of continuing the fight,'' was to subscribe to *The Stars and Stripes*, as there was nothing better to cure these ills (12 July 1918).

There is little doubt that *The Stars and Stripes* enjoyed something rare and fine; the time, place, personnel, and occasion came together and the results were a sparkling performance. The paper reflected journalism at a high level. It manifested class, style, verve, and vivacity. The World War I edition of the paper remains an American journalism classic, and perhaps a minor literary one as well. To be sure, much of what the paper printed came in from that apparently inexhaustible literary and journalistic fountain, the officers and men of the AEF. The editors felt so, in any case: "Probably no publication in the history of journalism ever received in a single year so many contributions, one and all submitted without any thought of remuneration. Famous writers, writers who will be famous, writers who will never be famous—they have all chipped in.'' In truth, they modestly averred, "the best things *The Stars and Stripes* ever printed were not written by any of its staff. They came in in the morning mail.'' Put another way, "The editorial staff just hung on to the coat-tails of the irresistible doughboys and was carried to glory. Any group of scribes who could not have got out a readable newspaper, with the American Infantry providing the news, would properly have been shot'' (7 February 1919). This is a bit of an exaggeration; the staff wrote some very fine things indeed, many of the editorials, for instance, being splendid brief essays, sparkling literary set pieces of considerable merit.

The paper's editors had, in the first issue, stated that *"The Stars and Stripes* is up at the top o' the mast for the duration of the war.'' It had stayed up well beyond that time, until the majority of the AEF had returned home. The paper then came to the end of its active career, "with malice toward none, with charity for all, and apologies to nobody'' (13 June 1919). However, while the paper ceased publication on 13 June 1919, this is not the end of its story. In the first place, there was the matter of its large accumulated profits. So efficient had it become, that at the end, it had on hand a tidy balance of 3,500,000 francs, or

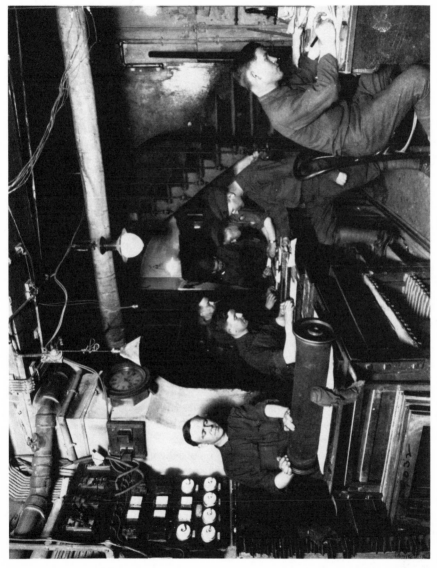

7. The staff "putting to bed" the Victory Edition of *The Stars and Stripes. Courtesy of National Archives.*

about $700,000.[10] These profits were originally intended to benefit company funds, but with many of these units being disbanded or shipped home, there was nowhere to go with the profits. It remained to find an acceptable substitute. General Nolan was of the opinion that the soldiers themselves should vote on their use. He suggested three propositions: the funds should go to the orphans' fund; the money should be turned over the American Relief Association for the care of children of U.S. dead and wounded; or a monument might be erected, perhaps in the Meuse-Argonne to commemorate the exploits of the AEF. He felt sure that the French government would contribute a site and a campaign could be launched raising the additional funding that such a project would require.[11]

However, the staff of *The Stars and Stripes* adamantly supported the view that the paper's profits must go to the orphans' fund. This was especially needed, since one of the paper's auxiliary publications, *Wally's Cartoons,* had been sold with the specific understanding that the profits would go to the fund. When the matter was raised with Brig. Gen. W. A. Bethel, the judge advocate of the AEF, he ruled that both the paper's profits and those of all of its publications, must go to the United States Treasury as miscellaneous receipts, since they were all produced by labor and materials of the United States government and any specific assurances as to the use of profits to the contrary were "totally unauthorized."[12]

Though it was understood that the judge advocate acted properly from a legal standpoint, his ruling caused consternation at the paper, and Watson was forced to print a correction, offering a refund for Wallgren's cartoons, if the purchasers desired it, and if they were not satisfied with the book on its own merits (28 March 1919).

This was not the end of the story, though. The editorial council of *The Stars and Stripes*, at the time consisting of Ross, Baldridge, Hawley, Wallgren, Winterich and Woollcott, drafted a petition to the Congress of the United States for the passage of a law enabling the paper to turn over its profits to the orphans' fund. This was necessary in part so that the paper's record might not "be smirched by such a disposition of its profits as would lay its founders open to suspicion of misrepresentation, however innocently incurred."[13]

The petition made its way to Watson, who recommended its being submitted to Congress, "with or without favorable indorsement." It subsequently went to Secretary of War Baker, who transmitted it to Senator James W. Wadsworth, Jr., chairman of the Senate's committee on military affairs.[14] It was introduced, however, in the House by Julius Kahn, congressman from California, as House Resolution 5499, and was referred to the military affairs committee, never to be heard from again—apparently dying in committee.[15]

If the paper ultimately had no success with the final disposition of its funds, it was as little successful regarding protecting the paper's name and preventing its subsequent use and abuse. While officer-in-charge, Viskniskki had consulted Charles E. Kelley of New York City, an expert on copyright and trademark law, in regard to protecting the paper's name. But numerous difficulties were adduced.

For example, if it were copyrighted in an individual's name, that person would be open to criticism for attempting to profit at the expense of the government since the paper was, after all, a quasi-governmental publication. One solution might have been for Congress to pass legislation providing for a copyright of the paper.[16] This was not pursued, however, and later, Col. E. C. McNeil, acting judge advocate of the AEF, advised Nolan that he doubted "the propriety of attempting to secure any such protection . . . [and] I do not think the fullest use by the public of such a government publication should be interfered with."[17]

Nevertheless, those close to the paper felt that any use of its name for crass business purposes was deplorable. When the Butterick Company of New York, having obtained the services of some of the paper's former staffers, proposed to commercially publish *The Stars and Stripes*, the American Legion, the Secretary of War and Pershing were all strongly opposed. So was Ross, who was induced to write an appeal to the U.S. Congress to stay such exploitation, urging a law to restrict the right of the name to the U.S. Army, "to be used by that Army if and whenever the need of the Nation calls for another such expedition as gave birth to *The Stars and Stripes*." This was in keeping with statements in the paper's last issue that "*The Stars and Stripes* was being hauled down to be folded and put away beyond reach of any trafficker in the publication market." Thus, he concluded, "*The Stars and Stripes* was so true an expression of the spirit of the American Expeditionary Forces and so proudly the property of the troops that no one at all sensitive to their struggle and sacrifice would wish to foster a paper under the same name—under the name of the American flag—in civilian America." The name, then, must "be bequeathed unimpaired and untarnished to the American Army," and set aside "as the rightful inheritance of the writers and artists in the ranks of the next American Expeditionary Forces."

Ross's memorial was heartily approved by Baker and Theodore Roosevelt, Jr., and other members of the national commission of the Legion, as did Pershing, the latter referring to the origins of the paper and its purposes, seriously doubting "if a paper of this character can be maintained except under the conditions which gave [it] birth," and strongly opposed its being commercially published.

Ross's memorial was taken in hand by Senator Wadsworth, who referred it to the committee on military affairs for consideration, and read it and its supporting documents into the *Congressional Record,* there to stand as an appeal to the consciences of those who might exploit the good name of *The Stars and Stripes*. However, no legislation was forthcoming on the matter, likewise dying in committee.[18]

The Butterick Company did not persist in its plans to use the name *The Stars and Stripes*. However, it did launch *The Home Sector*, a weekly magazine which ran from 20 September 1919 to 17 April 1920, and included on its staff Ross, Winterich, Baldridge, Wallgren and Woollcott. The venture was dedicated to the proposition that former members of the AEF would be interested in keeping alive their experiences in the war, relating them to their new civilian existence, and that the United States in general would continue its high interest in its men at arms. Such was clearly not the case; the nation's mood had turned cynical and bored, desiring only to forget the war and return to normalcy.

More successful was the independently established newspaper called, without apology, *The Stars and Stripes*, beginning publication in Washington, D.C., on 14 June 1919, the day after the official paper ceased publication in Paris. Published as a weekly by *The Stars and Stripes* Publishing Company, it continued until 2 January 1926, when it merged with *The National Tribune* five days later. This edition was one of the causes of Ross's memorial, which clearly failed to deter the Washington entrepreneurs.

There was one authorized reappearance of *The Stars and Stripes* between the wars. When, in September 1927, the American Legion held a huge convention in Paris, an American Legion Paris Convention edition of the paper appeared, written and edited by ex-members of the AEF. It was reproduced by the offices and presses of the Paris editions of *The Chicago Tribune* and *The New York Daily News* and ran from 17 to 25 September, as Vol. I, Nos. 1–10. When the convention adjourned the paper ceased publication.

There was more friction when ex-Regimental Sgt. Maj. Clayton Melvin Ryder established the AEF Publishing Company in Minneapolis to publish a bound collection of *The Stars and Stripes*. The War Department, concerned about it, recognized that there were no legal means which could be employed to stop it, but felt that perhaps the profits might go to the orphans' fund.[19] Watson and Viskniskki were sounded out by Col. Aristides Moreno, who had earlier been at Chaumont, and who was then with the general staff corps in Washington, as to their opinions, since he understood that "General Nolan's idea [was] that no republication should be made of this paper until you . . . had given approval."[20]

Watson, by then an editor for *The Ladies' Home Journal*, felt that it came down to a matter of taste, and concluded, resignedly, that "capitalizing on the name of *The Stars and Stripes* for purposes of gain and the publication of the full edition for gain, has wearied me so much that I have very little interest in what those boys from the old business office do." Since there were no legal restraints possible, and "as no amount of gentle talking by the War Department seems able to succeed in cultivating taste in them, I don't see that there is anything to be done except to grin and bear it." In fact, he begrudgingly admitted that "the re-publication is, I think, a good thing if anybody cares to buy it." However, he added, he would like to see the profits go to the orphans' fund.[21]

Viskniskki, then at *The Red Cross Magazine*, had more pronounced views: "So many persons formerly on the paper have been engaging in literary theft and falsehoods as to same, to say nothing of attempting the commercialization of the spirit of patriotism, that I suppose it will do no harm to let one more join the merry throng of buccaneers. In the long run I believe that they will bring about their own punishment in a full realization of the fact that 'all is not gold that glitters.' "[22]

Related to the protection of the name of the paper were the great concerns of many of the poets, writers and artists on the paper's staff, or who contributed to the publication, to protect their creations from pirating. This was especially true of those who had already published books as auxiliary publications under the auspices of *The Stars and Stripes*. Viskniskki was of the opinion that these should rely on public opinion to keep these books from being exploited: "Personally I feel that the extreme anxiety in various quarters that these books will be pirated is 99 per cent needless for several reasons and principally because of the peculiar position of *The Stars and Stripes*. I am of the firm conviction that the average person back home believes that the paper is very closely tied up with the government, and anyone with piratical literary inclination would hesitate a long time before hazarding the publication of a book of *Stars and Stripes* poems or *Stars and Stripes* cartoons." He went on to admonish them further: "It is my opinion that some of the writers and artists on the staff of *The Stars and Stripes* are overlooking the fact that it is not what they have written or drawn for [the paper] that will gain them monetary returns in civil life but that their work as civilians will be judged by what they do when they have resumed their former habits of life."[23]

But these views were not those of the staffers. *The Stars and Stripes* had published Wallgren's cartoons, Seth Bailey's *Henry's Pal To Henry*, and *Yanks: A Book Of A.E.F. Verse*, and planned to bring out another, tentatively entitled, "Summer Days." However, the latter was never published because of the confusion that arose about the disposition of the profits of the paper and its enterprises and the matter of the copyright, the latter of which disturbed the members of the staff to the very end. Watson planned to bring out Wallgren's cartoons in The United States so as to establish a copyrighted edition, with the profits to go to the orphans' fund, beyond the grasp of the U.S. government, and perhaps under the auspices of the Red Cross. However, Nolan refused to countenance this, not wanting *The Stars and Stripes* to compound its business interests at a time when the paper's liquidation was being considered. Furthermore, the feeling at Chaumont was that Wallgren and others should be permitted to republish their own stuff in the United States, taking advantage of the profits themselves with no obligations to support anyone else, certainly not the Treasury of the United States. They had done their duty by the AEF when they produced their work for *The Stars and Stripes*. After all, such men as Edward Streeter and Frederick Palmer had done very well commercially.[24]

And so it was decided, and the flood gates were thereby opened. *Yanks. A.E.F. Verse Originally Published In The Stars and Stripes The Official Newspaper Of The American Expeditionary Forces* was one of the first to appear— in 1919—published by G. P. Putnam's Sons. The same house, in the same year, also produced Baldridge's *"I Was There." With The Yanks On The Western Front, 1917–1919,* consisting of some of his best-known drawings that had originally appeared in *The Stars and Stripes, Leslie's Weekly,* and *Scribner's Magazine*. This was enhanced by a few of Hilmar R. Baukhage's poems. Woollcott soon weighed in with his *The Command Is Forward, Tales Of The A.E.F.*

Battlefields As They Appeared In The Stars And Stripes, published in 1919, by The Century Company. In 1921 *Buddies, A Sequel To Yanks: A Book of Verse, Originally Published In The Stars And Stripes* was published in Washington, D.C., by the Eastern Supply Company. Later, Winterich brought out his edited book, *Squads Write! A Selection Of The Best Things In Prose, Verse And Cartoon From The Stars And Stripes, Official Newspaper Of The A.E.F.* in 1931, published by Harper and Brothers. Finally, in 1933, Wallgren got around to publishing *The A.E.F. In Cartoon*, brought out by the Dan Sowers Company of Philadelphia, containing an engaging introduction by Woollcott.

The high caliber of many of the people associated with *The Stars and Stripes* has frequently been remarked upon. Many of the staffers had already established themselves in journalism before coming to France. Afterwards, the considerable accomplishments of these extraordinary people continued.

Of the officers, little is known of Viskniskki's subsequent career, though shortly after leaving the paper he was on the staff of *The Red Cross Magazine*. Major Watson, however, continued to develop as a journalist of some repute. For a brief time after his return home he was managing editor of *The Ladies' Home Journal*; in 1920 he became managing editor of *The Baltimore Sun*. From 1927 to 1941, he was the paper's Sunday editor, and from 1941, military writer for the paper. In 1945 he won the Pulitzer Prize for international correspondence. In 1947 he was a member of the Gen. Albert C. Wedemeyer Mission to China and Korea. He is the author of *Chief of Staff; Prewar Plans and Preparations,* a volume in the series The United States Army in World War II that came out in 1950 and of *The U.S. and Armaments,* published by the Foreign Policy Association in 1960.

Lieut. Adolph Ochs was soon back in harness at his family's paper, *The Chattanooga Times*. Capt. Stephen T. Early is best known for his serving as secretary for FDR for the years of his presidency. Capt. Richard H. Waldo became, in 1919, the organizing officer and secretary of the Inter-Allied Games held in Paris in that year. From 1921 to 1923, he published Hearst's *International Magazine*, and in 1928, became the president and editor of the McClure Newspaper Syndicate. Capt. Joseph Mills Hanson, following his military service, remained active in the field of military history, writing works such as *The World War Through The Stereoscope* in 1923 for the Keystone View Company which produced the familiar photographic records of the war, a firm he later joined. Still later, Hanson became an associate editor of the American Military Institute.

Better known was Franklin Pierce Adams—widely referred to as "F.P.A."—who returned to *The New York Tribune* (until 1921) as columnist and humorist. In 1922, he went to *The New York World*, remaining until 1931 when he joined the staff of *The New York Herald Tribune,* staying until 1938 when he became associated with *The New York Post*. He was the writer of the well-known column the "Conning Tower," the principal outlet for his views, poems and wit. In 1938 he also became a member of the cast of the popular radio program "Information Please." He published numerous books, such as a volume of poetry,

8. Lieut. Adolph Ochs (left) and Sgt. Maj. Frank U. McDermott (right), two members of the paper's staff. *Courtesy of National Archives.*

Christopher Columbus And Other Patriotic Poems, and *The Diary Of Our Own Samuel Pepys.*[25]

Another officer who served *The Stars and Stripes* to gain renown later was Grantland Rice, the sports writer. Until 1930 he was on the staff of *The New York Tribune.* In that year he launched the syndicated column "The Sportlight," and founded the motion picture firm Grantland Rice Sportlight, Inc. He published widely in the field of sports, as, for example, *Sportlights of 1923,* but also published poetry, as *The Final Answer And Other Poems.* His autobiography was entitled, *The Tumult And The Shouting: My Life In Sport.*[26]

The enlisted members of the editorial staff exceeded the accomplishments of the officers in later life. It is common knowledge that Harold Wallace Ross founded *The New Yorker* in 1925. Before that, he edited the short-lived *The Home Sector,* becoming editor of *The American Legion Weekly* from 1920 to 1924, and for a brief time in 1925 was editor of the periodical *Judge.* John Tracy Winterich went with Ross to *The Home Sector* as managing editor, moving with him to *The American Legion Weekly,* remaining in that capacity from 1920 to 1924 and taking over as editor when Ross left. This publication became *The American Legion Monthly* in 1926, and Winterich continued to serve it as editor until 1938. In 1940 Winterich became a major in the U.S. Army, staying at the War Department until the war's end in 1945. Discharged as a colonel, he became managing editor of *The Saturday Review of Literature* in 1945, continuing as contributing editor from 1946. He developed a parallel career as a bibliophile and author, publishing his esteemed *A Primer Of Book Collecting* at the Green-berg Press in 1926, a work that went through several editions. He also published *Books And The Man* in 1929; *Early American Books And Printing* in 1935; and his autobiography, *Another Day, Another Dollar,* in 1947.[27]

Perhaps the best known of the former editors was Alexander Humphreys Woollcott who made a name for himself as drama critic, raconteur, wit, play-wright, actor, radio personality, author, and general character. After the war he returned to *The New York Times* as drama critic, remaining until 1922, at which time he went to *The New York Herald* for a short period. From 1925 to 1928 he was at *The New York World.* His publications are numerous, including *Shouts And Murmurs: Echoes Of A Thousand And One First Nights*, published in 1922 by The Century Company, and *Enchanted Aisles,* produced by Putnam's in 1924. Both of these works are concerned with the world of the drama critic. He also wrote and edited various collections of literature and some plays. Mindful of his earlier military service, he assembled for members of the armed forces and the merchant marine the collection *As You Were; A Portable Library Of American Prose And Poetry,* in 1943.[28]

Some of the other staffers continued to write, as did Seth Thomas Bailey, who produced detective stories. And the artists continued to paint and draw. Baldridge became a book illustrator and writer, often collaborating with his wife, the writer Caroline Singer. Abian Wallgren later published, in 1934, another collection of drawings, *Happy Days Cartoons Of The C.C.C.,* published by the

Happy Days Publishing Company of Washington, D.C. This is reminiscent of his drawings of the AEF, in this instance caricaturing the antics and foibles of the Civilian Conservation Corps.[29]

Altogether, *The Stars and Stripes* was a remarkable sheet published by a group of outstanding men. In words of a later parlance, they "had it all together." In the midst of the chaos of a nation at war, they performed at a consistently high level. The chemistry was present to produce a bright journalistic light of considerable magnitude.

Under the erratic, egotistical, somewhat tyrannical, but able Viskniskki, and the steady, quietly competent Watson, the paper was enthusiastically launched and magnificently produced. The high command, though sometimes aching to intervene, with only a few exceptions let the paper run its course. It is clear that at times Chaumont even protected it. There were some parameters, to be sure, and it was not entirely left to its own devices, but the metes and bounds allowed considerable latitude of expression, which was one of its reasons for being. The paper remains, however, a sort of test case as to how far the high command would go in allowing freedom of expression in the military's essentially closed society. The issue would be raised once more in World War II with an Eisenhower, like Pershing, allowing considerable latitude. World War I did not have its equivalents of Patton and MacArthur to contend with. In addition, the World War I version lasted for only a comparatively short time; the numerous editions during World War II had to persist over a much longer time and appear in a much more complex world, making their publication more difficult and involved. They also encountered far more high-ranking officers.

There is no reason to believe that the enlisted staff at Paris was in serious disagreement with the way that the paper was set up and run. Certainly not if they could, as they did, evolve local policy, and essentially produce the paper. They understood as well as anybody that, in order to be viable, it must serve to help siphon off discontent among the rank and file; to let the men feel that they, as individuals, were not alone, and that they had an advocate and a mouthpiece. Their traditional rights of freedom of expression were not totally curtailed, not even in the army. Still, they were in that army, a fact never lost sight of.

Naturally, for all of its merits, *The Stars and Stripes* does not convey all aspects of the life of the doughboy in the AEF. Nevertheless, it does reveal, to a considerable degree, what life was like in the American Army in Europe at that time. For instance, in the early issues of the paper, the reader is able to ascertain the excitement experienced by the American troops, lately arrived in Europe, and perceive something of their fears, apprehensions and attraction for action as they drew near to the front. The paper sought to smooth the path for these men, helping to the extent possible to inform them as to what to expect. At the same time, they were encouraged to believe that their idealism was not misplaced; America was to have a significant impact on the course of the war. If the men would only have faith in themselves, their officers, their training and their heritage—even their sports background—they would measure up fully to battle's demands. Indeed, they could be expected to acquit themselves well, even heroically. They could even expect decorations recognizing their valor.

With light-hearted banter, the paper also hoped to persuade the men that the hard pre-combat training was necessary, and the delays in getting into the trenches were only temporary. They must endure the season's unexpected rigors—the winter of 1917–1918 was especially harsh—the endless mud, the cold, the billets in barn and shed, and the many other discomforts. Their time for action would come. Those men who patiently disciplined themselves in the soldierly virtues could be expected to succeed and persevere. Those men caught far behind the lines in the S.O.S. must likewise recognize the heroics of unloading ships and boxcars; those whose duties involved mundane office responsibilities were no less involved in the war effort. All branches of service were worthy—though the artillery and the infantry grabbed more column space—even those largely neglected in the pages of the paper, the Air Service and the Navy.

Beyond this, the allied nations must be properly venerated. In this regard, strange French customs and their frustrating language must be met somehow, and unity with them welded. The French war orphan's campaign played no small part in these things. The British, too, must be accepted; the old hates forgotten. The foe was appropriately excoriated, especially the Kaiser and his minions. The common people of Germany were extended sympathy at times; they would one day be freed of their shackles. The other Central Powers apparently mattered little, at least to *The Stars and Stripes*.

The paper followed the course of the war as America fought it. Discussions of the German successes in the spring of 1918 were printed but muted, and never with any panic or sense of urgency. As Americans began to make their weight felt, their battles began to be featured in detail, but with becoming modesty, though some features focused with pride on medal winners.

In the midst of these preoccupations, the Armistice came with a rush. The paper almost immediately switched to events involving the occupation of the Rhineland and the forces sent there were closely followed, the paper publishing several accounts of first impressions of Germany. A considerable number of articles appeared on leave and educational opportunites; sports once more came into their own, though featuring athletic events in the AEF rather than those at home. With some perspective now possible, even more detailed accounts of American military action, and histories of the combat divisions, appeared in the paper's pages. *The Stars and Stripes* also followed the peace negotiations, as well as events surrounding the organization of the American Legion. Perhaps most importantly, however, were the numerous, almost continuous, injunctions that the men persist in exercising discipline and patience while awaiting the ship for home, in many ways, the toughest battle of all. By way of encouragement, the paper published departure schedules and details as to what to expect at the base camps and ports.

The Stars and Stripes provides the student of the AEF with a running account of major events in its career from early 1918 to the end of the paper's life, and specific topics can be investigated, revealing certain details of life as well as attitudes. For instance, to some extent the paper was a rallying sheet for Americans on crusade against the Hun. It should be pointed out, however, that the majority of its readers did not need to be propagandized to embrace a patriotic zeal which this implied. Most were true believers in the proposition that the New World was destined to save the Old from its failures and to create the basis for a New Era in the history of the world. Along the same lines, democracy was held to be virtuous, the paper being fundamentally opposed to class distinctions. It was truly the hope that the war experience would break down class barriers and biases where they existed, and that this could be accomplished when men of all levels were brought to the same level as comrades in a common, fateful enterprise. Of course, the hierarchical structure of the army had to be reckoned with, but this was regarded as a necessary evil, tolerable if one understood the American system which provided for a civilian commander-in-chief who in turn was elected by the people.

The Stars and Stripes confronted the related problem of race. Regarding most ethnic groups, a more rapid boiling of the melting pot, another consequence of the military experience, seemed inevitable as well as desirable. As to the blacks, ambivalance was noted. While there was genuine praise for their martial accomplishments, the old attitudes died hard but it is significant that some protests did appear in the paper on their behalf.

Further, *The Stars and Stripes* reveals something of the American love affair with machines, which could easily carry over to a close relationship with the cold instruments of destruction. Though it might be readily understood that the cavalryman might love his horse, in an age of mechanized warfare there were acceptable substitutes and the alliance of a man and his equipment strengthened the American war effort and contributed to the American soldier's accomplishments. Accordingly, the paper conveys something of the nature of combat in the modern era, as well as those conditions of war that are seemingly changeless.

The paper also informs its readers as to cultural and intellectual matters such as the state of art in advertising, what the AEF was reading, what movies it was viewing and what songs it was singing, what its religious convictions were, what sports it played, and how the latter, in particular, seemed of considerable value in an era of conflict, and perhaps were destined to sweep the world in popularity. The emphasis placed on amateur theatrical productions is striking at this time, as is how readily the doughboy turned to poetry and doggerel as a means of expression. The reasons for the latter are not altogether clear, but the romanticism present was no inconsequential factor. More serious study is needed on this phenomenon.

In addition, details as to uniforms, decorations, chow, medical care, discipline, and dozens of other aspects of the general mode of service life, so difficult to capture in official documents and other accounts, are made plain. Add to this how the men regarded their allies and their foes, and one begins to perceive the doughboy as a flesh and blood character very much alive.

The considerable insight that the paper gives into the life and times of the doughboy encourages the conclusion that the newspaper could be used to supplement other studies for other periods of history where the press existed. While newspapers have not been altogether ignored in this respect, much more could be done to exploit them to recover aspects of the past that the press readily reveals, as already discussed, i.e., insights into intellectual, cultural, and social dimensions of life in particular.

Finally, *The Stars and Stripes* left certain legacies. One was its contribution to the subsequent careers of many of its staff. Though these men no doubt would have succeeded without having served on the paper, the experience was clearly an asset, and in some cases, perhaps, functioned as a catalyst. Others emerged from the experience as from a chrysalis to enter upon a stage of higher accomplishment.

Another legacy was the numerous editions that were published under its name in World War II. In this regard, the desires of such men as Ross came to pass. The old torch, laid aside, was picked up again. The temptation is great to compare and contrast the various editions, and to measure a Mauldin, say, against a Wallgren. However, such is fortunately beyond the scope of this study, though this author is tempted to conclude that the boots of the likes of Ross, Winterich and Woollcott, were simply too large to be filled by their successors. Certainly, no World War II edition succeeded in getting together in one office the conglomerate of concentrated talent that Viskniskki and Watson had the good fortune—and difficulty—of presiding over.

Though this brief résumé does not cover all aspects of the paper's career and its significance, in recapitulation it can be suggested that ultimately the importance of *The Stars and Stripes* is that it "forms an invaluable document, a human and living contemporaneous history of the part played by the American Army in the Great War,"[30] or, as it was more grandly stated in the paper itself, it was most important "as a chronicle of the comedy and tragedy of the greatest expedition since the world began" (2 August 1918).

Notes

INTRODUCTION

1. Telegram, Goudie to Pershing, 8 February 1918; letter, headquarters to Goudie, in reply, expressing thanks and appreciation for his help in launching the paper, 12 February 1918, in Record Group 120, "Records of the American Expeditionary Forces"; subseries, "Censorship and Press Division (G-2-D)"; Entry 223, "Correspondence Relating to *The Stars and Stripes*, 1917–19," in folder 40, hereafter cited as Entry 223/40 (Telegram, Goudie to Pershing, 8 February 1918).

2. This appeared in *The New York Globe*, issue of 2 July 1918, and was reprinted in *The Stars and Stripes* in the 27 September 1918 issue.

1. ORIGINS, PERSONNEL, AND OPERATIONS

1. Most of the references in this book are from documents in the National Archives in Washington, D.C., filed under Record Group 120. Entry 237 refers to the bound collection of *The Stars and Stripes* (Minneapolis: A.E.F. Publishing Association, 1920). Unless otherwise indicated, entry numbers refer to Record Group 120 documents.

2. Memorandum, Lieut. Guy T. Viskniskki to chief, press division, censorship branch of the general staff, 28 November 1917, Entry 223/47. Viskniskki had been a member of the 320th Infantry, 80th Division, an outfit made up primarily of men of Polish descendants, before being tapped for press work. A native of New Jersey, Viskniskki had been associated earlier with *McClure's Magazine* and the Wheeler News Syndicate.

Pershing was perhaps the real father of the paper. It grew out of his concern for the morale of his troops which he realized "should be kept up to a high pitch." See John J. Pershing, *My Experiences in the World War*, 2 vols. (New York: Frederick A. Stokes Company, 1931), I, 317–318.

3. See copy of "Rules of Press Censorship," 18 November 1918, in Record Group 120, "Records of the American Expeditionary Forces"; subseries "Censorship and Press Division (G-2-D)"; Entry 236, "General Correspondence of the Office of *The Stars and*

Stripes, 1917–19,'' Box 31, hereafter cited as Entry 236/31 (''Rules of Press Censorship,'' 18 November 1918).

4. There is a copy of Vol. I, No. 1, of *The Bayonet* in Entry 223/47. Its price was five cents. It was published every Friday as *The Stars and Stripes* was to be. The format of the latter was remarkably like this paper, which is, of course, not surprising.

5. These details are in Memorandum, Nolan to Pershing, 2 January 1918, Entry 223/41.

6. Memorandum, Nolan to the Chief of Staff, Brig. Gen. James G. Harbord, 7 January 1918, Entry 223/41. Harbord was soon to become head of the Services of Supply (S.O.S.), AEF. Nolan was shortly to be a brigadier general as assistant chief of staff, G-2, i.e., Intelligence. The Censorship and Press Division, of the Intelligence Branch— G-2-D—was at that time headed by Lieut. Col. Walter E. Sweeney. The Press Section of the Censorship Division was headed by Maj. Frederick Palmer, the well-known war correspondent, with his headquarters at Neufchâteau in eastern France. His book *America In France* (New York: Dodd, Mead and Company, 1918) gives some insight into the spirit of those times. Palmer was assisted very ably by 2d Lieut. Mark S. Watson in charge of press matters at G.H.Q. at Chaumont. Both Viskniskki and Watson were within a few weeks jumped to the rank of captain.

It is not certain whether Viskniskki gave the paper its name. Also, one wonders whether the one who came up with the name was aware that various sporadic editions of newspapers published during the Civil War by several army units bore the name *The Stars and Stripes*. See discussion in Richard F. Riccardelli, ''From Chatham to Coblenz: A Historiography of U.S. Army Newspapers from the Revolutionary War through World War I,'' unpublished Master of Science thesis, Ohio University, Athens, Ohio, 1972, pp. 55–56.

The reader should be aware that there is some confusion as to who really initiated the launching of the new paper. The anniversary edition of the paper, published on 7 February 1919, stated that ''*The Stars and Stripes* was born of the needs of the A.E.F. and the energy of . . . Viskniskki.'' Other accounts discount Viskniskki's role, asserting that the paper was solely the creation of the General Staff at Chaumont and that Viskniskki knew nothing of the plan until he was ordered to duty in connection with it. To be sure, Viskniskki was only formally ordered to take up the work of publishing the paper as its editor and officer-in-charge on 16 March 1918, but he was clearly in on the project from the beginning. See orders from General Headquarters, A.E.F., 16 March 1918, in Entry 236/33. There were many people, however, who were ill disposed toward Viskniskki; he made many enemies along the way. For a discussion of the various versions as to the establishment of the paper, see Harry L. Katz, *The History of the Stars and Stripes. Official Newspaper of The American Expeditionary Forces in France, From February 8, 1918 to June 13, 1919* (Washington, D.C.: The Columbia Publishing Company, 1921), p. 7. Katz, as a sergeant, was a staffer in the mailing department of the paper. His brief forty-seven-page study is especially useful since it presents the viewpoint of an insider.

There is a long article summarizing the paper's history in the last issue, Vol. II, No. 19 (13 June 1919). There is other historical information in the anniversary issue of 7 February 1919.

7. Letter, Lieut. Col. Walter C. Sweeney to Roderick Darblay, Entry 223/47.

8. Viskniskki and other officers also apparently expended some private funds in helping to launch the paper. They were perhaps reimbursed. The 24,724.65 francs were returned to G-2 on 6 September 1918. Memorandum, Capt. Donald L. Stone, acting

chief, G-2-D (Censorship and Press Division), to a Major Ruffin, Judge Advocate's Office, G.H.Q., AEF, 14 February 1919, in Entry 223/54.

9. There is a copy of Bulletin No. 10 in Entry 223/41.

10. Thus Viskniskki's scheme that the profits would go into a tobacco fund was altered. The document also detailed circulation and distribution plans.

11. Second indorsement by Viskniskki of a Memorandum, Brig. Gen. M. Churchill, Chief Military Censor, to Nolan, 27 September 1918, Entry 223/40.

12. Cable, Viskniskki to Muller, 10 January 1918, Entry 223/49. Muller was later released from his position; it is not clear who replaced him in this capacity. He was released following the publication of a book which he edited, *Two Thousand Questions and Answers About the War*, and the furor which it aroused. Muller was charged with being unpatriotic and no doubt with some fears about his name and his German ancestors. Leading the attack against Muller was the American Security League. In any case, the Chief Military Censor barred the book from the mails, from public libraries and all camps, cantonments and stations. It was soon withdrawn from sale, the problem being that some of the answers presented in the book were regarded as unpatriotic. Though Viskniskki sought to save his position, higher authorities in the AEF, so as to spare both Muller and the paper any embarrassment, ordered his replacement, at the same time "expressing keen appreciation of his dispatches, which have conveyed to the men of the A.E.F. much of the spirit of people at home and their determination to back them to the limit, helping to maintain the high morale of troops." In fact, G-2-D was "thoroughly convinced that Mr. Muller has performed as patriotic a service as has been performed by any of us who have been privileged to serve on this side of the water." See Letter, Maj. A. L. James, Jr., then chief, G-2-D, to Visknisski, 1 November 1918, in Entry 223/40. There are several other relevant documents in this folder as well. It is interesting that in view of Muller's reservations about George Creel, the latter had written an introduction to the controversial book.

13. Letter, Muller to Viskniskki, 15 May 1918, Entry 223/40; Memorandum, Sweeney to Chief of Staff, G.H.Q., 5 February 1918, Entry 223/49. Muller had explained that the Creel organization had been "thoroughly discredited in the United States during the past few weeks and the opposition to it is only on the edge of really beginning. I am justified now in speaking plainly, because it is no longer a matter of my own, perhaps too dignified and austere taste. Congress, the newspapers, even the common man in the streets are dead against it." He also noted that "a nasty three-cornered mud-slinging fight between Roosevelt and *The Tribune*, Hearst and *The American*, has Creel for the angle of it." He further recounted Creel's reference to Congress as a slum, to which Uncle Joe Cannon had retorted that Creel should be "taken by the slack of the breeches and thrown into space." He was not, of course, and though he continued to be controversial, he performed prodigies in the months ahead. In any event, *The Stars and Stripes* remained aloof from Creel who, as Muller had stated it, did not "get even so much as the tip-end of a little finger into *The Stars and Stripes*." Muller's counterpart in London was George T. Bye.

14. Memorandum, Capt. Donald L. Stone, acting chief, G-2-D, to a Major Ruffin, Judge Advocate's Office, G.H.Q., AEF, 14 February 1919, Entry 223/54.

15. Lord Northcliffe later wrote to Viskniskki that "when I saw the first copy of *The Stars and Stripes* I realized what a valuable vitalizer it would be for the American boys and how it would link up scattered units." See his letter, 7 November 1918, in Entry 236/31.

16. The anniversary issue of the paper, published on 7 February 1919, recounted that in the process of founding the sheet Viskniskki had to brush aside the multitude of people "high and low, well-meaning and otherwise," who said that establishing such a paper could not—or should not—be done. It had been pointed out by the doubters "that the same thing had been tried without success by every other army in Europe." In light of the documents in the files of *The Stars and Stripes* this seems an overstatement. Also, though apparently not as successful as *The Stars and Stripes*, there were several examples of newspapers in the Allied forces. One Italian troop paper was styled *La Giberna*, "The Cartridge-Box," also an eight-page weekly, financed by the Italian government. It was edited and written by disabled Italian soldiers. See *The Stars and Stripes* issue of 5 April 1918. The French 74th Infantry Division also published an infrequently-appearing paper, *Le Rire aux Eclats*, which meant "Explosions of Laughter," or "Laughter amid the Explosions," as one prefers. *The Stars and Stripes* reprinted selections from this paper in an entire page in its 17 January 1919 issue.

17. See Memorandum by Sweeney, 23 February 1918, establishing the board in Entry 223/41. The board's composition changed from time to time. For example, on 16 March 1918, Maj. E. R. W. McCabe replaced Lieut. Smith. See Memorandum, Sweeney to Viskniskki, 16 March 1918, Entry 223/41. In early August, Maj. A. L. James, Jr., replaced Sweeney; Maj. Rozeman Bulger replaced McCabe. See Memorandum, Chief of G-2-D, to Viskniskki, 8 August 1918, Entry 223/41.

18. Later, an unsigned memorandum to Watson, dated 23 January 1919, put it more bluntly: "We must expect a certain amount of 'must-go' stuff from G.H.Q., but it has got to be handled with extreme care to avoid its being obvious, and it cannot be in too large a proportion to the news. There must be enough news to carry it." See in Entry 223/42.

19. Minutes of Board meeting, 19 April 1918, Entry 223/41.

20. Memorandum, Nolan to Viskniskki, 8 September 1918, Entry 223/40. This appeared in the 13 September 1918 issue of the paper.

21. Telegram, Nolan to proprietor, *The London Morning Post*, 18 December 1918, seeking permission to reprint the article, Entry 223/40.

22. Memorandum, Capt. David Stone, assistant chief of G-2-D, to Nolan, 23 December 1918, Entry 223/40. Repington's article was reproduced in the 3 January 1919 issue.

23. Memorandum, Harts to Harbord, then commanding general of the S.O.S., and his superior officer, 17 September 1918, Entry 223/40. Harts included a copy of the 13 September issue with his complaint which contained some offensive examples. Harbord, in the first indorsement to Harts' Memorandum, forwarded the complaint to Pershing's offices.

24. Memorandum, Moreno to Watson, 17 January 1919, Entry 223/40.

25. Memorandum, Watson to chief, G-2-D, 23 January 1919, Entry 223/40.

26. Pershing's lengthy final report to the Secretary of War was printed in the 20 and 27 December 1918 issues of the paper.

27. Watson, a native of Plattsburg, New York, had begun his newspaper career with the *Plattsburg* (New York) *Press* in 1908. He then had been reporter and travelling correspondent for *The Chicago Tribune* from 1909 to 1914.

28. There were other instances of some conflict between Watson and the high command. *The Stars and Stripes*, in the 10 January 1919 issue, had published an article critical of abuse of some officers in collecting mileage allowances when engaged in

official travel. Some "mileage hounds" had appeared, some collecting more for mileage than their pay. Watson's retort to an official criticism of the paper on this occasion was a familiar one: the paper was simply not going to function "on the assumption that everything in the A.E.F. is perfect." If this were to be the case, the paper should be killed immediately, and he insisted that the commander-in-chief would suffer "incalculable harm" if the paper should ever become thought of as "an organ devoted to stifling the expression of the thoughts of the men of the A.E.F." Memorandum, Watson to chief, G-2-D, 20 January 1919, Entry 223/40.

Somewhat later, the paper was instructed not to publish any more articles describing the unsatisfactory conditions in the casual camps and at the ports of embarkation, "which are not all that they should be." The reason given was that the conditions were known to be bad and General Pershing was on an extended tour of inspection seeking to improve matters. Therefore, further articles would not serve the useful purpose of exposing a bad situation; they would only "prejudice officers and men going to these camps . . . before their arrival, which does not seem desirable." This line of reasoning seemed acceptable to the paper's editors. See Memorandum, Capt. Donald Stone, acting chief, G-2-D, to Lieut. Stephen T. Early, assistant officer-in-charge, *The Stars and Stripes*, 4 February 1919, Entry 223/40.

29. For a description of the setting and an account of those war correspondents mentioned, see Emmet Crozier, *American Reporters on the Western Front, 1914–1918* (New York: Oxford University Press, 1959).

30. Viskniskki had at first requested three rooms in the hotel for quarters for the paper but G.H.Q. ordered the paper to Nos. 1 and 3, Rue des Italiens, taking over offices to be vacated on 2 March by the Bureau of War Risk Insurance. The new location was also conveniently near the offices of the *Daily Mail* which did the paper's printing. See Memorandum, Viskniskki to Sweeney, 22 February 1918, and Orders, Pershing to Harbord, 26 February 1918, in Entry 223/47. Somewhat later, Viskniskki asked for and received additional space in the same building at Rue des Italiens. He noted that the staff was then at 192 men, with ninety of these in the offices. The paper would soon have 350 men and simply needed more space, for the purposes of the "obviation of pother and conflict in departments." In a business where men must concentrate on their work, "conditions are so cramped that it is necessary for men at work to rise from chairs in order to allow others to pass." See Memorandum, Viskniskki to Harts, 21 September 1918, in Entry 236/6.

31. The Paris branch of the American Chamber of Commerce was also located in the same building. The issue of 6 December 1918 was the first released from the new address.

32. The anniversary issue of 7 February 1919 is the source of much of the detail of the paper's founding and early efforts.

33. Katz, *The History of the Stars and Stripes*, pp. 8–10. See also Winterich's own *Squads Write! A Selection of the Best Things in Prose, Verse and Cartoon from The Stars and Stripes. Official Newspaper of the A.E.F.* (New York: Harper and Brothers, 1931).

34. See Memorandum, Watson to Capt. Donald L. Stone, acting chief, G-2-D, 31 January 1919, Entry 223/48. The other enlisted man cited was Regimental Sgt. Maj. Melvin Ryder, who was recognized for his excellent work in the circulation department, and was credited by Watson for being mainly responsible for building up the paper's circulation past the 500,000-mark late in its career. He was credited also with having gotten *The Stars and Stripes* into the Third Army area, in the German occupation zone,

when the Red Cross and the YMCA had failed. Regarding the latter, see numerous documents in Entry 223/42.

On Ross, see also Brendan Gill, *Here at The New Yorker* (New York: Berkley Publishing Company, 1977), pp. 12, 24, 202 and *passim*.

35. See Woollcott's amusing self-description in his introduction to Abian A. Wallgren, *The A.E.F. in Cartoon. From The Stars and Stripes Official Newspaper of the A.E.F.* (Philadelphia: Dan Sowers and Company, 1933).

36. Ibid. General Pershing himself referred to the "remarkable" group of editors Viskniskki had assembled in *My Experiences in the World War*, I, 318. Katz praised the editorials written in such a way that they were at once interesting, gripping, convincing and understandable. Not only did they condemn what they regarded as wrong, they clearly praised what was regarded as right. The editorials were also written in the characteristic snappy style that the paper was famous for. Katz, *The History of the Stars and Stripes*, p. 10.

37. Seth T. Bailey, *Henry's Pal to Henry. Reprinted from The Stars and Stripes* (Paris: *The Stars and Stripes*, 1919). The publication sold for three francs. See account book on sales in Entry 236/9, and orders for the book in Entry 236/21, together with correspondence regarding this publication.

38. Katz, *The History of the Stars and Stripes*, pp. 11–12. Bailey's letters were no doubt inspired by the fabulously popular and successful "Dere Mable" letters originated by Lieut. Edward Streeter. See his collection entitled *Love Letters of Bill to Mable. Comprising Dere Mable: "That's Me All Over, Mable"; "Same Old Bill, Eh, Mable!"* (New York: Frederick A. Stokes Company, 1919). There are several editions of Streeter's works. Streeter contributed the oft-repeated expression of that day, "That's me all over, Mable." His letters were illustrated by G. William Breck.

39. The designation "third lieutenant" facetiously referred to graduates of officers' training schools whose commissions had been held up for one reason or another.

40. Katz, *The History of the Stars and Stripes*, pp. 19–20. There are many examples of letters sent in by soldiers—and others—in Entry 236/5, and Entry 236/40. Viskniskki also spent a great deal of time answering letters which contained all sorts of requests. For example, in October 1918, he received a letter from Charles H. Willoughby, advertising manager of *The Albany Evening Journal*, requesting that the paper obtain a German helmet for his daughter. He enclosed a dollar in payment. See his letter, 12 October 1918, in Entry 236/40. Viskniskki replied: "I can assure you that it takes us all of our time in getting out the official Army newspaper, and there is no chance for us to devote time in endeavoring to secure trophies of the war." He returned the dollar. See his letter of 31 October 1918 in Entry 236/40. The paper's files contain numerous letters from readers in the United States seeking information of lost loved ones. These were referred to various departments and services so that the writers would hopefully receive some answer eventually. Many of the inquiries were sent to the Central Records Office of the AEF; others were forwarded to *The New York Herald*, Paris Edition, which published a daily column of personal inquiry. Others were sent to the Red Cross. There is a large folder of such inquiries in Entry 236/5. The paper also handled letters from soldiers with ideas and inventions, as one, for example, from Sgt. J. J. Blevins, of the 110th Ammunition Train, who had invented a combination bacon and condiment can. Viskniskki duly forwarded it to the ordnance department and received a reply from a Brigadier General Wheeler who promised Viskniskki that the can would be thoroughly

tested and warmly thanked him for bringing it to his attention. These documents are in Entry 236/35.

41. Among others of note who served on the editorial staff were Sgt. J. W. Rixey Smith of the 110th Field Artillery, and *The Baltimore Sun*; Sgt. Tyler H. "Tip" Bliss of the 161st Infantry, who also wrote poetry for the paper; and Sgt. Robert I. Snajdr of the 308th Ammunition Train and *The Cleveland Plain Dealer*, one of the paper's far-ranging reporters, making his way to Berlin immediately after the war to report conditions there. A complete list of all members of the AEF who served the paper in some capacity is included in the final issue, 13 June 1919. This list has been reproduced in Katz, *The History of the Stars and Stripes,* pp. 42–46, and in Winterich, *Squads Write!,* pp. 321–335.

Bliss also wrote, for a time, a humor column entitled the "Dizzy Sector," which ranged from advice to the lovelorn to the notes of an expert on correct military dress.

42. See Woollcott's introduction in Wallgren, *The A.E.F. in Cartoon.* See also Entry 236/31 for letters and orders.

43. Katz, *The History of the Stars and Stripes*, pp. 13–15.

44. Ibid., p. 15.

45. See documents on the inspection of the books following Miltenberger's death in Entry 223/41.

46. See lengthy reports in Entry 223/40. It is not known where Viskniskki was transferred. In any case, he played no subsequent part in the life of the paper.

47. See, for example, Letter from Lieut. Stephen T. Early to Captain Stone, 31 January 1919, Entry 223/48, in which he recommended his chief for the DSM, stating that "Mark Watson is, in my opinion, one of the biggest institutions this AEF boasts." Stone followed through, but there is no indication that Watson got the decoration which seems likely in view of the fact that this award was rarely given to officers below the rank of colonel. See other relevant documents in Entry 223/48.

48. See Memorandum, Nolan to Chief of Staff, G.H.Q., 12 February 1918, requesting that Adams be sent to *The Stars and Stripes* if possible. It was desired that this news-paperman whose national reputation, especially as a humorist, which he had made at *The New York Tribune*, report as soon as possible, it being deemed "very advantageous to have his services, if they may be secured." See in entry 223/40.

49. Rice was asked, when he returned to civilian life, where he resumed his work at *The New York Tribune*, to send over some "sporting copy" for the paper's use. It is not clear whether he in fact did so. Letter, Watson to Rice, 1 April 1919, in Entry 236/32.

50. Hanson also wrote verse for the paper. The arguments raged hot and heavy as to the prowess and accomplishments of the various combat divisions. Countless letters came in to the paper on these matters and on the related one of "Who won the war?" Typical was the letter labelled by the editors as "Question No. 4,176,502" which went as follows:

I wish to take advantage of the knowledge of the staff of your paper by having them settle the question that is causing so many arguments in the A.E.F. and elsewhere. Which division did the best fighting on the front? Kindly publish in your paper at your earliest opportunity the standing of the different combat divisions. In doing this you will please the men of the A.E.F. and the folks back home. Signed: Cpl. M. J. Donoghue.

The editor's response: "We have two men in the hospital now. Can't stand any more casualties at present." As quoted in Katz, *The History of the Stars and Stripes*, p. 26. See also letters in Entry 236/5.

51. See Letter, Lieut. Col. E. R. W. McCabe, Chief, G-2-D, to Capt. Bruce Bairnsfather, 22 June 1918, thanking him for his contributions to *The Stars and Stripes*, in Entry 223/40. Bairnsfather was in British Military Intelligence and was at the War Office, London.

In another note regarding officers, two men, Pvt. Hilmar B. Baukhage and Regimental Supply Sgt. J. Palmer Cumming, were commissioned 2d Lieutenants while on the staff of the paper. These were the only ones to be so; others on the staff had opportunities to obtain commissions but preferred to remain in the ranks so as better to serve the enlisted men of the AEF.

52. Memorandum, Viskniskki to Watson, 27 September 1918, Entry 223/41. Viskniskki also noted that the cost would be about the same but the quality would be greatly improved. The *Daily Mail* would not be in any way disturbed by the move; indeed, they needed their own facilities more and more and hence both parties were satisfied with the new arrangement. The move would facilitate the bundling of the papers as from the *Mail's* presses they had to be transshipped to a warehouse for bundling. Finally, the composition and makeup could now be done in the daytime, eliminating the night shift.

53. The paper's engraving work was done by the firm of Ateliers Victor Michel, in Paris. See large folder pertaining to this business in Entry 236/35.

54. The problem of the paper supply was an urgent one and the paper's files contain numerous documents on this subject. See Entry 236/40; Entries 223/41 and 47.

55. See Watson's indorsement to Memorandum, Early to chief, G-2-D, 5 March 1919, Entry 223/42. Watson's indorsement is dated 17 March. It concerned a plan whereby the Knights of Columbus would circulate *The Stars and Stripes* free of charge to the men. He recommended "very strongly against letting them get the idea that they receive the paper except as a result of their own efforts. With any idea other than that which they have at present, the paper's influence on the men would, in my opinion, fall off seriously." Only the Hospital Edition was free.

56. See Memorandum, Waldo to Viskniskki, 18 April 1918, Entry 223/41. See copies of Waldo's flow charts and sample coupons in Entry 223/42.

57. Minutes, Board of Control meeting, 27 April 1918, which approved Waldo's scheme in Entry 223/41. Also in this entry is a copy of Bulletin No. 26 that bears the date of 11 May 1918. It concluded that "the most hearty and prompt co-operation of all organization commanders is desired in order that the official newspaper may continue to reflect the greatest possible credit on the American E.F."

58. Memorandum, Viskniskki to McCabe, 5 August 1918; Memorandum, McCabe to Viskniskki, 7 August 1918, in Entry 223/51. Viskniskki observed that the 2 August 1918 issue had reached a circulation of 155,831. See also Memorandum, Sweeney to Nolan, 7 May 1918, Entry 223/41.

59. Memorandum, Watson to the Board of Control, 19 September 1918, Entry 223/52. There are several documents on the question of Waldo's being relieved from duty at the Paris office, though none is clear on the matter. See Entry 223/51.

60. Hudson Hawley once informed Viskniskki that the paper was most eagerly received in the hospitals. It was read from beginning to end, and in general "jollies them along," cheers up the patients and "helps them immeasurably on the road to recovery." When the papers were passed out in the wards, there was "one continual grab for them,"

"one unanimous expression of delight." See Memorandum, Hawley to Viskniskki, 3 July 1918. This made its way through channels to Pershing, who minuted, "and the C-in-C fully agrees with all that Hawley says. He himself is about as eager to get the S and S." See in Letter, Nolan to Viskniskki, 8 July 1918. These documents are in Entry 223/40. See also folder in Entry 236/44.

61. There are several versions of this story and it may well be apocryphal. The 7 February 1919 issue describes the scene in which the two field agents were captured on Armistice Day. The 13 June 1919 issue identifies the person involved as Sgt. William Hale of the 2nd Idaho Infantry, and indicates that he was alone. Katz says that the person involved was Sgt. Joe Daly, the head of the transportation department of *The Stars and Stripes*. See in his *The History of the Stars and Stripes*, p. 33. For other data on the field agents see Entries 236/37, 38, and 46.

62. In Entry 223/42, there is a copy of the distribution list of issue No. 41, for 15 November 1918. It has details of all the field agents, as to numbers of copies they received and other relevant matters. The total press run of that issue was 379,000 copies. There are other details as to field agents in Entries 236/1 and 37. The paper's files contain much material on subscriptions, such as lists of subscribers. See Entries 236/3, 4, 6, 9, 23, 30, 33, 34, 35, 36, 38, 41, 42, 43 and 45.

63. There is an extensive file devoted to the Hachette Company in entry 236/1. Lieut. Ayers, the paper's business manager, felt that Louis Teyssou of the Hachette Company merited a decoration and he accordingly recommended him for a Distinguished Service Medal. It is not known whether or not he received it. See Letter, Ayres to Watson, 4 January 1919, Entry 223/48.

64. Though the paper eventually obtained the autos and trucks it needed, it always seemed to be a struggle to get them, at least in the early months. The paper's files contain many documents on this problem. See, for example, Entries 236/31 and 40; Entries 223/42 and 54. The paper often ran up against the fact that combatant troops' needs were naturally given first consideration.

65. The paper's staff was most unhappy that the U.S. Post Office Department decided that the paper must pay second-class postage on papers mailed to the United States. The argument had been made that the paper was a government publication and should be exempted from postage charges. The postal authorities, however, pointed out that the paper printed advertising and hence was only quasi-official. See several documents in Entry 223/53.

66. Memorandum, Viskniskki to chief, G-2-D, 23 June 1918, Entry 223/40.

67. Memorandum, Watson to Nolan, 26 December 1918, Entry 223/42. The same folder contains an interesting analysis of certain issues of the paper as to content—set forth in inches—regarding news, sports, and advertising, among other features. The sheet never expanded to twelve pages.

68. There are numerous communications on this and other matters pertaining to the planned American Edition in Entry 236/31.

69. Memorandum, Viskniskki to Watson, 30 September 1918, Entry 223/41.

70. Memorandum, Viskniskki to Watson, 11 October 1918, Entry 223/41.

71. Memorandum, Nolan to chief of staff, G.H.Q., AEF, 15 August 1918, Entry 223/41.

72. Memorandum, Nolan to the chief of staff, G.H.Q., AEF, 15 October 1918, Entry 223/41. Also at the last minute, Nolan decided to cancel the agreement with the Red Cross and deal with a reputable publishing firm. Erickson was to be instructed to set this

up, withholding the signing of a contract pending War Department approval. See Memorandum, Maj. A. L. James, Jr., chief of G-2-D, to Viskniskki, 26 October 1918, Entry 223/41.

73. Letter, Viskniskki to Erickson, 25 November 1918, in Entry 236/31.

74. Memorandum, Cartinhour to Capt. Waldo, 3 September 1918, Entry 223/51.

75. Memorandum, Waldo to Viskniskki, 11 September 1918, Entry 223/51.

76. Memorandum, Viskniskki to Waldo, 14 October 1918, and Waldo's indorsement returned to Viskniskki, 21 October 1918, Entry 223/51.

77. Memorandum and cable, Viskniskki to Waldo, 8 November 1918, Entry 223/42.

78. Memorandum, Ayers to Cartinhour, 8 November 1918, Entry 223/42. This document also summarizes each man's qualifications.

79. See Biddle's indorsement of orders, sent to Harbord, 18 November 1918; Harbord's indorsement returned to the commander-in-chief, AEF, 23 November 1918, Entry 223/42. See also telegram, Viskniskki to Waldo, 18 November 1918, Entry 236/31.

80. Memorandum, Watson to the Board of Control, 3 October 1918, Entry 223/41.

81. Memorandum, Viskniskki to McCabe, 23 June 1918, Entry 223/40.

82. Memorandum, McCabe to Viskniskki, 25 June 1918, Entry 223/52.

83. *The Stars and Stripes. Yanks. A.E.F. Verse. Originally Published in The Stars and Stripes, The Official Newspaper Of The American Expeditionary Forces* (New York: G. P. Putnam's Sons, 1919), pp. v–vi. This book was originally published as *The Stars and Stripes. Yanks; A Book Of A.E.F. Verse* (Paris: *The Stars and Stripes*, 1918). The ninety-two-page book was immensely popular, selling far more than any of the other auxiliary publications of the paper. See final account sheet, 2 May 1919, which reveals that 44,189 copies were sold at 2.50 francs per copy. This netted the paper $65,833.60 in profits. See in Entry 236/9. See also orders for the book in 236/14, 16, 17, 18, 19, 20, 21, 23, 24, 25, 26, 45, and 49. The entire Paris Edition was sold out.

84. Katz, *The History of the Stars and Stripes*, p. 15.

85. From the introduction dedicating a special page to the Army's Poets, in 16 August 1918 issue. Nearly every issue had a special column devoted to poetry which was introduced in the 3 May 1918 issue. It subsequently became the most widely read column in the paper. The editors did, however, desire that the poetry submitted be in better shape than some of it was. Accordingly, an editorial in the 8 March 1918 issue, entitled "Dress Up That Line!", emphasized that the editors hated to polish someone else's poetry wanting it "dressed up" henceforth.

The reference to "slum" is to "slumgullion," the Army's perennial catch-all meal; "cooties" refer to the infernal plague of fighting men in all armies in World War I—the lowly, omnipresent louse.

So great was the quantity of poetry submitted that the editors used many means of eliminating that which would not be published. As a matter of course, with few exceptions, poetry submitted by those other than members of the AEF was rejected out of hand. Though Entries 236/32 and 236/39 contain many of the rejections, most unwanted items were simply thrown in the trash. See Entry 236/6 for a folder of accepted works and letters and other documents concerning them.

86. There are other examples of plagiarisms noted in Entry 236/39.

87. Katz, *The History of the Stars and Stripes*, p. 36. See also folder in Entry 236/7.

88. Memorandum, Lieut. William K. Michael to Viskniskki, 8 April 1918; Memorandum, Viskniskki to chief, G-2-D, 8 October 1918, Entry 223/52.

89. Memorandum, Nolan to chief of staff, G.H.Q., AEF, 11 October 1918; Memorandum, Viskniskki to chief, G-2-D, 8 October 1918, Entry 223/52.

90. Memorandum, Pershing to Harbord, 10 October 1918, Entry 223/52.

91. Memorandum, Lieut. Col. H. W. Fleet, inspector general, District of Paris, to Brig. Gen. W. W. Harts, 31 October 1918, Entry 223/52. This investigation, following Pershing's orders, was not really necessary as Viskniskki had acted on his own. This served to intensify the tension between Harts' office and *The Stars and Stripes*.

92. Memorandum, Watson to adjutant general, District of Paris, 22 January 1919; Report, Capt. Harry L. Parker to chief, G-2-D, 27 February 1919; and numerous documents signed by individual soldiers listing stolen personal property, in Entry 223/52.

93. Report, Parker to chief, G-2-D, 27 February 1919, Entry 223/52.

94. Memorandum, Watson to Capt. Donald L. Stone, G-2-D, 28 February 1919, Entry 223/52.

95. Memoranda, Watson to G-2-D, 7 March 1919; and Capt. Harry Parker to Nolan, 6 March 1919, Entry 223/52.

96. Memorandum, Nolan to chief of staff, G.H.Q., AEF, 6 March 1919, Entry 223/52.

97. Memorandum, Capt. P. G. Mumford, G-2 inspector for *The Stars and Stripes*, to Judge Advocate, AEF, 11 March 1919, Entry 223/52.

98. Memorandum, Col. Eltinge, deputy chief of staff, AEF, to Nolan, 19 March 1919, Entry 223/52. This document did provide a compromise to the paper in that if the expenses thus incurred in feeding these men on the scale of army rations, "no better, no worse," exceeded commutation allowances, *The Stars and Stripes* could bear the excess as part of their running expenses. See also Memoranda, Nolan to chief, G-2-D, 19 March 1919; Mumford to Nolan, 24 March 1919; and copy of contract drawn up with the Duval restaurant, in Entry 223/52.

99. Memorandum, Capt. Donald L. Stone to Lieutenant Colonel Moreno, 28 March 1919, Entry 223/52. See several requests for commutation status in Entry 223/52; Entries 236/1 and 2.

100. There are documents pertaining to the courier service in Entry 236/6.

101. Among some of the untoward events associated with the paper's career were deaths and courts-martial. As to the latter, only a few minor cases are on record. Four members of the staff died in the course of their service on the paper. All victims of disease, they were buried in the American military cemetery at Suresnes, on a hillside overlooking Paris and the Seine. The relevant documents regarding the courts-martial are in Entry 236/48. Katz, in *The History of the Stars and Stripes*, p. 47, presents his "Roll of Honor" for these dead. Other details are in *The Stars and Stripes*, the 13 June 1919 issue.

102. Memorandum, Capt. P. G. Mumford to Nolan, 14 March 1919, Entry 223/40. The staff at that time consisted of 218 officers and men, a far cry from Viskniskki's original group.

103. This was *The Amaroc News*, founded as the official publication of the Army of Occupation in April of 1919.

104. Special Orders No. 112, 22 April 1919, Entry 223/48; Letter, Watson to Erickson, 12 May 1919, Entry 236/31. Watson was by this date a major.

105. Letter, Watson to Erickson, 12 May 1919, Entry 236/31. Since it had proved impossible for such men as Ryder and Ross to obtain DSMs, Capt. Donald L. Stone, then acting chief of G-2-D, sought to obtain letters containing commendations or citations

of merit on behalf of the "old guard of enlisted forces on *The Stars and Stripes*." He hoped that either Nolan or Pershing might oblige. Though this is probable, there is no evidence of such documents in the paper's files. See Memorandum, Stone to Nolan, 23 April 1919, Entry 223/48.

106. Memorandum, Early to Nolan, 8 May 1919, Entry 223/41.

107. There is a copy of Nolan's Memorandum reproduced in Katz, *The History of the Stars and Stripes*, p. 40.

108. The bound collection used in this study does not include the pictorial supplement.

109. Katz, *The History of the Stars and Stripes,* p. 36, discusses the departure of the staff for the United States.

2. ADVERTISING

1. Minutes of the Board of Control, 19 April 1918, Entry 223/41. Somewhat later, when Governor Walter Evans Edge of New Jersey, wanted to insert an ad in the paper, Viskniskki observed that the rule against political matter was a hard and fast one and "I think that the reason for this rigid rule is obvious to you." Letters, George W. Kettle of the Dorland Agency to Viskniskki, 29 October 1918, and Viskniskki's reply, 30 October 1918, in Entry 236/4. The problem of ad placement would cause some friction also as will be noted later.

2. See a special folder devoted to correspondence with Quainton in Entry 236/4.

3. The files of *The Stars and Stripes* contain a voluminous correspondence on advertising. See especially the folders in Entries 236/4, 5, 6, 16, 17, 19, 26, 31, 39, 40, 41, 43, and 46.

4. Cable, Viskniskki to Erickson, 10 January 1918, Entry 223/49. Viskniskki obviously knew Erickson earlier when the former was engaged in publishing before going to war.

5. Letter, Erickson to Viskniskki, 11 July 1918, Entry 236/41.

6. Cable, Erickson to Viskniskki, 11 July 1918, Entry 236/41.

7. Letter, Erickson to Viskniskki, 14 October 1918, Entry 236/4. The paper attempted to remedy the situation. In the issue of 31 January 1919, American advertising totalled 278 1/4 inches. See letter to Erickson, 30 January 1919, in Entry 236/4.

8. Letter, Erickson to *The Stars and Stripes*, 12 May 1919, Entry 236/19.

9. Letter, Erickson to *The Stars and Stripes*, 19 December 1918, Entry 236/4.

10. See Viskniskki's indorsement of 21 October 1918, to chief, G-2-D, to Memorandum, Brig. Gen. M. Churchill, the chief military censor, to assistant chief, G-2, 27 September 1918, Entry 223/40.

11. Memorandum, Viskniskki to Watson, 27 September 1918, Entry 223/41. At this time, the French rate was three francs per line and the British was three and one-half francs per line. The British rate was higher because of higher commission rates.

12. See Letters, Capt. Harold J. McClatchy, then the paper's business manager, to Erickson, 30 December 1918, and 28 January 1919; Memorandum, Sgt. George E. Mulvaney to Lieut. Ayers, 27 January 1919, Entry 236/4. Apparently the $14.00 rate was reached in any case.

13. Letter, Erickson to 1st Lieut. William K. Michael, 24 May 1918, Entry 236/19. There is some evidence, though, that Erickson instructed the paper's business staff on computation methods.

14. Letter, Erickson to Viskniskki, 3 January 1919, Entry 236/4. Apparently Erickson was not yet apprised of Viskniskki's departure.

15. Letter, Erickson to *The Stars and Stripes*, 28 April 1919, Entry 236/19.

16. Letter, Erickson to Viskniskki, 3 January 1919, Entry 236/4.

17. These details are in Letters, Erickson to Watson, 22 April 1919, and Watson to Erickson, 12 May 1919, Entry 236/31. Erickson certainly could not understand that a *real newspaper* would be devoid of advertising.

18. Letter, H. P. Somner to Lieut. Michael, 6 March 1918, Entry 236/31. Somner was an American.

19. See large folder with much correspondence on these matters in Entry 236/4. The Dorland Agency also had offices in Paris, Rome, Brussels, and in the United States, in New York City and New Jersey, and so was acquainted with American advertising methods as well.

Peggy Quainton signed her letters "P. Quainton," and it was not known for some time in the Paris office that she was a woman. This led to some amusing exchanges. See several items in Entry 236/4.

20. Letter, Quainton to Michael, 10 June 1918, Entry 236/4.

21. Letter, Michael to Somner, 10 June 1918, Entry 236/4.

22. Letter, Michael to the Dorland Agency, 16 May 1918, Entry 236/4.

23. Letter, Somner to Michael, 4 June 1918, Entry 236/4.

24. Letter, Quainton to Michael, 10 June 1918, Entry 236/4.

25. Letter, Quainton to Michael, 8 June 1918, Entry 236/4.

26. Telegram, Kettle to *The Stars and Stripes*, 5 December 1918, Entry 236/31. Perhaps Viskniskki acted as he did because he was himself relieved on that day.

27. Letters, Quainton to Viskniskki, 4 December 1918; Mulvaney to Quainton, offering her the usual 20 percent commission, 5 December 1918, Entry 236/4.

28. Cable, Mulvaney to Quainton, 11 December 1918, Entry 236/4.

29. Letter, Prosser to Mulvaney, 14 January 1919, Entry 236/4.

30. Letter, apparently from Mulvaney to Quainton, 15 January 1919, Entry 236/4.

31. Letter, Somner to Mulvaney, 10 January 1919, Entry 236/31.

32. Letter, *The Stars and Stripes* to the Dorland Agency, 4 April 1919; Memorandum of settlement between the Dorland Agency and *The Stars and Stripes*, 5 April 1919; Letter, Mumford to Nolan, 9 April 1919, Entry 223/41.

33. Letters, the Dorland Agency to *The Stars and Stripes*, 8 April 1919; Watson to the Dorland Agency, 10 April 1919, Entry 236/31.

34. Memorandum, Viskniskki to the staff of *The Stars and Stripes*, 15 August 1918, Entry 236/22.

35. There is a brief discussion in Katz, *The History of the Stars and Stripes*, p. 31.

36. Another "ad" stated: "To prevent gas attack—Give the Boche no quarter. Then he can't work his meter." See the 21 June 1918 issue.

37. Erickson had said that the soap was not for sale in France; the advertising implied otherwise, but perhaps the publicity was all that was desired, in any case.

38. Junior's also had stores in Aldershot and Dublin. Curiously, Harrods of London, that famed provider of luxury goods to British troops, did not publish an ad until 13 September 1918. Similarly, the equally well-known Le Printemps department store on Boulevard Hausemann, Paris, did not place an ad in *The Stars and Stripes* until after the Armistice on 15 November 1918, after which it made frequent appearances.

39. Letter, Richards to H. P. Somner, 17 June 1918, Entry 236/4. The firm's ad was on the back page; its next one was on page five.

40. Letter, Viskniskki to Somner, 25 June 1918, Entry 236/4.

41. Letter, Mulvaney to Quainton, 11 December 1918, Entry 236/4.

42. The popular Montgomery Ward Company hoped to be of service to supply officers, company clerks and YMCAs if they needed things that they could not obtain in France.

43. Another of the Tapioca Company's ads featured men of the black regiments which, according to rumor, were "not at all satisfied with the weapons furnished by Uncle Sam for trench work. True to instinct, they are reported to be carrying their trusty razors during night expeditions through no man's land, where they get in quiet but deadly work. It seems that these dark-skinned troops spend much of their time every evening before taps sharpening these wicked instruments of destruction until the blades are exceedingly keen." This was not meant to denigrate, but to praise the blacks, who acquitted themselves very well in combat, to the surprise of many (15 November 1918).

44. There is a small folder in Entry 236/5, containing some correspondence relating to the Filene establishment and some letters from soldiers who wrote directly to *The Stars and Stripes* with their requests, rather than to the store's representatives in Paris. There is also information as to some subscriptions from the United States generated by the various stores discussed.

Another source of exotic foods was Robert Jackson and Company of London, which specialized in such American delicacies as sweet pickles, maple syrup, clam chowder, fruit cakes, Tunis figs, Welch's grape juice, lime juice, and cherries in Crème de Menthe, among other things.

45. Murads, of Turkish tobacco were made by S. Anargyros Tobacco Company, which also sold Egyptian tobacco. Turkish cigarettes were referred to as "Turkish atrocities" by the men.

46. Letters, J. F. Bresnahan to Waldo, 24 September 1918; Waldo to Bresnahan, 21 October 1918, Entry 236/31. The former contains the clipping from *The New York Times*.

47. At least one doughboy missed ice cream sodas, leaving behind a poem on the subject. See the 19 April 1918 issue. No doubt others missed them as well.

48. In July of 1918 the Wells Fargo Company transferred its Foreign Service Branch to the American Express Company.

49. The Red Cross had established this Service for soldiers of the Allied Armies in 1915. Its well-known director was Mrs. Alice S. Weeks.

50. The American University Union also set up a purchasing service for the use of the members, who could send in a remittance and requests for purchases to be made and sent to them.

51. This appeared in the 6 December 1918 issue of the paper; its sentiments were a bit dated by that time, attesting to the time lag in getting ads printed.

52. Memorandum, Dawes to Harbord, 20 December 1918, and Harbord's first indorsement sent to Pershing, 21 December 1918, Entry 223/49.

53. Memoranda, Watson to chief, G-2-D, 27 December 1918; Stone to Nolan, 28 December 1918; Nolan to chief of staff, G.H.Q., AEF, 1 January 1919, Entry 223/49.

54. See Brewster's report, 30 January 1919, and several other relevant documents, including the contract between the association and *The Stars and Stripes*, in Entry 223/49. It is not known whether the general order was forthcoming. Interestingly, Brewster had said that officers could "anticipate arrangements to enter civilian life," whatever that might mean. By Pershing's order, Waite was advised that "acts on the part of officers

or enlisted men of the American Expeditionary Forces which might be interpreted to imply that in their official capacity they have any connection with a private business enterprise are regarded as improper.'' See Memorandum, the adjutant general, AEF, to Capt. H. G. Waite, 31 January 1919, Entry 223/49.

55. Memorandum, Watson to the business manager, 10 March 1919, Entry 223/47. It should be noted that Watson ventured the opinion that Harbord was wrong and the Judge Advocate was right in the matter. See his being quoted in Memorandum, Capt. Donald L. Stone, assistant chief, G-2-D, to Nolan, 28 December 1918, Entry 223/49.

3. ARMY MESS AND UNIFORMS

1. Not all of the eats were bad. Also, the relief organizations, such as the Salvation Army, attempted to supplement army chow—at a price—with more acceptable items. Some of these auxiliaries established canteens quite close to the front. There was one mention in the paper of the Salvation Army's issuing hot cocoa to troops just prior to their going into action. On this occasion, ''the company advanced successfully against the enemy. After the war the S.A. will be justified in telling folks how many miles the boys got to the gallon'' (24 May 1918).

2. Wally drew one of his funniest cartoons on the subject of soldier-farmers. They appeared in his sketch as a most inept lot (15 March 1918).

3. In the 27 September 1918 issue.

4. There is a short discussion of steel helmets in the 3 May 1918 issue. The men were allowed to keep these and their gas masks after release from the service, as souvenirs. There is a short article discussing this in the 6 December 1918 issue.

5. For several accounts regarding the campaign hat, see the issues of 22 November 1918, and 3 and 10 January 1919.

6. ''A Doughboy's Dictionary'' once defined a Christmas Box along these lines: ''A broken-into parcel partly filled with wristlets, mufflers, heavy sox, knit helmets, mittens, kidney pads and tummy bands that arrives in France about the middle of July'' (15 February 1918).

7. A *bon mot* in the 18 April 1919 issue observed that the biggest lie to come out of the war was the one claiming that ''my spirals never came down.''

8. A poem in the 3 May 1918 issue, ''The Supply Sergeant,'' contains these details. It was one in a series under the general heading, ''As We Know Them,'' which eventually included many ranks and professions, as the Medical Officer, the Chaplain and others.

9. See article in the 6 September 1918 issue. One can perhaps sympathize with the airmen. A close study of the photographs of both the officers and men in the American Army in World War I reveals a great number of shoddy, ill-fitting uniforms. Only a few of the soldiers seem to have overcome this, appearing rather nattily turned out; many were plainly seedy looking.

10. There are numerous references to this, as in the issues of 21 June, 5 July and 2 August 1918. There was later some additional irritation among the officers when further orders were issued that the belt could not be worn in the United States, and the officers going home had to accept that the obvious streak visible on their uniforms amounted to a service stripe, indicative of overseas duty (24 January 1919).

11. See especially issue of 23 May 1919. There is also an interesting article in the 8 March 1918 issue comparing and contrasting the U.S. Congressional Medal of Honor, the British Victoria Cross (the VC as it was commonly called), and the German Iron

Cross. Other articles of interest on the subject of medals and how they were won are in the issues of 22 and 29 March 1918, and a lengthy feature article, "How You May Win Our Army's Decorations," in the 17 May 1918 issue.

The Distinguished Service Cross was introduced at this time, but the National Sculpture Society objected to the original design as "too regal to be in keeping with the democratic nature of the Government which confers it, and that something simpler, something a little more Spartan, might conform better to the nature of the deeds performed to win it, and to the spirit in which it is bestowed." The Society asked that American artists be charged with designing a new one (21 June 1918). This was subsequently done. See picture and text in the 4 October 1918 issue.

12. The men could also wear other decorations of the Allied armies. As to authorized U.S. decorations, the following were recognized: The U.S. Medal of Honor, the Distinguished Service Cross, the Philippines Congressional Medal, the Civil War Campaign Badge, the Indian Campaign Badge, the Spanish Campaign Badge, the Philippines Campaign Badge, the China Campaign Badge, the Army of Cuban Occupation Badge, the Mexican Service Badge, the Congressional National Guard Medal, and the Distinguished Service Medal. Though it came too late for some, a victory medal was also at length authorized for all members of the AEF who had served in France. Each member could attach a bronze star to its ribbon for each of the twelve official major engagements that the American Army participated in and a silver star for each official citation for which no medal had been awarded (16 May 1919). A chart and discussion of the twelve battles is located in the 30 May 1919 issue.

13. Circular 18 of the War Department, 1919, was amended by direction of the Secretary of War, stating that the divisional insignia could be worn by all officers and men returning from overseas for discharge either with their units or as casuals. However, if they were returning for reassignment, they must remove their patches (28 February 1919).

14. As evidence that the Army was not indifferent to uniforms and their condition, it was appreciated that shipboard travel on the troopships was not conducive to keeping uniforms clean and neat. Men on shipboard were accordingly issued blue denim overalls to wear, donning their uniforms just prior to landing, giving rise to the little ditty: "In a suit of denim blue / I'll come sailing back to you." A short article in the 11 April 1919 issue discusses this.

4. RANK, FILE, AND BRASS

1. A poem by an unknown poet in the 16 August 1918 issue had further comment on the "midnight oil" at headquarters, noting that the colonel's lamp was shining because "an earthlier task his mind engages / he's sewing buttons on his pants."

2. The 12 July 1918 issue, just in time for Bastille Day, published lengthy articles on General Rochambeau, described as the commander of the "F.E.F." in America, and on Lafayette's career. Both men, naturally, manifested the ideals of high command worthy of emulation.

3. This poem, in the 16 August 1918 issue, was collectively by the Third Platoon, Company L, of an unnamed infantry unit as censorship at this time prevented its mention.

4. One of Wallgren's famous cartoons, appearing in the same issue, further emphasized how to—and not to—salute.

Even late in the career of the AEF, demands for proper saluting were still being repeated.

If officers did not properly salute the M.P.s at Brest, in response to the latter's snappy versions, they were to be given a card issued by Headquarters stating the regulations and the M.P. was to report them.

5. Napoleon's remark was also referred to in connection with several instances in combat when sergeants took command of units when their officers were killed or incapacitated. See editorial, "Napoleon Was Right" (20 September 1918).

6. Some of these men were subsequently commissioned as openings occurred.

5. HOSPITAL, CHAPEL, AND MORGUE

1. This paucity of material was noticed by those concerned. See, for example, letter to the editor asking for more recognition in the paper for Medical Corps people in the 31 May 1918 issue.

2. Many instances of the courage of the wounded are recorded in an article, "When The Wounded Come In," in the 2 August 1918 issue.

3. See, for instance, a lengthy article in the 22 February 1918 issue, which discussed an official AEF bulletin on the subject.

4. This naturally affected morale. There is a special folder on troop morale, containing items revealing their concern with the VD problem, in Entry 236/35.

5. There is an interesting article in the 22 March 1918 issue pertaining to delousing. It was not until late in the career of the AEF that the problem became manageable. One report indicated that at the time of the Armistice, some ninety percent of the divisions were lousy; by early spring of 1919, only ten percent were still infested (4 April 1919).

6. These last shots were to be typhoid inoculations which were given just prior to sailing, or failing that, upon arrival in the United States. The paper reported that a new French-invented oil base inoculant was to be used, said to be relatively painless, as the oil slowed the absorption rate. The Medical Corps was pleased to observe that the AEF had recorded less than 1,000 cases of typhoid, a rate much less than that common in such major American cities as Chicago, New York City and Philadelphia (21 February 1919).

7. There is a lengthy, interesting article on chaplains and their role in the military by Bishop H. C. Brent in the 10 May 1918 issue of the paper. There was no mention of Jewish chaplains, however.

8. Regarding "do-gooders," the paper could affect a lighter tone on occasion. When it was announced that Billy Sunday was travelling to Europe "to fight the devil in the trenches," the paper asserted, "all together boys—Gawd help Kaiser Bill!" (5 April 1918).

9. However, the YMCA also found strong supporters. For example, Pvt. Joseph Sikora, an infantryman, had nothing but the warmest praise for one Dave Duncan, a Y man who was right up front in the hottest action rendering what assistance he could to the men (22 November 1918). But Sikora's letter was rebutted in turn by several dissenters who had strong negative feelings about the organization (14 March 1919).

10. *The Stars and Stripes* received hundreds of letters from the United States written by people wanting information about their dead loved ones. These were usually turned over to the AEF's auxiliary organizations for action or response. There is a large folder of such communications in Entry 236/37.

11. This attitude toward the dead was often commented upon, indeed, was a sort of fascination for some. For example, a coast artilleryman was singularly touched when he

buried a mere youth and marveled: "He fell with his face towards the Hun, one hand gripping the small of the stock of his Springfield. They knocked the life out of the little fellow, but they couldn't knock that smile off his face. He died with it there" (29 November 1918).

12. This was by Virginia A. G. Nelson of the YMCA (6 December 1918).

13. *The Stars and Stripes* felt similarly toward what was regarded as abuses surrounding Memorial Day observances in 1918. The editors deeply deplored "the avowed intention of certain officers and men of the A.E.F. to celebrate the coming Memorial Day with a program of field sports and baseball." While such games were very well in their place, their "holiday nature" was distinctly out of keeping with the spirit of America's great commemorative day. This was "doubly true in a time like the present, when almost every hour is adding to the list of those who 'die to make men free.' " The day had been originally intended as one for prayer, thanksgiving, and "solemn thought-taking." Memorial Day was therefore a "holy day," not a "holiday." It must be kept so (24 May 1918).

14. The editorial page of the issue of 29 March 1918 featured a reprinting of St. John 20:1–31, describing the first Easter.

6. MORALE AND ESPRIT

1. "Don't swear here; it sounds like hell," was an old barroom classic the men were reminded of. By the same token, they should not "swear...over much about the virtues of one's own unit." All should keep in mind, rather, that with few exceptions, every member of the AEF, "did everything that was asked of him—or died or was wounded trying; and man can do no more" (10 January 1919).

2. On numerous occasions the paper lauded the American troops, as, between the Marne and the Ourcq, they had "fought with such splendid dash and such high, exalted courage that today every other American in France salutes them reverently." In that battle, in fact, "they have so borne themselves that every other American soldier wears his uniform a little more proudly, and to his eyes the dear star spangled banner gleams more brilliant in the morning sunlight" (9 August 1918).

3. America was, of course, also the home of immigrants, another source of pride. When the first French decorations began to be bestowed upon American troops, one of the paper's editors observed that the names of the recipients revealed that the men were from a great variety of origins, even Germany. Thus, plainly, "it was all the world that went to war with Germany when America came in" (10 May 1918).

4. Another editorial, "Those Gloomy Gusses," concluded: "The [American] newspapers and magazines should remember that the pessimist on America inevitably goes broke" (24 May 1918).

5. It was also remarked that the Australians had arrived "nameless in France." They had at first been called "Anzacs," but later tired of it, and adopted "Aussie." There is a short discussion in the 29 March 1918 issue.

6. This is discussed in a letter from an unnamed American from the North who had resided in the South for some years, to an unknown recipient in France, reprinted in the 13 September 1918 issue.

7. One letter to the editor indicated that the term *doughboy* had originated in the Philippines; that after marching on the extremely dusty roads of that place, the troops were covered with a dust and sweat mixture creating a "dough." Their lucky companions,

the mounted cavalry, called them rather obviously, "doughboys." See the 25 April 1919 issue.

8. Letter from a cavalryman, "camouflaged as artillery," in the 7 March 1919 issue. The Marines, of course, were also sensitive to any attack on their honor. When in the 14 February 1919 issue a cartoon appeared which seemed to insult the Corps, the editor received a scathing letter from Cpl. John S. Johnson, 79th Company of the 6th Regiment, USMC, in which the guilty party was asked to "remember that the Marine Corps is as always a *man's* outfit and stands ready to repel assault whether by hostile fire or insidious misrepresentation." His letter is in Entry 236/31.

9. This is in the 19 April 1918 issue. The editor justified even calling General Pershing a doughboy.

10. There is a deposition attesting to these facts from Capt. R. T. Heard, 6th Field Artillery, to Watson, 16 February 1919, in Entry 236/35. This was signed by several of the participants listed. Watson's letter to Heard, 3 March 1919, is in the same source. Watson observed that he had "a hunch that there probably are fifteen or twenty of the 'genuine first shell fired' scattered about France and the United States," but he apparently accepted Heard's document as authentic and accurate.

11. This poem is by Cpl. Albert Jay Cook and appeared in the 13 September 1918 issue.

12. See also *The Army Times. The Yanks Are Coming. The Story of General John J. Pershing* (New York: G. P. Putnam's Sons, 1960), p. 128.

13. There is a lengthy article on heavy tank operations in the 1 November 1918 issue.

14. There are additional kudos for the Navy in the 27 December 1918 issue.

15. On one occasion an editor felt constrained to say a word for the unsung, unchronicled observation aircraft pilots, who, unlike the flashy combat pilots, never appeared in the headlines (26 July 1918).

16. Letter, Holmes to *The Stars and Stripes*, 19 November 1918, Entry 236/31. There is no indication as to Holmes' race.

17. Letter, Viskniskki to Holmes, 23 November 1918, Entry 236/31.

18. Memorandum, Nolan to the chief of staff, AEF, 6 March 1919, Entry 223/40. Nolan simply recommended the filing away of the relevant correspondence and the informing of Harts of this action.

If the blacks received some attention, so did the American Indians on occasion, and the paper rather gleefully reported that Sioux Indians had been used to foil German wiretappers of telephone lines by transmitting messages in their own language (10 January 1919).

19. Letter, Army Field Clerk Ben Gershon to the editor, 14 March 1919, Entry 236/31.

20. Letter, Col. Harry Cutler to Watson, 20 March 1919; Memorandum, Watson to Gershon, 22 March 1919, Entry 236/31.

21. The issue of 29 November 1918 has many of the details.

22. The letters column in the 20 December 1918 issue contains a typical hotcake yarn and other "mostest" items.

7. FRIENDS AND FOES

1. The *Aussie* was first known as *The Honk*, the first issue of which came out on shipboard with the coming of the first Australian troops to France. Its name was later

changed to *The Rising Sun*, and finally, to *Aussie*. The same editor—not identified—was responsible throughout. He was a former newspaperman from Sydney.

The Canadian troops also had their publication, a four-page daily review, mainly of news from home. It was published in London by the War Records Office and was called *The Canadian Daily Record* (5 April 1918).

2. A limerick addressed the peculiarities of the French language:

There was a young man from Marseilles
Who went out for an airing one deilles,
      But a wicked M.P.
      Said, "Hey, Jack, come with me!"
And he'd nothing to do but obeilles.

                                Anon.
                        (3 January 1919)

3. Memorandum, Stone to Nolan, 31 January 1919, Entry 223/48.

4. The issue of 6 December 1918 contains an article and picture illustrating Mlle. Marin Perrin, head of *The Stars and Stripes*'s Bureau of the American Red Cross in charge of the orphan program. She was French by birth and American by adoption. She had earlier been a member of the faculty of the Ethical Culture School in New York City.

There are numerous folders containing all sorts of information about the orphans in Entries 236/3, 12, 13, 14, 15, 41, and 45.

5. The Department of Public Information of the American Red Cross in Paris published a booklet, *From French Mascots to Their American Godfathers*, which described the orphan program and included fifty of the best letters written by the orphans to their benefactors and a list of all adopters. It cost one franc, though adopters got a free copy.

6. On this occasion, *The Stars and Stripes*, on its editorial page, raised a toast: "Gentlemen, To France!", continuing, "In the hour of victory, what member of the A.E.F. could hope to express in mere words the feeling of eternal comradeship and eternal gratitude of the men of the A.E.F. for France?" All should "drink deep to her unquenchable spirit of liberty, equality, fraternity [and] to her undismayed and unconquerable *poilus*."

7. One interesting anti-German article appeared in the 27 September 1918 issue of the paper. It was a stinging rebuttal to an article in an English-language propaganda newspaper published at Frankfurt am Main. This issue of that paper, *America in Europe*, included a cartoon with the editor of *The Stars and Stripes* on the "Pillory for Liars," with the observation that "a casual perusal of any of its numbers will convince the reader that the editors, in contradistinction to all gallant and chivalrous soldiers, have made it their general object to throw mud at their enemies in war. We absolutely refuse to believe that real American fighters are in any way responsible for the mad howl against the Huns set up in the columns of *Stars and Stripes* and for the sake of America's good name we protest against this disgraceful employment of our beloved emblem."

8. "There is only one way to deal with the Hun," another issue of the paper wrote, and "thank God, we have learned that way!" (31 May 1918).

9. The paper once asked the men to remember "when the days seem very long and when the powers that be seem to have forgotten that your outfit ever existed, remember

what might have been. Remember what came painfully near to being," namely the victory of German arms (21 March 1919). This issue, appearing on the anniversary of the massive, concerted German attacks in the West, observed that, if successful, they well might have meant an end to the war and a German victory. The day 21 March 1918 to contemporaries seemed almost as significant as 11 November 1918.

10. Memorandum, Woollcott to Watson, 24 December 1918, Entry 236/38.

11. Memoranda, Watson to chief, G-2-D, 26 December 1918; Stone, assistant chief, G-2-D, to Nolan, 28 December 1918, Entry 236/38.

8. SPORTS AND ENTERTAINMENT

1. The title of this piece was "Great Expectations."

2. The action taken by *The Stars and Stripes* was not well received in certain quarters in the United States. An article in *The Sporting News*, published in St. Louis, for instance, retorted that the "cutting out [of] all reference to sports [was] narrow minded to [the] point of making [the] perpetrators ridiculous." *The Stars and Stripes* was also attacked for the same reasons by the Camp Upton's edition of *Trench and Camp*, the training camp weekly published at various camps in the United States. Clippings and other relevant documents are in Entry 236/31.

3. The 18 October 1918 issue of the paper featured a picture and short article on Sgt. Hank Gowdy, referred to as "our kind," a big league ballplayer who had not scuttled into an easy job with a shipyard ball team. Nor did he protest that baseball was an essential war industry. Also, "he didn't suddenly remember a whole flock of relatives dependent upon him for support."

4. General Order 27, G.H.Q., AEF, 1919, stipulated that there would be no more afternoon drills for troops of the AEF, except when on maneuvers or exercises. The afternoons would henceforth be turned over to educational and athletic activities (28 February 1919).

5. However, if boxing became steadily more popular, football soon eased out boxing as the AEF's most popular sport. There is a statistical presentation and discussion in the 18 April 1919 issue.

6. Pvt. H. M. Hargrave of the Medical Corps, was disturbed that apparently black soldiers were neither "allowed to dance in public dance Halls on pass," nor to obtain furloughs, writing to the paper for information. The editor replied, noting that "you are advised that there is no distinction in color in the American Expeditionary Forces. We Americans came over here for the same cause, to defeat the Hun, and the colored soldiers have the same privileges as the white." He was referred to the standing orders pertaining to leaves and passes. His letter of 21 April 1919, and the paper's response dated 25 April, are in Entry 236/42.

7. There are several mentions in *The Stars and Stripes* as to the titles of songs that were at the time being hummed, sung and whistled. These included, "One, two, three, four, sometimes I wish there were more"; "Sweet Adeline"; "I found you among the roses"; "Caroline"; "On Moonlight Bay"; "You're mammy's coal black rose"; "Pretty baby"; "Where the River Shannon flows"; "Sweet Rosie O'Grady"; "Rings on my fingers and bells on my toes"; "Little Annie Rooney"; "By the old mill stream"; and "Don't wake me up, let me dream, dream, dream," among many others (9 August 1918).

8. Lord Northcliffe took it upon himself to send a copy of the issue containing this

poem to Kipling, and "he was naturally pleased." Letter, Northcliffe to Viskniskki, 7 November 1918, Entry 236/31.

9. The 700 players from theaters in America did not include those appearing in the over 100 French vaudeville acts playing in the twenty-six leave area vaudeville theaters.

10. There is an article in the 8 March 1918 issue discussing Elsie's arrival in France. Her memoirs were published as *So Far, So Good!* (New York: E. P. Dutton and Company, 1932), of which pages 182–235 are devoted to her stay with the AEF.

11. Letter, Viskniskki to Clarence F. Jones, Y secretary at Libourne, France, 11 May 1918, Entry 236/32; Janis, *So Far, So Good!* p. 194.

12. *The Army Times. The Yanks Are Coming,* p. 100.

13. There are several letters and other documents devoted to doughboy troupes and related matters in Entry 236/3.

9. EDUCATION

1. These educators were able to build upon a report about the AEF's educational needs that had been drafted by Dr. Anson Phelps Stokes, secretary of Yale University, who had visited France for that purpose in the winter of 1917–1918.

The ALA had already collected about three million books in the United States for shipment to France. There is an interesting article on this effort in the 14 June 1918 issue of *The Stars and Stripes.*

2. The AEF already had one impressive school in existence, the bandmaster's school at Chaumont. In the new educational scheme, it was to be expanded into a conservatory of music to benefit many more musicians (6 December 1918).

3. An innovation in business education was introduced at Bordeaux. There, Base Section No. 2 had established a business course which was conducted in cooperation with the Bordeaux Chamber of Commerce, and was designed to interest the men in trade and commerce in France and in trade between America and France (7 March 1919).

4. There were more than 1,000 buildings in the old hospital complex, some 400 being taken over by the new univesity, which had the facilities to expand to accommodate 40,000 were the need to arise. Some 400 German prisoners-of-war were used as part of the laboring force at Beaune also (16 May 1919).

5. There are articles pertaining to the correspondence course program in the 25 April and 9 May 1919 issues of the paper.

6. One of the things that interested *The Stars and Stripes* was that the doughboy students at the various French universities soon began publishing their own news sheets. For example, the University of Beaune launched the *11th Regiment Bulletin*; students at the University of Rennes produced *As You Were*; those at the University of Nancy came out with the *Lorraine Sentinel*; the *Soldier-Student* was the product of the students at the University of Montpellier; *Qu'est-ce Que C'est* was the name of the paper of the students at the University of Toulouse; *Les Beaux Jours* was published by their fellows at the University of Poitiers (25 April and 2 May 1919).

10. DÉNOUEMENT

1. War Department. *Annual Reports,* 1919, Vol. I (in 4 parts) (Washington, D.C.: U.S. Government Printing Office, 1920), Part 1, p. 640.

2. There is a discussion by Clayton M. Ryder in the foreword of the bound collection of *The Stars and Stripes* (Minneapolis: A.E.F. Publishing Association, 1920). Ryder, attached to the 22nd Field Signal Battalion, had served *The Stars and Stripes* ably in circulation matters.

3. Katz, *The History of the Stars and Stripes*, p. 27.

4. Baker, on a visit to France, wrote to *The Stars and Stripes*, in a letter dated 12 March 1918, wishing the paper good luck and observing that if it were wisely managed, it could be a forum for the ideas of the troops, and "a means for each part of the American front to speak to all the others, a means for drawing closer together all the soldiers of the A.E.F." (15 March 1918). In the autumn of 1918, he was pleased to see and to applaud the paper's obvious success: "I have been delighted to find how valuable the work of *The Stars and Stripes* is to our soldiers. It is welcomed in every camp I visited and seems to be not only the most popular reading matter available to our men, but a great source of interest, comfort and pleasure to them." See Letter, Baker to Viskniskki, 4 October 1918, Entry 223/54.

5. Baker had also been asked for his cabled congratulations. The several relevant documents are in Entry 223/40.

6. Memorandum, Stone to Nolan, 28 January 1919, Entry 223/48.

7. Memorandum of a telephone conversation, Nolan to Early, 8 February 1919, Entry 223/48.

8. Among those who praised the paper was a Colonel Avalés of the Spanish General Staff, and other Spanish officers. Obtaining the paper as a courtesy from Maj. John W. Lang, the U.S. military attaché at Madrid, the Spaniards expressed their admiration for the paper's excellence and its value "from the standpoint of a builder of morale and *esprit de corps*." In short, Lang reported, "*The Stars and Stripes* has made a big hit in Spain." Memorandum, Lang to Watson, 28 February 1919, Entry 236/31.

9. She especially applauded a story in the 26 July 1918 issue, "One Man and a Battle Sixty Miles Long," as a classic one, so powerful, but yet "dramatically simple" (18 October 1918).

10. The 13 June 1919 issue of the paper revealed that the paper, in the course of its career, had expended 21,433,357 francs by check and 4,723,564 by cash, for a total expenditure of 26,156,921 francs.

11. Memorandum, Nolan to chief of staff, AEF, 19 January 1919, Entry 223/41.

12. Memorandum, Bethel to assistant chief, G-2, 11 March 1919, Entry 223/47; and another from Bethel to deputy chief of staff, AEF, 25 February 1919, Entry 223/41. This was approved by headquarters on 27 February 1919, and the funds were, after the business office of the paper closed, which occurred on 20 June 1919, to be turned over to the AEF's Chief Quartermaster for transmission to Washington as miscellaneous receipts. Subsequent claims against the paper would be handled by the director of military intelligence at the War Department. There is a discussion in the 13 June 1919 issue of the paper.

13. Petition, the editorial council of *The Stars and Stripes* to the Congress of the United States, through military channels, 3 April 1919, Entry 236/48.

14. These documents are in Entry 223/47.

15. U.S. Congress. *Congressional Record*, 66th Cong., 1st sess., 1919, Vol. 58, Part 1, 1007.

16. Memorandum, Viskniskki to chief, G-2-D, 18 February 1919, Entry 236/16.

17. Memorandum, McNeil to Nolan, 6 May 1919, Entry 223/41.

18. U.S. Congress. *Congressional Record*, 66th Cong., 1st sess., 1919, Vol. 58, Part 4, 3618; Letter, Ralph Hayes, assistant to the secretary of war, to Lieut. Col. Erick Fisher Wood, of the national commission of the American Legion, 10 June 1919, Entry 223/47.

19. Confidential Memorandum, Ralph Hayes to Col. Aristides Moreno, G.H.Q., AEF, 15 February 1920, Entry 223/47.

20. Letters, Moreno to Watson and Viskniskki, 19 February 1920, Entry 223/47.

21. Letter, Watson to Moreno, 27 February 1920, Entry 223/40.

22. Letter, Viskniskki to Moreno, 2 March 1920, Entry 223/40. The National Tribune Corporation of Washington, D.C., also produced a bound copy of the 1918–1919 edition of *The Stars and Stripes*, in 1926.

23. Memorandum, Viskniskki to chief, G-2-D, 18 February 1919, Entry 236/16.

24. Streeter, of course, gained much from the publication of his books on the "Dere Mable" theme. Frederick Palmer, among other things, published his widely-read *America In France* (New York: Dodd, Mead and Co., 1918).

25. Franklin Pierce Adams, *Christopher Columbus And Other Patriotic Verses* (New York: Viking, 1931); *The Diary Of Our Own Samuel Pepys* (New York: Simon and Schuster, 1935).

26. Grantland Rice, *Sportlights of 1923* (New York: G. P. Putnam's Sons, 1924); *The Final Answer, And Other Poems* (New York: Barnes, 1955); *The Tumult And The Shouting: My Life In Sport* (New York: Barnes, 1954).

27. John Tracy Winterich, *Books And The Man* (New York: Greenberg, 1929); *Early American Books And Printing* (Boston: Houghton Mifflin Co., 1935); *Another Day, Another Dollar* (Philadelphia: J. B. Lippincott Co., 1947).

28. The literature on Woollcott is considerable, but see his own *Going To Pieces* (New York: G. P. Putnam's Sons, 1928); Beatrice Kaufman and Joseph Hennessey, eds., *The Letters Of Alexander Woollcott* (New York: The Viking Press, 1944); and Samuel Hopkins Adams, *A. Woollcott. His Life And His World* (New York: Reynal and Hitchcock, 1945). The *Portable Library* referred to was published by Viking in 1943.

29. This collection was with Ray Evans and Grant Powers.

30. Clayton M. Ryder, from the foreword to the bound collection of *The Stars and Stripes*.

Bibliographical Essay

The major part of this study is based on *The Stars and Stripes* itself. However, there is a large documentary collection in the National Archives in Washington, D.C., pertaining to the newspaper and its affairs. The documents in Record Group 120, relating to American Expeditionary Forces, contain in those concerning the AEF a subseries entitled, "Censorship and Press Division (G-2-D)." Three entries in this subseries have direct bearing on *The Stars and Stripes*: Entry 223, "Correspondence Relating to *The Stars and Stripes*, 1917–1919"; Entry 236, "General Correspondence of The Office of *The Stars and Stripes*, 1917–1919"; and Entry 237, a bound, complete file of the paper.

The author has drawn heavily from Entries 223 and 236. The former consists of about 2,000 items arranged in several folders concerning such topics as organization, advertising, postage, personnel, financial reports, and a few reports of the directing board and the like. Entry 236 consists of forty-nine file boxes—about twenty linear shelf feet—pertaining to all aspects of the paper's operations and is far too large to list or describe conveniently. Though Entry 236 has its own filing system, a researcher will not find it reliable, as the records are not always to be found according to its guide, many files and folders are not correctly marked, and numerous documents are haphazardly placed in the file boxes. It is far simpler to refer to an individual document and denote the number of the file box in which it is located. This system of citation has been used in this study.

Other government publications having bearing on *The Stars and Stripes* include the *Congressional Record*, 66th Congress, 1st session, 1919, Vol. 58, Parts 1 and 4, and the War Department's *Annual Reports*, 1919, Vol. I, which contains a brief discussion of the paper.

Some perspective on the American involvement in the war can be obtained in Laurence Stallings' classic study *The Doughboys: The Story of the AEF, 1917–1918* (New York: Harper and Row, 1963). Also useful is Edward M. Coffman's *The War to End All Wars: The American Military Experience in World War I* (New York: Oxford University Press, 1968); and Frank Freidel's *Over There* (Boston: Little, Brown and Company, 1964).

Studies of American society during the war and the attitudes manifested by Americans, both at home and abroad, include the following: Steven Jantzen, *Hooray for Peace; Hurrah for War* (New York: Alfred A. Knopf, 1971); Allen Churchill, *Over Here! An Informal Re-Creation of the Home Front in World War I* (New York: Dodd, Mead and Company, 1968); and the superb book by David M. Kennedy, *Over Here. The First World War and American Society* (New York: Oxford University Press, 1980).

Regarding journalism history, the standard study is Frank Luther Mott, *American Journalism—A History: 1690–1960*, 3rd ed. (New York: The Macmillan Company, 1962). Edwin Emery and Michael Emery, *The Press and America. An Interpretative History of the Mass Media*, 4th ed. (Englewood Cliffs, N.J.: Prentice-Hall, 1978) is a lively account which includes a useful chapter on the press in modern war with a brief discussion of *The Stars and Stripes*. More specifically as to World War I, there is Emmet Crozier's fine *American Reporters on the Western Front, 1914–1918* (New York: Oxford University Press, 1959), which is especially useful for descriptions of the war conditions from the newspaperman's point of view at the time of the launching of *The Stars and Stripes*, with a brief account of the paper's founding.

The only systematic historical account of *The Stars and Stripes* in World War I is Harry L. Katz, *The History of the Stars and Stripes. Official Newspaper of the American Expeditionary Forces in France, From February 8, 1918 to June 13, 1919* (Washington, D.C.: The Columbia Publishing Company, 1921). This forty-seven-page study amounts to a useful summary of the paper's career by a member of its mailing department and therefore has the merit of having been written by an insider.

The Stars and Stripes has been assiduously mined for its many treasures, especially its poetry and cartoons. *Yanks. A.E.F. Verse. Originally Published in The Stars and Stripes, the Official Newspaper of the American Expeditionary Forces* was published by the newspaper itself in 1918. The following year, Seth T. Bailey's famous fictitious letters were published as a collection of *Henry's Pal to Henry. Reprinted from the Stars and Stripes*, also in Paris. *Yanks* was reissued in 1919 by G. P. Putnam's Sons and in Washington, D.C., The Eastern Supply Company published *Buddies. A Sequel to Yanks: A Book of Verse, Originally Published in The Stars and Stripes* in 1921. Cyrus Leroy Baldridge, one of the artists, published a collection of his work as *"I Was There." With the Yanks on the Western Front, 1917–1919* (New York: G. P. Putnam's Sons, 1919). His colleague, Abian A. Wallgren, followed suit later with *The A.E.F. in Cartoon. From The Stars and Stripes Official Newspaper of the A.E.F.* (Philadelphia: Dan Sowers and Company, 1933). John Tracy Winterich later excerpted much from the paper in his publication, *Squads Write! A Selection of the Best Things in Prose, Verse and Cartoon from The Stars and Stripes, Official Newspaper of the A.E.F.* (New York: Harper Brothers, 1931), a book which also contains interesting information regarding the paper and its operations. Alexander Woollcott published a collection of prose pieces as *The Command is Forward. Tales of the A.E.F. Battlefields as they appeared in The Stars and Stripes* (New York: The Century Company, 1919). Other selections are in Theodore Roosevelt, Jr., and Grantland Rice, compilers, *Taps: Selected Poems of the Great War* (Garden City, N.Y.: Doubleday, Doran and Company, 1932); and Herbert Mitgang, ed., *Civilians Under Arms. The American Soldier—Civil War to Korea—as he revealed himself in his own words in The Stars and Stripes army newspaper* (Cleveland: Pennington Press, 1959).

Two journal articles which conjure up something of the paper's spirit are Calder M. Pickett's "A Paper for the Doughboys: *Stars and Stripes* in World War I," *Journalism Quarterly*, Vol. XLII, No. 1 (Winter 1965), 60–68; and Alexander Woollcott, "The Miracle of *The Stars and Stripes*: How the Official Paper of the A.E.F. Achieved Success," *Everybody's Magazine*, Vol. XLII, No. 1 (January 1920), 61–68. Woollcott's article emphasizes the freedom from official constraint that the paper enjoyed, overstating the case a bit. He also herein makes an appeal to the U.S. Congress to grant the paper's request that the considerable profits gained by the enterprise be transferred from the U.S. Treasury to the paper's famous orphan's fund, which proved to be a lost cause, however.

Several theses and dissertations have been written on *The Stars and Stripes* and regarding various aspects of the military press. Among the most useful are: David H. Burpee, "The American Expeditionary Force and *Stars and Stripes*: The American Military Reports World War I," University of Kansas, Master of Science thesis, 1975; Max Lawrence Marshall, "A Survey of Military Periodicals," University of Missouri, Master of Arts thesis, 1953; Richard F. Riccardelli, "From Chatham to Coblenz: A Historiography of U.S. Army Newspapers from the Revolutionary War through World War I," Ohio University, Master of Science thesis, 1972; and for a great deal of information on the paper's doughboy readers, see Fred Davis Baldwin, "The American Enlisted Man in World War I," Princeton University, Ph.D. dissertation, 1964.

Although not primarily accounts of *The Stars and Stripes*, certain biographies, autobiographies and memoirs relating to several of the paper's staff worthy of consideration include: Samuel Hopkins Adams, *A. Woollcott. His Life and His World* (New York: Reynal and Hitchcock, 1945); Grantland Rice, *The Tumult and the Shouting; My Life in Sport* (New York: Barnes and Noble, 1954); John Tracy Winterich, *Another Day, Another Dollar* (Philadelphia: J. B. Lippincott, 1947); Alexander Woollcott, *Shouts and Murmurs; Echoes of a Thousand and One First Nights* (New York: The Century Company, 1922); his *Enchanted Aisles* (New York: G. P. Putnam's Sons, 1924); and his *Going to Pieces* (New York: G.P. Putnam's Sons, 1928). For information on Harold Ross, see Dale Kramer's *Ross and The New Yorker* (Garden City, N.Y.: Doubleday and Company, 1951), which devotes a short chapter to Ross and *The Stars and Stripes*, and the much better book by Brendan Gill, *Here at the New Yorker* (New York: Berkley Publishing Company, 1977).

Index

About the Author
ALFRED E. CORNEBISE is Professor of History at the University of Northern Colorado. He is the author of *The Weimar in Crisis, The Amaroc News,* and *Typhus and Doughboys.* His articles have appeared in *Proceedings of the American Philosophical Society, European Studies Review,* and other journals.

Recent Titles in Contributions in Military History